MARS
AND
MINERVA

MARS AND MINERVA

World War I and the

Uses of the Higher Learning

in America

CAROL S. GRUBER

LOUISIANA STATE UNIVERSITY PRESS/BATON ROUGE

ISBN 0–8071–0096–X

Library of Congress Catalog Card Number 74–82004

Copyright © 1975 by Louisiana State University Press

Manufactured in the United States of America

Designed by Albert R. Crochet

Grateful acknowledgment is made for permission
to quote from material owned by the following institutions:

Bentley Historical Library, Michigan Historical
Collections, University of Michigan

Columbia University Archives

Columbia University Libraries

Harvard University Archives

Harvard College Library

President and Fellows of Harvard College

State Historical Society of Wisconsin

University of Chicago Archives

University of Minnesota Libraries

University of Oklahoma Library

Yale University Library

For the memory of my father,
Selig Signer,
who thought of others to the very end.

Contents

Acknowledgments

SCHOLARSHIP IS a collective as well as a solitary enterprise, and the preparation of this book has put me in the debt of many individuals and institutions whose assistance it is a pleasure to acknowledge.

This study began as a doctoral dissertation at Columbia University. My interest in the history of higher education and the academic profession grew out of my work as Professor Richard Hofstadter's research assistant. As sponsor of my dissertation, Professor Hofstadter provided intellectual stimulation and personal encouragement and support that helped me maintain confidence in a study that proved to be more controversial and problematic than I had supposed at the start. I was fortunate in having Professors Walter P. Metzger, Lawrence Cremin, and Sigmund Diamond on my dissertation examining board. Their careful and constructive criticism was an invaluable aid in revising the manuscript for publication.

I have profited from the expertise, cooperation, and friendliness of archivists and librarians at many institutions, particularly at the William L. Clements Library of the University of Michigan, Columbia University Archives, Harvard University Archives, Houghton Library of Harvard University, Library of Congress, Michigan Historical Collections of the University of Michigan, National Archives, Special Collections of

Columbia University, State Historical Society of Wisconsin, University of Chicago Archives, University of Minnesota Archives, University of Oklahoma Library, University of Pennsylvania Archives, University of Wisconsin Archives, and Historical Manuscripts Collection of the Yale University Library.

A grant from the National Endowment for the Humanities made it possible for me to take a year off from teaching and begin revising the manuscript. The revisions were accomplished with the aid of many individuals whose thoughtful comments helped me rethink my approach to the book's fundamental issues. Three friends, in particular, deserve special mention. Eugene Genovese, Christopher Lasch, and Warren Susman read this book in both its original and revised manuscript versions. Each in his own way subjected the study to penetrating criticism and analysis; if I have not been entirely successful in implementing their suggestions for improvement, it is not because of their lack of effort or ability. I am grateful to Robert McCaughey, Dorothy Ross, and Michael Wreszin for useful criticisms of the entire manuscript and to Ann Lane, David Lowenthal, and Michael Sokal for reading and commenting on individual chapters. My editor Marie Carmichael worked very hard to eliminate errors and infelicities from my writing style.

I am indebted to Helmut Gruber more than to anyone else. He has been a sounding board for my ideas and a critic of the various versions of this book; more important, however, have been his commitment and contribution to our shared sense of the seriousness and joy of the life of the mind.

C. S. G.
New York City, 1975

Introduction

IN THE SUMMER of 1927 the *American Mercury* printed two articles excoriating American college professors, particularly historians, for the role they had played during World War I.[1] The pages of the journal fairly bristled with indignation at the legion of learned men who had engaged in "shouting maledictions upon the Hun" and who had prostituted themselves by offering "their intellectual gifts upon the altar of the nation."[2] Both articles were sprinkled liberally with samples of mindless and hate-filled imprecations against Germany. "The Higher Learning Goes to War" presented example upon example of witch-hunts conducted against professors who were suspected of disbelief in the Holy Cause, witch-hunts which had been undertaken with the sanction of their colleagues and the academic freedom committee of the American Association of University Professors (AAUP).[3] "The Historians Cut Loose" indicted practitioners of the historical discipline in particular for accepting as truth the most violently distorted fulminations of war propagandists and for themselves becoming propagandists for the government's "information" agency as well as for private and semiofficial pro-

1. Charles Angoff, "The Higher Learning Goes to War," *American Mercury*, XI (June, 1927), 179–91; C. Hartley Grattan, "The Historians Cut Loose," *American Mercury*, XI (August, 1927), 414–30.
2. Angoff, "The Higher Learning Goes to War," 178, 181.
3. *Ibid.*, especially 187–91.

paganda organizations. These men, C. Hartley Grattan argued, most of whom had received their Ph.D. degrees from German universities and whose professional lives hitherto had been models of "immaculate taste" and gentlemanly etiquette, had distinguished themselves by hurling anathema against the Germans and thereby becoming fit subjects for students of pathology.[4] Not only did the historians read Germany out of civilization, Grattan continued, they rewrote history from an Anglo-Saxon perspective as part of a deliberate campaign "to promote amorous embraces between the eagle and the lion." Finally, Grattan made the historians (who had been well represented on the Inquiry, the group of scholars that helped formulate American policy for the peace conference) personally responsible for what he characterized as "some of the most vicious and imbecile schemes adopted at Versailles." The "new map of Europe," he concluded, as well as the files of unofficial and official propaganda agencies, was shameful evidence of "Clio's debauch in the arms of Uncle Sam."[5]

Charles Angoff and C. Hartley Grattan were writing in the takeoff period of the revisionist controversy about the war,[6] and their hyperbolic articles, neither of which was a comprehensive or scholarly treatment of its subject, are of interest chiefly to illustrate how the Great Crusade could come to appear tawdry in the revisionist aftermath. But, to the extent that they describe conditions that did in fact exist, while suggesting but not providing reasons for a profound disapproval of them, the articles provoke thought.

It is clear that Angoff and Grattan expected of professors a very different response to the challenge of war, but precisely what they expected must be inferred, since they never stated explicitly why the professors' behavior offended them so deeply. Underlying both articles is the plain assumption that there was an awful contradiction between ideal at-

4. Grattan, "The Historians Cut Loose," 414–15, 423. Describing the decorum that ordinarily characterized the American Historical Association, Grattan observed that "a Rotary Club session was a congress of hyenas compared to its business meetings and sectional dinners."

5. *Ibid.*, 427, 430.

6. For World War I revisionism see Warren I. Cohen, *The American Revisionists: The Lessons on Intervention in World War I* (Chicago, 1967).

tributes of the life of the mind and the manner in which American professors rallied to the flag in wartime, a contradiction that was given a slightly obscene tinge by the use of sexual imagery. More specifically, repeated reference to the professors' German training implies that their professional and personal experience should have made them immune to prevailing vulgar, stereotypic characterizations of the enemy. The references to academic freedom suggest that professors violated the essence of intellectual life by insisting upon absolute conformity of opinion and that their acquiescence in outright persecution of nonconformists was the ultimate shame. The charge against the historians was more concrete. The methodology that made history a science, Grattan argued, demanded objectivity, close scrutiny of evidence, and eschewal of racial and national bias; clearly, the conduct of historians during the war cost them their claim to professionalism. In general, Angoff and Grattan portrayed a twofold contradiction: the obvious contradiction expressed in the loss of reason by men whose professional lives were characterized by critical analysis and the more subtle contradiction involved in the wholehearted devotion of men, who professionally exemplified human rationality, to the purpose of war, the most irrational of human activities.

But there was another kind of contradiction that might help to explain the behavior of American professors during the war, a contradiction between the role of disinterested scholars dedicated to the pursuit of truth and that of patriotic citizens committed to supporting their country in a time of grave national crisis. The process by which these roles came into conflict and the capacity of professors to recognize and resolve the conflict are as important to the story of their response to the war as are Angoff's and Grattan's chronicles of their mental collapse.

In the early stages of American involvement in World War II, Merle Curti wrote an article examining the role of scholarship in previous American wars. His conclusions about the First World War were substantially the same as those of Angoff and Grattan. He, too, described the enthusiasm with which war was greeted by scholars, an enthusiasm so overwhelming that it drowned out contrary opinion.

Before we formally entered the war American scholars by and large were already in it. . . . Thus, before the final decision of April 5, 1917, American intellectuals had for the most part chosen their places and used such influence as they possessed to launch their fellow-citizens on the great crusade to make the world safe for democracy. . . . The voices of those who dissented, who urged adherence to the scholarly canons of judicious and reasonable analysis, were unheard amidst the blare of trumpets.

Curti proceeded to describe the toll taken by war on scholarship and the search for truth, on academic tolerance and fair play, on intellectual values. But he introduced a subject that added a new dimension to the problem. By devoting themselves to the purposes of the warfare state, Curti argued, scholars helped to break down "the traditional gulf between the thinker and the actor, between idea and practice." He concluded that the role of scholarship in war, particularly in the First World War, was important "in promoting the ideal of the scholar as a servant of society."[7] By putting his finger on the service ideal in American scholarship, Curti was pointing to yet another possible area of exploration for understanding the response of American professors to the challenge of the Great War.

That response is the subject of this book. In dealing with it, I have broadened the focus to include the institutional context within which professors worked; otherwise, explanations for their attitudes and activities would be incomplete. The subject is an important part of the history of America during the First World War and deserves to be studied for that reason alone; but it derives an even greater significance from what it reveals about the relationship between the higher learning and society in modern America. The challenge of war evoked a response that exposed basic assumptions about the uses of knowledge and of the university that remain live issues today.

7. Merle Curti, "The American Scholar in Three Wars," *Journal of the History of Ideas*, III (June, 1942), 241–64. Curti applauds this ideal and regards closing the gap between scholarship and life as one of the essential tasks of American democracy. See his "Intellectuals and Other People," *American Historical Review*, LX (January, 1955), 259–82, and his *American Paradox: The Conflict of Thought and Action* (New Brunswick, 1956), especially 93, 102–103.

If at times I appear, like Angoff and Grattan, to disapprove of the behavior of professors, I would like to make it clear at the outset that I
am fully aware that the choices imposed on the academic community by
the challenge of war were, in fact, problematic ones. Institutions of
higher learning were faced with a particular kind of challenge. Imbued,
as they were, with an ideal of social service—which had been expressed
for years in the donation of faculty as expert advisers to municipal,
state, and federal agencies and in the establishment of experimental sta-
tions and extension divisions for service to the surrounding community—their service to the state at war was not a departure from the past
practice but a logical culmination of what had gone before. Yet, because
of the uniqueness of the social crisis of war, there were new dangers to
the institutions of higher learning in performing a customary service
role.

Because the very life of a nation is threatened in time of war, military
victory becomes a first priority to which other social goals are bent. Social service in time of peace posed no threat to the institutions of higher
learning; indeed, it may have contributed to their health and vitality.
But, in wartime, that vitality was threatened by the universities becoming a resource to accomplish the overriding goal of victory. The
problem that confronted the universities was a real one, which beggared
simple solutions: they could not have been expected to remain aloof
from the social crisis of war; yet, to the extent that they inevitably became "instruments" at the disposal of the government, their own health
was endangered and so, ultimately, was the health of the society that, in
the broadest sense, they served. Service to society was a mutually benefi-
cial goal; service to the state contained the danger of becoming servi-
tude, to the detriment of both the institutions of higher learning and the
society at large. Unfortunately, during war the ordinarily thin line between society and state seems to disappear, and confusing the two is the
trap the institutions of higher learning were unable to avoid.

For professors as individuals, the war posed equally difficult choices,
because it placed them in roles that were conflicting and at times contradictory. The critical detachment and independence that are the hall-
marks of the scholar could appear to be peacetime luxuries when war

demanded dedication and total commitment from citizens. This is not to say that the roles of scholar and citizen during the war were always, or necessarily, mutually exclusive, but the inherent conflicts and contradictions were real enough to demand close scrutiny and analysis if professors, too, were not to fall into a trap. The trap for them was not so much having to decide to sacrifice scholarly detachment to patriotic commitment as it was denying that a conflict between the roles existed and making a virtue of what might have been seen as a necessity.

In studying the apparent contradiction between the ideal characteristics of men of knowledge and their behavior during the war, it is instructive to look at a similar charge of contradiction leveled against the American clergy, whose martial fervor was so much at odds with their avowed principles that the obvious conclusion seemed to be that the men of God suffered a psychic lapse under the extreme pressure of wartime. That is the explanation suggested by Ray Abrams' study, *Preachers Present Arms*.[8] The contradiction between the clergy's principles and practice was real indeed; but a glance at the history of the Western world, which shows war and religion marching hand in hand from the time of the Crusades, suggests that the incompatibility between them is only skin-deep. Abrams himself provides material for a less superficial interpretation when he demonstrates that the American clergy's wholehearted participation in the war effort accomplished a rapprochement between church and state, increased the prestige of the clergy, and infused the pulpit with new life and vigor.[9] Other writers perceptively have noted the similarity between the psychological states engendered by war and religion, such as exaltation, millennialism, mysticism, fatalism, and self-sacrifice.[10] To call attention to the unbecoming contradiction between Christian doctrine and the clerics' devotion to the martial

8. Ray H. Abrams, *Preachers Present Arms* (New York, 1933).
9. *Ibid.*, 79.
10. See Caroline E. Playne, *Society at War*, 1914–1916 (Boston and New York, 1931), 188, and John Dewey, "The Post-War Mind," *New Republic,* XVII (December 7, 1918), 157–58. See also Benjamin W. van Riper, "War and Religion," *Unpopular Review,* VIII (October–December, 1917), 235–42. Carlton J. H. Hayes makes a similar point when he characterizes nationalism as the dominant religion of the nineteenth and twentieth centuries. See his *Nationalism: A Religion* (New York, 1960).

purposes of the state is an important but only partial service; to understand the sources of the contradiction requires an analytic rather than a descriptive approach. The same holds true for the subject of the American professors' response to the war. The method of critics like Angoff and Grattan leaves us with the choice of being charitably disappointed or smugly indignant. When the subject is probed deeper, it is apparent that the response of professors to American intervention in the First World War was neither so simple nor so surprising as such critics would have us believe.

This book is not based on a quantitative survey of professors' opinions and responses to the war and does not pretend to portray the reaction of the entire academic community to the war itself and the problems it raised. The study is concerned, instead, with the impact of the war as a crisis situation that brought to the surface key problems of defining the nature, function, and social value of higher learning in America. Those professors who did not see in the war a challenge of this sort, who proceeded with business as usual, have been ignored. This is not to say that it is unimportant to understand what sorts of social, intellectual, and institutional factors influenced those who were able to keep their professional lives in a separate compartment and who went quietly about their business during the war. But that is a subject for another book. Nor does this study explore in depth the cases of those who clearly opposed the prevalent views, concerning either the justification for the war itself and American participation in it or the appropriate response of the higher learning to the challenge. To have slighted the dissidents in no way reflects a judgment on the significance or worthiness of their position. They play a small role in this book partly because of the difficulty of studying their views, which were submerged in the consensus of opinion that supported the American cause and the idea that the intellectual and physical resources of the higher learning should be mobilized in its behalf, and largely because it is the consensus itself that interests me.

One may question whether the consensus can be established by studying those individuals who were most vocal and visible in devoting their talents and energy to the prosecution of the war. Even if these men had stood alone, their wartime attitudes and activities are important, because most of them were leaders in their disciplines, in their institutions, and in the academic profession. They included among their numbers department chairmen; founders, presidents, and future presidents of professional associations; and editors and future editors of professional journals. They represented leading public and private institutions of higher learning in the country. Certainly, the wartime role of Richard T. Ely, for example, a founder of the American Economic Association, charter member of the AAUP, and head of the Department of Economics, Political Science, and History at the University of Wisconsin, is of interest in itself. The same can be said about many of the other subjects of this study, among them George Burton Adams, Charles A. Beard, Carl L. Becker, John Dewey, William E. Dodd, Henry W. Farnam, Guy Stanton Ford, Albert Bushnell Hart, J. Franklin Jameson, Arthur O. Lovejoy, Andrew C. McLaughlin, and Frederick Jackson Turner. However, although these individuals were outstanding among their colleagues, the record indicates that they were representative of them in their response to the war. Their correspondence, the observations of contemporaries, and the files of various associations and war agencies reveal that less prominent colleagues, who did not have their contacts or access to national publications and places of power, were performing similar wartime roles on a local level throughout the country. So, too, it is possible to get an overall picture of the response of the nation's institutions of higher learning to the challenge of war from observations by contemporary spokesmen, policies and statements of national educational associations, reports by the AAUP, and the history of the government's Students' Army Training Corps (SATC).

Historians figure prominently in the study because their talents lent themselves to explaining and publicizing the background and issues of the war; thus their kind of service made them especially visible. Beyond this reason, the role of historians during the war is interesting because it exposed tensions within the discipline surrounding an issue that continues to be a subject of debate: is history valuable for what it teaches about the past or mainly because it is a tool, even a weapon, for understanding the present and for manipulating and changing it?

The Great Crusade was not the first war to pose the issue of the public role of men of knowledge in America.[11] But it was the first war in which there occurred a conjunction of the needs dictated by a technological, total war and of the universities, scholarly disciplines, and academic professionalism that were sufficiently developed and defined to be considered resources for serving those needs. The response of the higher learning to the First World War must be seen against the background of its emergence into its modern form. This book begins with that background.

11. See, for example, Curti, "The American Scholar in Three Wars"; George M. Fredrickson, *The Inner Civil War: Northern Intellectuals and the Crisis of the Union* (New York, 1965); and Robert L. Beisner, *Twelve Against Empire: The Anti-Imperialists, 1898–1900* (New York, 1968).

I

Backdrop

IT IS COMMONPLACE to describe the emergence of the modern university in post–Civil War America as a phenomenon of revolutionary proportions, marked not only by the erection of great new institutions of higher learning but by the thorough transformation of the existing liberal arts college as well. The decades from the late 1860s to the turn of the century saw the rise of new universities, the construction of universities on the base of existing colleges, the founding of centers of professional, technical, and graduate training, and the invasion and profound alteration of the curriculum of the college itself.[1] "By contrast with England and the Continent, the problem [in America] was one of

---

1. The indispensable source for the subject is Laurence R. Veysey, *The Emergence of the American University* (Chicago, 1965). See also Richard Hofstadter, "The Revolution in Higher Education," in Arthur M. Schlesinger, Jr., and Morton White (eds.), *Paths of American Thought* (Boston, 1963), 269–90; Frederick Rudolph, *The American College and University: A History* (New York, 1962); John S. Brubacher and Willis Rudy, *Higher Education in Transition: A History of American Colleges and Universities, 1636–1968* (New York, 1958); George W. Pierson, "American Universities in the Nineteenth Century: The Formative Period," in Margaret Clapp (ed.), *The Modern University* (Ithaca, 1950), 59–94; and Richard J. Storr, *The Beginnings of Graduate Education in America* (Chicago, 1953). The following account is based largely on these sources; citations will be given only in the case of quotations or if otherwise indicated.

creation, not capture or redirection."[2] To be sure, the ideas and institutional devices were imported from abroad, but not before the social and material preconditions were established in the United States, and the product that resulted was stamped with the unmistakable imprint of the American environment.

The old liberal arts college that dated from colonial times was an adaptation of the English model. Its inspiration came from Oxbridge; but, because the American land was so vast and financial resources were so few and because of local and sectarian rivalries, the English pattern of great universities composed of clusters of independent, autonomous colleges never was duplicated. Instead, the American college assumed its own character, which it retained, not unchallenged but essentially unchanged, until the university revolution of the late nineteenth century.

The American liberal arts college was a sectarian institution designed to perpetuate a class of educated gentlemen. Staff members either already wore the cloth or were in training for the ministry. Its curriculum was prescribed and reflected the view that knowledge was a fixed body of truth to be acquired by rote through the discipline of the faculties of which the human mind was held to be composed: reason, memory, imagination, judgment, and attention. It was thought that these faculties could be developed best by drill in the classics, which consequently made up the heart of the curriculum. Because the course of study was fixed and because teaching chiefly was by recitation, there was no need for teachers to be specialists, and it was not uncommon for a tutor to take his students through the whole curriculum for the year (or longer, if he remained at the institution). Discipline, also under the tutor's charge, was enforced rigorously; attendance in class and chapel was compulsory and a tight rein was held on the students' behavior. The college, with its rigidly prescribed general education, its tone of moral piety, and its exclusive constituency, was isolated from the world around it. There was little, if any, articulation between college and career, school and society. Richard Shryock has observed that, in their educational level, their isolation from each other, and their pattern of lay government, pre–Civil War American colleges resembled the public schools

2. Pierson, "American Universities in the Nineteenth Century," 62–63.

(preparatory schools) of England more than its universities. "For more than two centuries," he concluded, "there was nothing 'higher' about American higher education."[3]

Beginning in the early nineteenth century there were serious attempts to reform the American college in conformity with the expansion of knowledge and changing social conditions and needs, but the attempts met with enormous resistance and were brought to an end by the Civil War. The commitment to general education was too firm, the colleges were too poor to restructure even if they had had the will to do so, and the business community, which might have supplied some of the necessary funds, saw no relationship between higher education and its own interests. College still was viewed as a luxury for a minority, whose needs were met by traditional liberal education.

Following the Civil War, several material and social factors converged to produce a change in conditions and convictions sufficient to precipitate the restructuring of American higher education. The acceleration of urbanization and industrialization and the settlement of the continent created a demand for scientific and technical knowledge by both business and the federal and state governments. The accumulation of great fortunes made private capital available just at the time that the business community was beginning to identify education with material success. The increasing recognition by federal and state authorities of the social value of higher education made public funds available as well. The level of original and experimental work in science and engineering began to be sufficiently high to command respect in comparison with the classical curriculum, and the expansion of knowledge exposed the limitations of that curriculum to increasingly critical view. The challenge to the classical curriculum and the intellectual foundations on which it rested further was facilitated by an erosion of religious influence and an advancing secularism to which the impact of Darwinism contributed. All of these factors made American educational theorists receptive to the influence and example of university developments in Europe, particularly in Germany.

3. Richard Shryock, "The Academic Profession in the United States," *American Association of University Professors Bulletin*, XXXVIII (Spring, 1952), 38.

We have been cautioned against viewing the modern university of the 1870s, 1880s, and 1890s as a totally new type of institution established on foreign models. Laurence Veysey reminds us of the important legacies left by the old-time college, and Arthur Bestor insists that the university revolution essentially was a process of assimilation and integration of already present ingredients.[4] Granting the legitimacy of these caveats, it nevertheless is true that the modern university fundamentally was different in character and purpose from the college it superseded. The small, residential, closely regulated undergraduate colleges were supplanted by educational centers comprised of professional schools in law, medicine, theology, and higher arts and sciences, whose ideal intellectual climate was one of free inquiry. These centers were dedicated to the education of a mass society, to the expansion rather than mere perpetuation and transmission of knowledge, and to the teaching of technical and vocational skills. Their curricula were diversified and specialized, with scientific, technical, and vocational subjects assuming equal rank with liberal humanistic studies. The new objectives in higher education gave rise to new teaching techniques and special facilities, such as laboratories and research libraries. The universities recruited specialists in the new branches of knowledge, and the faculties were organized into departments along the lines of the various scholarly disciplines and technical and vocational subjects.

These developments were not confined to the university; they spilled over into the college itself, which was transformed in the process. Beginning with the reforms of Charles W. Eliot at Harvard in the 1870s, the new and higher studies were gradually introduced into the college curriculum. By the turn of the century, and after considerable controversy, the required classical curriculum had been invaded even in the most conservative colleges; it gave way to a program of varied studies from which the student could choose his courses. Adopting the elective system brought about the modernization of the undergraduate college along the lines laid down by the university revolution.

4. See Veysey, *American University,* 55, and Arthur E. Bestor, Jr., "The Transformation of American Scholarship, 1875–1917," *Library Quarterly,* XXIII (1953), 164–79.

By 1900 the great changes had been accomplished. New university centers had been built across the country—Cornell in 1869, Johns Hopkins in 1876, Clark in 1889, Chicago in 1890, and Stanford in 1891; established institutions like California, Michigan, Minnesota, Wisconsin, Columbia, Harvard, Yale, and Princeton had been turned into modern universities; and the character of the undergraduate college had been transformed. Within these institutional changes and in reciprocal relationship to them, equally profound changes had taken place in the various branches of knowledge and in the profession of their practitioners. Two distinct but inseparable processes of professionalization had occurred: the professionalization of knowledge characterized by the emergence of discrete scholarly disciplines and the development of an academic profession characterized by the definition of standards of preparation, performance, protection, and rewards.

The professionalization of knowledge in part reflected the impact of science on American thought. The grip of theology and ethics on all branches of knowledge was weakened by the belief in rational causation, discoverable by induction from data accumulated by observation and experimentation. As knowledge expanded, it became defined and specialized into discrete subject areas. The process began with the professionalization of science itself in the second half of the nineteenth century; simultaneously, philosophy sloughed off its allegiances to theology; psychology was grounded on an experimental basis; the hodgepodge curriculum in moral philosophy broke up into the new disciplines of economics, political science, and sociology; and history, moving away from literature and philosophy, attempted to establish itself on a scientific basis.[5]

Specialists in the disciplines were trained in the new graduate schools

5. See Edward Lurie, "Science in American Thought," *Journal of World History*, VIII (1964–65), 638–65, and "An Interpretation of Science in the Nineteenth Century," *Journal of World History*, VIII (1964–65), 681–706; Dorothy Ross, *G. Stanley Hall: The Psychologist as Prophet* (Chicago, 1972); Geraldine Joncich, *The Sane Positivist: A Biography of Edward L. Thorndike* (Middletown, Conn., 1968); Jurgen Herbst, *The German Historical School in American Scholarship: A Study in the Transfer of Culture* (Ithaca, 1965); John Higham *et al.*, *History* (Englewood Cliffs, 1965); and Merle Curti (ed.), *American Scholarship in the Twentieth Century* (Cambridge, Mass., 1953).

of arts and sciences, where they were imbued with the ideal of research and instructed in its techniques. University presses and scholarly journals were founded to provide outlets for the results of their investigations. Finally, an institutional framework for the newly professionalized disciplines was provided by the establishment of associations to define standards and goals in the various fields of learning. Supplanting the pre–Civil War learned societies that were local in membership, generally open to anyone who wished to join, comprehensive in scope, and sometimes confused between scientific and humanitarian aims, the new professional associations functioned like guilds, setting standards for admission and performance on a national scale and giving the scholar a new persona as a practitioner of his discipline.[6] Organizations such as the Modern Language Association, American Historical Association, American Economic Association, American Psychological Association, and American Sociological Society, established between the last decades of the nineteenth century and the first years of the twentieth century, were indications of the professionalization of scholarship. The founding of the American Association of University Professors in 1915 signified a professional consciousness that transcended discipline boundaries to define the academic occupation.

As the academic setting changed with the emergence of the modern university, so did the character and vocation of the faculty. The academic career previously had been relatively unstructured and accessible; it was available to cultivated men of letters who did not need to give evidence of special training or competence in scholarly subjects. The professionalization of knowledge and diversification of the curriculum created the need for a specially trained and certified faculty, which led to the establishment of standards for entry into the profession, itself becoming increasingly structured and defined. Specialized training was provided by the graduate schools of arts and sciences and the Ph.D degree became the certificate of entry into the profession, whose division into ranks provided a structure for measured advance. Finally, reflecting

6. For the pre–Civil War learned societies see Merle Curti, *The Growth of American Thought* (New York, 1943), 570–71; for the guildlike character of the professional associations see Herbst, *German Historical School*, 40.

these changes, the general character of the calling also was changed. A vocation that previously had been confined to the teaching function was infused with the ideal of research and scholarship. The teacher no longer was an isolated instructor of immature minds; he was a member of a community of scholars dedicated to the expansion of learning as well as to its preservation and transmission.[7]

The uncertainties in the new profession, as well as its clearly emerging outlines, created a need to define its relationship with the constituent members of its own community and with the outside world. The AAUP was founded in 1915 to satisfy this need. When John Dewey defended the new association against charges of "trade unionism" and "sordid economic self-interest" by likening it to the American Medical Association and the American Bar Association,[8] he was voicing the emergent professional consciousness of the academic community. By the second decade of the twentieth century, professors had overcome their habitual individualism sufficiently to organize into a pressure group to protect their professional status. They were acknowledging that the revolution in higher learning had turned their vocation into a profession. The president of the AAUP announced at the second annual meeting:

> The truth is that we are a single profession—the most responsible branch of that profession which Fichte forever exalted with his inspired essay on 'The Nature of the Scholar.' And, to adapt a phrase of his from 'The Vocation of Man,' 'It is the vocation of our profession to unite itself into one single body, all the parts of which shall be thoroughly known to each other and all possessed of similar intellectual standards.' . . . Separated as we have been by the distinctions of our several sciences, and sundered as we still are and will be by distances of space and by independence of institutions, the professional bond of the University Scholar and Teacher must become and remain the strongest; for it is the one common and fundamental element in our careers. We need no charter to unite us; this

7. For the emergence of the academic profession see Walter P. Metzger, "Expansion and Profession" (Paper delivered before the Committee on the Role of Education in American History, Symposium on the Role of Education in Nineteenth-Century America, Chatham, Mass., June, 1964).

8. See Robert P. Ludlom, "Academic Freedom and Tenure: A History," *Antioch Review*, X (March, 1950), 18–19.

bond is stronger and freer than a chartered law. Circumstances, and the ripeness of the times, have destined us to this union.[9]

Any description of the sources and contours of the university revolution that omits the German influence must be incomplete. To be sure, change could not occur before the ground was prepared at home; nevertheless, there was no single influence on the direction that change would take as great as that provided by the example from Germany. The influence was exerted directly on American students who, beginning in the early nineteenth century, went to the universities of Germany to acquire the professional and advanced education that was not yet available at home.

Between 1820 and 1920 almost nine thousand Americans studied in German universities—the majority during the last decades of the nineteenth century—either receiving advanced training as part of an American doctoral program or, more typically, taking a German Ph.D. degree. Among them were men who would become architects of the modern university in America, including Andrew Dickson White, Daniel Coit Gilman, and G. Stanley Hall. They returned to America inspired by the idea of the university as a community of students and scholars engaged in the free transmission and expansion of knowledge, and they proceeded to translate the idea into institutions modeled after the German example. The erection of the graduate school of arts and sciences reflected the Germanization of American higher education, as did the introduction of such teaching techniques and research devices as lectures, seminars, libraries, and laboratories. The establishment of knowledge on a scientific basis also reflected the influence of Germany, for it was there that the pioneering work was done in the various scholarly disciplines, and it was there that Americans learned to apply the methods of science to the accumulation and analysis of data. It was there, too, that they were introduced to the concept, which would become a foundation of their profession, that knowledge can be advanced only in a climate of absolute intellectual freedom. Finally, Americans who earned German

9. John H. Wigmore, "Presidential Address," *American Association of University Professors Bulletin*, II (March, 1916), 8–9.

Ph.D. degrees returned home as fully trained professionals in their disciplines. Their view of the vocation of scholarship contributed to the establishment of an academic profession, with precise standards and goals and with a high sense of social value.[10]

The German influence was particularly great on the American social sciences. It promoted not only a scientific methodology but also a conviction that knowledge has a social function, and it impressed upon scholars in the new disciplines a keen sense of responsibility to the public welfare.[11] Many of the pioneering American social scientists of the late nineteenth and early twentieth century—including the economists Richard T. Ely, Henry W. Farnam, and E. R. A. Seligman, the sociologists Albion W. Small and E. A. Ross, and the historians Herbert Baxter Adams, John W. Burgess, and James Harvey Robinson—did graduate work in Germany. German-trained social scientists were in the vanguard of those who developed graduate departments in their disciplines and founded professional associations and publications. They dominated the faculties of the social sciences departments of the new universities.

That Germany was the nation to vitally influence the emergence of the modern American university is not difficult to explain. From the early nineteenth century until the advent of Nazism, the excellence of the German universities and their high level of achievement made them "model academic institutions."[12] The prestige of a German doctorate was very high, and the degree was relatively easy to acquire. Americans were drawn by the intellectual vitality of nineteenth-century German university scholarship and by the reputation of individual scholars.

10. See Herbst, *German Historical School;* Charles F. Thwing, *The American and the German University: One Hundred Years of History* (New York, 1928); and Walter P. Metzger, "The German Contribution to the American Theory of Academic Freedom," *American Association of University Professors, Bulletin,* XLI (Summer, 1955), 214–30.

11. See Herbst, *German Historical School,* and Ernest Becker, *The Lost Science of Man* (New York, 1971).

12. Joseph Ben-David and Awraham Zloczower, "Universities and Academic Systems in Modern Societies," *European Journal of Sociology,* III (1962), 47. The authors argue that the unique success of the German university sprang less from the "idea of the university" in Germany than from circumstances that historically had shaped it, particularly the decentralization of the higher educational system.

Furthermore, the cost of living in Germany was attractively low. By comparison, the universities of France and Britain had little to offer.[13] Indeed, although British universities were emerging from a period of "torpor and ossification" and were beginning to improve in the early twentieth century and to attract American attention,[14] the advances they made were influenced by the German example.[15] Josiah Royce beautifully described the centrality of the German experience during the formative years of university building in America. Speaking of the late 1870s, he recalled a professor at Johns Hopkins telling him that "when he dealt with young American scholars he found them feeling as if not England, but Germany, were their mother-country. . . . One went to Germany," he continued, "still a doubter as to the possibility of the theoretic life; one returned an idealist, devoted for the time to pure learning for learnings' sake determined to contribute his *Scherflein* to the massive store of human knowledge, burning for a chance to help build the American University."[16]

Americans did not hesitate to acknowledge the influence of German higher education and scholarship. For example, in 1904 the University of Chicago for its fiftieth convocation chose the theme "Recognition of the Indebtedness of American Universities to the Ideals of German Scholarship." The principal address of the occasion, delivered by Professor John M. Coulter, held up the German university as "a model to other nations." The great principles on which the German university rests, Coulter said, must be the basic principles of universities everywhere.[17] In his letter of greeting to the assemblage, President Theodore Roosevelt hailed Germany as "the mother of modern science and learning."[18] The following year, an annual exchange professorship between

13. See Herbst, *German Historical School,* Chap. 1.
14. Veysey, *American University,* 196.
15. See George H. Haines IV, *Essays on German Influence Upon English Education and Science, 1850–1919* (Hamden, Conn., 1969).
16. Josiah Royce, "Present Ideals of American University Life," *Scribner's,* X (1891), 383.
17. John M. Coulter, "The Contribution of Germany to Higher Education," *Chicago University Record,* VIII (March, 1904), 348.
18. *Ibid.,* 354.

German and American universities was established, expressing a mutual desire to preserve and promote the affinities between the higher educational world in the two countries.

In 1914 German representatives in the United States counted on these affinities to make American university scholars sympathetic to Germany's cause in the war. These representatives founded the German University League, with the purpose of uniting "those who have enjoyed the privilege of a German university education" in efforts "to strengthen the regard for the Germans and for their aims and ideals, and to secure for them . . . fair play and proper appreciation."[19] A letter from the philosophers Rudolf Eucken and Ernst Haeckel to the universities of America was distributed with the league's first announcement, expressing confidence in "the friendly feeling of the American universities," whose members, as a result of their training in Germany, the exchange of scholars, and the bonds created by scholarly research, "know what German culture means to the world." Eucken and Haeckel concluded with the expectation that American scholars would reject the Allied interpretation of the war and accept that of the Central Powers.[20]

This expectation, aside from overlooking the influence of the war's political and diplomatic issues on American scholars, was based on a mistakenly simple view of the influence of Germany on American higher education. What had been involved was a complicated process of interpretation, even misinterpretation, selection, and alteration to adapt the German example to the American environment. Americans transported the organizational structure of German scholarship—the graduate school and the instructional techniques and research devices associated with it, the professional association, and professional publications—and the new scientific methodology almost intact; but they eschewed the idealist context in which these operated in Germany. Walter P. Metzger observes, "Most Americans who went to study in Germany . . . took home the methods of her seminars and laboratories, but left the

---

19. Hugo Kirbach to "Dear Sir," January, 1915, in Richard T. Ely Papers, State Historical Society of Wisconsin.

20. Rudolf Eucken and Ernst Haeckel to the universities of America, August 31, 1914, sent with O. J. Merkel to A. Lawrence Lowell, December 26, 1914, both in A. Lawrence Lowell Papers, Harvard University Archives.

Anschauung of idealism behind."[21] According to Veysey, Americans who, under the influence of Germany, became dedicated to scientific research missed "the larger, almost contemplative implications of *Wissenschaft*" and transformed the German ideal of "pure learning," unaffected by utilitarian demands, into an American version, "pure science," assuming that "investigation meant something specifically scientific." The Germans' lofty evocation of underlying spiritual unity was ignored by research-minded Americans, who found the inspiration for their academic theorizing on the level of German practice and became deeply inspired by the rigorous and precise examination of phenomena. "An insufficiently differentiated Germany, partly real and partly imaginary," Veysey concludes, "became the symbol for all scientific claims upon American education."[22]

Furthermore, the process of cultural transfer was ambivalent, particularly in the social sciences. Jurgen Herbst demonstrates that it was largely the influence of German methods of empirical research and inductive generalization that professionalized history in late nineteenth-century America. But, he continues, the philosophic assumptions and political ideas that were central to German historical writing at the time were incompatible with American tradition and values. Consequently, the attempt to transfer to the United States a German science of history and politics failed in the long run.[23] The writings of the first generation of German-trained historians, chief among them Herbert Baxter Adams and John W. Burgess, applied German ideas and values—statism, rejection of natural rights and the social contract, Aryan superiority—to the history of the United States. In order for the next generation of American historians to understand the dynamics of a democratic society, they had to reject the approach of Adams and his followers. Herbst declares that Adams himself came to realize the incompatibility of German ideas

21. Metzger, "German Contribution to Academic Freedom," 227.
22. Veysey, *American University*, 128.
23. Herbst, *German Historical School*, Chap. 5. He concludes that the failure was a direct consequence of the Americans' misunderstanding of *Ideengeschichte*. Had they correctly read Wilhelm von Humboldt and Leopold von Ranke, he maintains, "they would have realized that not only the facts but the ideas of American history had to come from American sources." (p. 128).

with American history and ended his contacts with his German mentors, drawing closer to "democratic" colleagues in England. Herbst quotes W. Stull Holt's conclusion from this fact that "the orthodox account of the dominant influence of German scholarship in America during this period [1876–1901] may need revision."[24]

Herbst maintains that it was easier to accomplish cultural transfer in the fields of economics and sociology, where the object of inquiry was society and not the state and where, consequently, the problem of antagonism between the individual and the state did not necessarily have to be confronted.[25] But even in these disciplines Americans responded with discrimination to the influence of German scholarship. For example, Joseph Dorfman points out that, although the German historical school had a seminal influence on modern economics in America, the Germans' political philosophy of centralized authority was rejected by Americans, who substituted ideas more congenial to a pluralistic society.[26]

Finally, the manner in which Americans simultaneously adopted the German principle of academic freedom and adapted it to the American environment illustrates the selectivity of the process of cultural transfer. The German ideal of the free pursuit of knowledge, without religious, political, or administrative control, exacted both praise and envy from Americans from the time they first began to study in German universities.[27] By the time they organized the AAUP, professors in America had concluded that academic freedom was the prerequisite of the profession. But their application of the principle was vastly different from that of the Germans. For one thing, unlike the Germans, they were relatively unconcerned with the issue of student freedom (*Lernfreiheit*) and restricted their efforts to the definition and protection of the freedom of the faculty (*Lehrfreiheit*). Furthermore, the Americans restricted a pro-

24. *Ibid.,* 126.
25. *Ibid.,* Chap. 6.
26. Joseph Dorfman, "The Role of the German Historical School in American Economic Thought," *American Economic Review: Papers and Proceedings,* XLV (May, 1955), 17–28.
27. See Metzger, "German Contribution to Academic Freedom," 220. For an interesting development of the observation that academic freedom always was severely limited in Germany, see Ben-David and Zloczower, "Universities and Academic Systems," 56–61.

fessor's freedom within the classroom, insisting that he confine his subject matter to his field of competence and that he maintain a "neutral" posture in presenting it. At the same time they extended the definition of academic freedom to protect freedom of expression outside university walls, insisting that a professor should no more be penalized for exercising his constitutional right of free speech than any other citizen. In this fashion, academic freedom in the United States became associated with civil liberty.[28]

One aspect of the experience of American students in Germany should at least be mentioned in connection with any evaluation of the German impact on American scholars. It was not uncommon for Americans who received their professional training in Germany and who were enormously impressed by German scholarship and culture to be at the same time disturbed, even repelled, by other traits of German society, particularly the high esteem accorded to the military establishment and the authoritarianism that characterized German political and social life. A high regard for German learning and culture, in other words, could go hand in hand with a rejection of other German values and institutions.[29]

Taken together, the increasing discrimination with which Americans came to view German education and scholarship and the simultaneous improvement in American graduate education led to a waning of German influence on American higher education after the 1890s. Veysey concludes that, "despite the inauguration of exchange professorships between the two countries, American and German academic circles increasingly lost contact with each other well before the advent of the First World War."[30] Nevertheless, by this time an acknowledged prior debt to Germany was part of the record of American higher education and, in the case of individual American professors, there were warm

28. See "Report of the Committee on Academic Freedom and Academic Tenure," *American Association of University Professors Bulletin*, I (December, 1915), 20–43. Metzger's "German Contribution to Academic Freedom" provides a detailed exposition of the reasons for the modifications of the German model in America.

29. See Melvin Small, "The American Image of Germany, 1906–1914" (Ph.D. dissertation, University of Michigan, 1965), 118.

30. Veysey, *American University*, 131.

professional and personal relationships with German scholars and their families that had been established when the Americans had studied abroad and that endured during the early years of the twentieth century.

Professors Eucken and Haeckel and the founders of the German University League erred not only in viewing the influence of Germany on American higher education with an undiscriminating eye, but also in failing to consider other influences on American higher education and other deep and enduring influences on American culture that would help determine American sympathies in the war. Although the erection of the modern university in America was a process of Germanization, the base on which it was imposed derived from England, and the traces of the English college and the values it represented never disappeared from the American system. Historically, from the time of its inception in the seventeenth century, the American college had belonged to the English type. In its dedication to education rather than training and to the cultivation of moral and social as well as intellectual attributes, the American college exemplified the English ideal of liberal education.[31] It was this ideal that had to be combated by the proponents of the modern university. A French observer of the American educational scene in the late nineteenth century described it as a great battlefield on which English (liberal education) and German (laboratory science) influences fought.[32] Richard Hofstadter demonstrates that, although the German ideals of scholarship and academic freedom were at the heart of the university revolution, English influences persisted even after the revolution had been accomplished. He describes these influences as follows: concern with the development of character in undergraduates and with "atmosphere" in the institutions; a passion for imposing buildings, separated if possible from the urban community; an emphasis on teaching as opposed to research; a commitment to the centrality of the college among the various parts of the university; an aim of creating a

31. For a description of English higher education in the nineteenth and twentieth centuries see Charles C. Gillispie, "English Ideas of the University in the Nineteenth Century," in Clapp (ed.), *The Modern University*, 27–55, and Albert H. Halsey, "British Universities," *European Journal of Sociology*, III (1962), 85–101.
32. See Veysey, *American University*, 196–97n.

broadly educated leadership as opposed to a body of specialists; and a zeal for undergraduate sports. These influences, he concludes, remained "especially strong in the better colleges and in some universities, like Yale and Princeton."[33] The regular attendance of American Rhodes Scholars at Oxford University beginning in 1902 suggests that British ideals of higher education continued to be relevant for Americans even after they had revamped their universities largely along German lines.

The cultural and intellectual affinities between America and Britain stretched far beyond the area of educational influences and interchange and present an even more complicated picture of cultural transfer than that already described between Germany and America. Only the broad outlines of that picture can be sketched here. In his study *The American Image of the Old World,* Cushing Strout demonstrates that Americans traditionally experienced acute ambivalence toward England. From the time of the Revolution, he argues, England provoked a kind of schizophrenic response from America; it was both America's oldest and most detested enemy, the prime target of America's antipathy toward the Old World, and the mother country, the source of America's language, culture, and many of its most cherished institutions.[34] Throughout the nineteenth century, Anglophobia lay at the heart of American patriotism; its persistence was demonstrated every Fourth of July and was revealed in virtually every school text in American history. This Anglophobia was reinforced by the fact that it was England with whom America was engaged in the most frequent and most dangerous diplomatic controversies. But there also was a strong strain of Anglophilia in nineteenth-century American culture, which was shared by those who recognized America's profound cultural debt to Britain and by trading and financial interests that had close economic ties with England.

Toward the end of the century, as a result of developments in both countries, relations between America and England began perceptibly to improve. Anglophilia in America was strengthened considerably as white Protestant Americans became increasingly fearful of the effects of

33. Hofstadter, "The Revolution in Higher Education," 565n.
34. Cushing Strout, *The American Image of the Old World* (New York, 1963), 134.

the new immigration and as popularizers of Anglo-Saxonism played on the racial and cultural affinities of the English and American peoples. When the United States joined the ranks of imperialist powers, with its own overseas possessions and expanding interests in Latin America and the Far East, Americans grew increasingly aware of the necessity to cement the relationship with Great Britain, potentially the country's most dangerous foe. Britain was interested in improved relations because of its own imperial problems, particularly the threat of an expanding Germany. The possibilities of mutual benefit were demonstrated when Britain's benevolent neutrality in the Spanish-American War forestalled intervention by hostile European powers and Secretary of State John Hay reciprocated during the Boer War by making sure that America would take no action that would hurt the British cause.[35]

Bradford Perkins concludes that, in spite of the persistence of antipathy to England in the American popular imagination, during the years 1895–1914 a "great rapprochement" had taken place between America and Britain. With most of the concessions being made by Britain in response to challenges it faced elsewhere and with the American political elite in advance of American public opinion, the slate of more than a century of antagonism and conflict was wiped clean after the Spanish-American War, and a new spirit of understanding and accommodation between the two countries came to prevail.[36] A recent study of the intellectual roots of this Anglo-American "alliance" demonstrates that the turn-of-the-century accord reflected more than the political, economic, and strategic considerations from which it originated. Concentrating on the ideas of Theodore Roosevelt and some of his English correspondents, David H. Burton portrays a shared conviction that, despite superficial differences between England and the United States, there were deep, underlying political and cultural similarities between the two countries. The accord, these Anglo-Saxonists believed, was a "natural" response to the threats of the alien culture and polity of the dynamic,

35. See *ibid.*, Chap. 8, and Harry C. Allen, *Conflict and Concord: The Anglo-American Relationship Since 1783* (New York, 1959), 221–24.
36. Bradford Perkins, *The Great Rapprochement: England and the United States, 1895–1914* (New York, 1968).

new German Empire, the uncertain future direction of the Russian state, and the chaotic conditions in China. St. Loe Strachey spoke for Anglo-Saxonists in both countries when he said: "We speak the same language, recognize the same common law principles in our law and administration, and are inspired by the same political and moral ideals."[37]

American Anglo-Saxonists were in a good position to combat continuing popular tendencies in their country to twist the lion's tail, for they were well represented in the sectors of society that influenced foreign policy opinions and decisions—in presidential administrations, in the army and navy, in the leadership of Congress, and among the intelligentsia.[38] Anglophilia flourished in America's pressrooms and publishing houses and on American campuses. Among professors the close intellectual tie with England exerted great sway, "stretching in memory," as Veysey observes, "all the way back to the first importation of 'liberal education' from Cambridge to Harvard in colonial times."[39] It was the persistence of the English gentlemanly social ideal among professors that ultimately intertwined with the newer impulse toward professionalization. Finally, the concept of "civilization," which was so important to American professors' interpretation of the war, meant to them the political, legal, economic, and cultural accomplishments of the English-speaking peoples and the prospective benefits to the rest of the world from the spread of their influence.

After the influences from Germany and England have been acknowledged, the fact remains that the character of American universities from the time of their origin has been unique and has stemmed from the special circumstances of the American environment. Compared to universities elsewhere in the Western world, American institutions of higher learning have been exceptionally responsive to conditions in the surrounding community. This is partly a result of the American departure from the pattern of national universities. The concomitant decentraliza-

37. See David H. Burton, "Theodore Roosevelt and His English Correspondents: The Intellectual Roots of the Anglo-American Alliance," *Mid-America,* LIII (January, 1971), 12–34.
38. See Small, "American Image of Germany."
39. Veysey, *American University,* 196.

tion of decision making in American institutions of higher learning (that is, their freedom from central planning) and the extreme heterogeneity of their quality and character have made them responsive to social and economic forces in their local environments.[40] Furthermore, American universities, Allan Nevins points out, always have been peculiarly regional, in the sense of having "relevance to a special community." The idea that universities in America should have a regional function took root from the beginning, Nevins observes, as Harvard was planted for the special inspiration of Massachusetts Bay and William and Mary for the Old Dominion. The country was so large that as higher education spread westward it had to find a state or regional pattern. This pattern was most characteristic of state universities, but not confined to them alone.[41] Finally, American universities have been particularly responsive to outside influence because of their pattern of lay government and their dependence for funds on donors in the case of private institutions and on legislative bodies in the case of public institutions.

Because the emergence of the modern university in America was associated so closely with the needs of a democratic, industrializing society, it is not surprising that its function should be defined largely in terms of serving those needs. The singularity of American institutions of higher learning stems more from the ideal of service with which they are permeated than from any other factor in their history. Although there never has been agreement about goals within the academic community, the ideal of service was pervasive in educational circles at the time of the university revolution and afterwards; it continues to be a distinguishing feature of American higher education. Indeed, Veysey makes it clear that the initial impetus toward the modern university came from those—like Charles W. Eliot of Harvard and Andrew Dickson White of Cornell—who viewed its function as serving the surrounding community. The concept of service sprang in part from the recognition by administrators of their need for support from public and private sources, from prevailing the-

40. See Martin Trow, "The Democratization of Higher Education in America," *European Journal of Sociology*, III (1962), 232–34.

41. Allan Nevins, *The State Universities and Democracy* (Urbana, 1962), 18, 19.

ories about the nature and function of knowledge, and from moral idealism in the faculty.[42]

The service-oriented educators made the primary assumption "that the patterns of behavior which flourished outside the campus were more 'real' than those which most often prevailed within it." "Reality" increasingly was defined as "democratic" and given a vocational tinge, and the university was to mirror that democratic reality in several ways: by establishing all fields of learning on an equal basis; by treating all students as equals; by providing easy admission; by portraying itself as an agency for individual success; by emphasizing its function to widely diffuse knowledge throughout society; and by embracing the idea that it should take its orders directly from the citizenry.[43] The commitment to service was reflected in student bodies drawn not from an intellectual elite seeking initiation into the mysteries of pure science, arts, and letters, but from those among the general population interested in acquiring an increasingly functional degree; in curricula that were highly differentiated and offered a wide range of practical training (extending downward in the education hierarchy from training for the professions of medicine, law, and engineering to training in the "science" of business administration and the "economics" of homemaking); and in faculties whose members freely donated their talents as expert advisers to municipal, state, and federal agencies.

The articulation of interest between the university and society was both appreciated and promoted by the federal government. Beginning in 1862 with the passage of the first Morrill Act and continuing with the Hatch Act of 1887 and the second Morrill Act of 1890, the federal government pledged its support to the promotion of education in the useful—agricultural and mechanical—arts, for the common man. The first Morrill Act was designed to provide improved techniques and trained operatives for the industry and agriculture upon which the northern na-

42. See Veysey, *American University*, Chap. 2. Although Veysey prefers the term "utility" to "service," I choose to retain the latter because it was the term used by the professors with whom I deal. The very ambiguities in the concept of "service" are a clue to understanding the role of the academic community during the war.

43. *Ibid.*, 61–64.

tional economy rested.[44] Grants of land under the act went both to existing institutions (in Wisconsin, for example, the state university was the
beneficiary) and to newly established agricultural and technical colleges,
and it was these land-grant colleges and other state institutions that
came particularly to stand for the "all-purpose" curriculum and for service to the community.[45] Clark Kerr describes the Morrill Act as "one of
the most seminal pieces of legislation ever enacted" and states,
"Nowhere before had universities been so closely linked with the daily
life of so much of their societies."[46]

The "Wisconsin Idea" was one of the earliest, most fully developed,
and best publicized expressions of the service ideal and has come to
stand as its archetype.[47] To be sure, the Wisconsin Idea neither significantly affected state politics nor ensured harmonious relations between
the university and the legislature, educational authorities, and other officials in the state.[48] But the wide-ranging extension program and the substantial faculty advisory service to the many branches of the state government testified to the university's highly developed commitment to an
organic relationship between itself and its surrounding community.
However, the service ideal should not be associated exclusively with
land-grant and state institutions or with universities, like Wisconsin, that
established carefully planned and executed programs to put the ideal
into practice. Even private institutions and those that had a more traditional focus on undergraduate liberal education or research-oriented
graduate work in the pure sciences and in arts and letters appeared before the public in a garb of social service. It was not uncommon to use
the idea of "service," loosely defined, to legitimize the American university.[49]

44. See Curti, "The American Scholar in Three Wars," 260.
45. See Brubacher and Rudy, *Higher Education in Transition*, 158.
46. Clark Kerr, *The Uses of the University* (Cambridge, Mass., 1963), 46–47.
47. For a detailed description of the Wisconsin Idea by one of the participants
in its development, see Charles R. McCarthy, *The Wisconsin Idea* (New York,
1912).
48. See Merle Curti and Vernon L. Carstensen, *The University of Wisconsin*
(Madison, 1949), II, 99–104. See also Veysey, *American University*, 108.
49. See, for example, Woodrow Wilson, "Princeton in the Nation's Service,"
Forum, XXII (December, 1896), 450–66, and "Public Service of University Officers," *Columbia University Quarterly*, XVI (March, 1914), 169–82.

Since the revolution in higher learning was a process and not an event, it is not possible to say precisely when it was completed. But we can safely say that by 1910 the period of greatest change in the world of higher learning had taken place. By then the period of new university building had passed its peak, as had the influence of the elective principle on the undergraduate curriculum, and a professional outlook had come to characterize the scholarly disciplines and the academic vocation. That a great transformation had been accomplished, however, is not to say that a uniform product had emerged capable of clear definition or characterized by inner harmony and tranquillity. The opposite, in fact, was true. The modern university in America did not have clear goals or a common sense of purpose; aspects of the university revolution stood in contradictory relationship to each other and resulted in dysfunctional tension and antagonism; and, although the professional disciplines and a professional consciousness had been born, they were in their infancy and their future direction was unclear.

To speak at all of "the college" or "the university" in America at the time of the great transformation and down to the present can be misleading. In a country so vast, where there came to be such a great emphasis on skill and where education became identified with success, there was room for an apparently unlimited number of higher educational institutions of very uneven character and quality. The world of higher education presented a varied face. In addition to the new and re-formed private universities, the reformed liberal arts colleges, and the state institutions and their far-flung extension divisions, there were various vocational and technical schools, municipal colleges, separate schools for Negroes and for women, and the old-style denominational colleges, which, no longer in the mainstream, continued to exist. Higher educational institutions were, and remain, so heterogeneous in character and quality that a contemporary observer has concluded that "there is a college somewhere in America for everybody."[50] Too, the rate of development in the period of growth, particularly among the state institutions, was uneven, reflecting the uneven material and cultural progress

50. Trow, "Democratization of Higher Education," 234.

of their states and the particular political and social circumstances in their environments.[51] Within this decentralized and continually expanding world of higher education, and particularly among the "successful" institutions, a state of keen competition came to prevail for financial support, students, faculty, and prestige.[52]

A salient fact emerges from the history of the university revolution: it failed to replace the unified pattern of the old-time college, which it shattered, with a clear pattern of its own. Veysey's work is a massive elaboration precisely of this point. It demonstrates the competing goals that characterized the early period of the university revolution, when the proponents of liberal culture, of research, and of utility struggled to stamp their vision on the face of the new institution. The debate over goals had quieted by about 1890, he concludes, but never was settled; rather than a clear sense of purpose, only "unacknowledged confusion," "hazy generalities," and an accommodation of conflicting purposes under the general rubric of social service had resulted. To this day the university remains in a state of "uneasy balance" from its embodiment of conflicting ideals: the German ideal of research and graduate and professional education; the English ideal of liberal culture and undergraduate education; and the American ideal of "lesser professional" (other than legal and medical) education and public service.[53] "The university is so many things to so many people," concludes Kerr, "that it must, of necessity, be partially at war with itself."[54]

Tensions that sprang from the internal development of the university as a social system were as significant as those that resulted from the lack of a unified sense of purpose within and between the institutions of higher learning. The chief tensions resulted from the bureaucratization of the university in the last decades of the nineteenth century. As the university grew in size and complexity, the old "familial" pattern of management was replaced by a bureaucratic structure embodied in an

51. See Nevins, *The State Universities and Democracy*, 78–79.
52. See Veysey, *American University*, 317–32.
53. See Kerr, *The Uses of the University*, 17–18, and Trow, "Democratization of Higher Education," 234.
54. Kerr, *The Uses of the University*, 8–9.

elaborate administrative hierarchy.[55] By the early 1900s the universities had come to look like business corporations, with their directors (trustees), executives (administrators), and employees (faculty).[56] Within this process of bureaucratization the changing role of the president had the most dramatic consequences. Although the president's legal rights had not expanded since 1870 (legally he still was the chief executive of the trustees), his stature had grown enormously with the expansion of the institutions and their administrative personnel. So, too, had the nature of the office changed, from the president being "first among equals," who shared with his faculty a religious purpose, a teaching function, a common intellectual background, and an intimacy of daily contact, to his becoming managerial overlord of a complex organization.[57]

The change in the presidential office destroyed the homogeneity of academic society by dividing it into two vocations—administration and teaching—with clearly demarcated spheres of influence. The faculty was given hegemony over the classroom, but vital policy decisions affecting the functioning and future development of the institution were the province of the administration, even though it might assign the faculty an advisory role in these areas. During the first decades of reform, the innovative presidents and the faculty often were allies against resistant conservative forces; but significant faculty resistance to presidential authority had developed by the early twentieth century, when a new generation of managerial consolidators occupied the presidential office.[58]

Tensions between the faculty and the president reflected more than competition for power over decision making; they reflected the deeplying and often subtle tensions that grew out of the peculiar position of the faculty member as both professional and employee. The concept of professionalism resists easy definition, but sociologists seem to agree that autonomy—control by professionals themselves of the development and

55. For a description of the rise of administration, see Veysey, *American University*, 305–17; Metzger, "Expansion and Profession," 27–31; and Shryock, "Academic Profession," 43–50.

56. Shryock, "Academic Profession," 45. Thorstein Veblen's *The Higher Learning in America* (New York, 1957) is the classic contemporary discussion of this development.

57. Metzger, "Expansion and Profession," 27.

58. *Ibid.*, 29–30.

application of their field of special competence—is its essential condition. Because authority in an organization is enforced through "superordinate control," tension inevitably arises when professional roles confront organizational necessities.[59] These confrontations occurred frequently in academia; not only were subtle forms of rendering the faculty subservient involved, but head-on collisions as well.[60] The dual professional-employee position of the faculty has implications beyond the confines of the institution of higher learning. When he discusses the relative social status of university professors and other professional men like physicians and lawyers, Shryock observes that the general prestige of professors is lowered by their "quasi-employee" status.[61]

The simultaneous emergence of the modern university and professionalization of scholarship and the academic vocation offers a clue to internal tensions in the system. In many respects the two revolutions, in university structure and professionalism, were complementary, even interdependent. The new disciplines and their practitioners needed the resources of the new universities to become established, gain recognition, and extend their influence. They were enormously strengthened by being recognized in the expanding curriculum, being given departmental status (with separate budgets and considerable control over standards and staffing), and having laboratory and library resources at their command. So, too, did the universities depend on the professionals for their advance. A faculty with a high professional reputation commanded students, financial support, and prestige for its institution. In another respect, however, the two revolutions were contradictory. For, as the university revolution climaxed in the triumph of administrative bureaucracy, with its descending lines of command, this bureaucracy conflicted with the increasing professional consciousness of the faculty. Indeed, the

59. Bernard Barber, "Some Problems in the Sociology of the Professions," *Daedalus*, XCII (Fall, 1963), 679. That the academic profession possesses the common attributes of the major professions is demonstrated in Logan Wilson, *The Academic Man: A Study in the Sociology of a Profession* (London, 1942), 114.
60. For an excellent treatment of the theme of subserviency and dependency see James McKeen Cattell, "Academic Slavery," *School and Society*, VI (October, 13, 1917), 421–26.
61. Shryock, "Academic Profession," 54.

more accomplished and professionally distinguished the faculty, the more it would resist the enlarged powers of the president, insist on a voice in university management, and demand greater freedom. The tensions created by the dual professional-employee status of the faculty were an important factor in the academic freedom cases of the late nineteenth and early twentieth centuries.

It should not be concluded from the above observations that by the early twentieth century the academic vocation was characterized by a fully developed sense of group solidarity and professional élan or that there were no tensions and strains within the academic profession itself. The division of the vocation into ranks was one index of professionalism;[62] but the establishment of a rank hierarchy introduced considerable differences of status and outlook between individuals in the lower and higher positions. The individuals on the lower rung of the occupational ladder, instructors and assistant professors, were in a precarious occupational position characterized by uncertainty and insecurity.[63] Their number among the nation's professoriate had undergone a marked proportional increase between the late nineteenth and early twentieth centuries.[64] Their lot, according to a 1910 study of a selected group of assistant professors, was one of retarded advancement and exploitation, which benefited their seniors.[65] And it was the small core of senior professors who exercised whatever influence and power the faculty had.[66]

The history of the founding of their professional association itself reveals the problematic professional solidarity of university scholars, which persists to this day. Discussing the origins of the AAUP, Metzger points out that, although there was an enormous variety of proposals for the direction the new association should take, there was consensus about what the association should *not* do: deal with the question of salaries. "Collective bargaining was unthinkable," he says; "even a collective

62. Metzger, "Expansion and Profession," 52n.
63. For a description of the occupational implications and psychological consequences of rank divisions see Wilson, *The Academic Man*, 60–70.
64. Metzger, "Expansion and Profession," 17.
65. Guido Marx, "The Problem of the Assistant Professor," *Association of American Universities Journal of Proceedings and Addresses*, XI (1910), 18–32.
66. Veysey, *American University*, 304.

statement was presumed to suggest trade union tactics."[67] Although this response may, in part, suggest the presence of a professional self-image, the opposition to a united front on remuneration also suggests an absence of professional solidarity. Logan Wilson quotes a study that explains this opposition as a product of the preprofessional "tradition of dignity" inherited from the professor's previous ecclesiastical function, with its resulting notions that a gentleman does not bargain, that learning is its own reward, and that the life of a scholar necessarily is one of poverty and sacrifice. The study attributes the opposition further to a spirit of individualism among professors that indicates, it says, little conception of cooperative or unified welfare. This spirit was encouraged by rank cleavages, which produced a different occupational outlook between individuals in the lower and higher ranks, and by the departmental structure, which resulted in each department seeking to advance its own interests. That the AAUP operates under much heavier odds than the American Medical Association or the American Bar Association, Wilson observes, can be attributed to the absence of an overriding commitment to broad, professional interests among university scholars. Typically, a scholar's primary professional interest is his own discipline.[68] The limited resources and facilities of the AAUP, Shryock concludes, reflect "the fact that the first interest of professors is usually in their special fields, while their concern for the academic profession as a whole is secondary. The academic guild is, in a sense, a collection of a score or more of distinct professions." He contrasts this situation with "the solidarity of medical men who are physicians first and specialists thereafter."[69]

The scholarly disciplines themselves were in an inchoate condition in the early years of the twentieth century. Only recently established on a scientific basis and in a rudimentary state, they were characterized not only by a lack of clear definition of the substance and nature of the dis-

67. Metzger, "Expansion and Profession," 19.
68. Wilson, *The Academic Man,* 140, 132-33.
69. Shryock, "Academic Profession," 68. It remains to be seen whether the present financial crisis in the colleges and universities and the tensions it spawns will be sufficiently threatening for professors to overcome their resistance to professional solidarity.

ciplines, but also by a lack of certainty about their limits and the lines of demarcation between them. The problems of definition and demarcation were most apparent in the social sciences, the "new body of studies" as Dewey called them, that emerged out of the moral philosophy curriculum in the late nineteenth century. John Higham locates the origin of the ill-conceived, post–World War I "schism in American scholarship" between the humanities and the social sciences partly in the fluidity of categories in the subjects of the human studies and in the embryonic organization of scholarship during the early years of the century. The division between the modern humanists and social scientists, he argues, began in the effort of the new disciplines to define themselves as the classical curriculum broke down in the late nineteenth century. A student of the new science of sociology has described "the whole atmosphere of social science" between about 1885 and 1915 as "one of struggle for legitimacy against adversaries."[70]

In the attempts during the late nineteenth and early twentieth centuries to define and delimit the disciplines, historians found themselves in an ambiguous position: on the defensive against assaults on their legitimacy by the new social scientists and divided among themselves about the nature of their discipline and its proper relationship to the social sciences. Higham attributes considerable significance to the prewar quarrel among historians about the extent to which they should ally themselves with social scientists, seeing in the disagreement a premonition of the larger schism in American scholarship that would develop after the war.[71]

History in America became professionalized by differentiating itself from philosophy and literature and establishing itself on a scientific basis. The first generation of professional historians adopted not only the methods of science—empirical research, a critical approach to evidence, and inductive generalization—but its spirit as well: the repudiation of romantic idealism and its search for ultimate meaning. Misreading Leopold von Ranke, they drew a sharp distinction between the science and

70. John Higham, "The Schism in American Scholarship," *American Historical Review,* LXXII (October, 1966), 1–21, and Becker, *The Lost Science of Man,* 9n.
71. Higham, "The Schism in American Scholarship," 13.

the philosophy of history, eschewed an interpretive approach and a search for laws to explain historical development, and confined themselves to a rigid factualism in an effort to recreate the past as it actually was.[72] Scientific history soon drew fire from the social sciences on the grounds that it was, in fact, highly unscientific, if not thoroughly meaningless. For example, at a session of the American Historical Association (AHA) annual meeting in 1903 devoted to the relation of history to the social sciences, Albion Small "contended that the historians ... spend all their time in indexing dreary, profitless details about inconsequential folk, in developing their technical skill for the discovery of insignificant objects, in learning so much about how to investigate that they have forgotten what is worth investigating." Continuing the assault, Lester Ward charged that history was not a science because it was not concerned with causation, only with facts. Delivering the coup de grâce, "he declared [history] to be an agreeable occupation and a pleasant pastime."[73]

Considering the severity of the attack, it is not difficult to understand the heated tone in which George Burton Adams defended orthodox scientific history in his presidential address to the AHA in 1908. Using the language of conflict, he characterized the approach to history of political scientists, geographers, economic determinists, sociologists, and social psychologists as "a hostile movement," an "aggressive and vigorous school of thought" that threatened to drive the traditional historian from the field. This "disturbance in our province," he declared, represented a passing from the age of investigation to the perilous age of speculation (from which, he might have added, the first generation of professional historians had labored so assiduously to emerge). "What should the historian do," Adams asked, "in view of the threatened invasion of his domain by ideals and methods not quite his own?" He answered, in essence, that the historian must stick to his task of scientifically gathering the facts because, in the final analysis, if ever a philosophy of history was to emerge it could do so only on a firm foundation of fact. "At the beginning of all conquest of the unknown," he declared,

72. Higham et al., History, 92–103.
73. "What Is History?" American Historical Review, IX (1904), 449, 450.

"lies the fact. . . . The field of the historian is, and must long remain, the discovery and recording of what actually happened."[74]

The assault on scientific history came not only from hostile outsiders; by the early twentieth century there was defection within the ranks, as historians themselves divided along the lines suggested by the social scientists. A comparison of the address of Adams with those of his fellow historians at the International Congress of Arts and Science in St. Louis in 1904 offers evidence of this division. The remarks of Woodrow Wilson, James Harvey Robinson, and Frederick Jackson Turner at the congress were collectively a plea for interpretive history, for a rejection of narrative political history in favor of the study of history as a neverending process of social development, which could be understood only by studying all aspects of human life and relying on all the allied sciences of human behavior. In contrast, Adams' paper amounted to an argument that history is fixed, there to be discovered by the historian, who mines the facts and from them constructs a narrative good for all time.[75]

The sources of the challenge by historians to scientific history, dubbed "the new history" by Robinson in 1912, were varied. Nurtured in the Progressive era and reflecting its spirit of democratic reform, infused with a "softened," nonideological version of Marxism, which was apparent not only in its emphasis of economic factors but in its view of causation and law in history, the new history was responding also to the prospect of the desertion of history by the social scientists. In its main outlines the new history comprised a deliberate subordination of the past to the present by selecting and emphasizing those aspects of the past most relevant to present needs; a widening of the scope of history away from the institutional focus of scientific history to embrace all aspects of human affairs; and an enthusiastic alliance with the social

74. George Burton Adams, "History and the Philosophy of History," *American Historical Review*, XIV (January, 1909), 224, 227, 229, 235, 236.
75. Cf. Woodrow Wilson, "The Variety and Unity of History," James Harvey Robinson, "The Conception and Methods of History," Frederick Jackson Turner, "Problems in American History," and George Burton Adams, "The Present Problems of Medieval History," all in Howard J. Rogers (ed.), *Congress of Arts and Science, Universal Exposition, St. Louis, 1904* (Boston and New York, 1905–1907), II, 3–20, 40–51, 183–94, 125–38.

sciences, with a view toward discovering laws of human development.[76] Particularly in their emphasis on the present, the new historians were expressing their conviction that the discipline derived its legitimacy from being a "useful" science. This conviction was expressed perfectly in a frequently quoted sentence from the introduction to James Harvey Robinson and Charles Beard's *The Development of Modern Europe*. Admitting that they "consistently subordinated the past to the present," the authors averred that it had been their "ever-conscious aim to enable the reader to catch up with his own times; to read intelligently the foreign news in the morning paper; to know what was the attitude of Leo XIII toward the Social Democrats even if he has forgotten that of Innocent III toward the Albigenses."[77] The new historians self-consciously emphasized the practical utility of their discipline; they "wanted history to prove itself."[78]

The orthodox and reform historians shared the field before World War I and frequently were united in "the common cause of superseding amateur scholarship." Furthermore, in many areas the reformers accepted the basic principles of orthodoxy.[79] Nevertheless, their attack on scientific history was sharp, even belligerent, and the discipline clearly was divided. In the emerging split between the humanities and the social sciences, history stood somewhere in the middle, unsure of its essential character. Paradoxically, those who opposed the "adulteration" of history with social science were speaking in the name of "scientific" history; those who argued in favor of an alliance with the social sciences were speaking of introducing meaning (*i.e.*, value) into history; all the while, the social sciences themselves deliberately were moving away from the realm of value into that of empiricism.

The issue of the relationship between fact and value was a large one in early twentieth-century American thought; in almost all its branches there was a quest for a means to unite science and ethics in the interest of social reform. To be sure, the "new" social theorists in economics, so-

76. Higham *et al., History,* 104–16, 171–82.
77. James Harvey Robinson and Charles Beard, *The Development of Modern Europe* (New York, 1907–1908), I, iii.
78. Higham *et al., History*, 112.
79. *Ibid.*, 183, 104, 114–15.

ciology, philosophy, political science, history, and jurisprudence sought
first to divorce science from morality, to make science "objective,"
because the two united traditionally had been an instrument of conservatism. But their objective was to establish morality on a scientific
foundation by making science the arbiter of ethical problems. As non-
revolutionary critics of "the glaring evils of capitalism," the "new"
scholars sought to apply the scientific method to social problems and
thus to formulate a science of reform.[80]

Similar concerns about the nature and function of knowledge were reflected in efforts to reestablish the unity of knowledge after the great
fragmentation and specialization of the late nineteenth century. The urgency of the problem of unification was suggested by the attempts in
nearly every field of thought to reconcile factual and normative knowledge and to consider the significance of rapidly accumulating "facts,"
their relationship to each other, and their place in the whole realm of
knowledge and experience. The 1904 International Congress of Arts
and Science, which brought together leading scholars in all fields of
thought to consider the problem, approached it from an idealist perspective: reconciliation was to be accomplished by recognizing the "inner
unity" of all branches of learning and acknowledging the human intellect and "psychical" causes as the chief social determinants.[81]

Theorists who rejected the idealist view were equally committed to
the quest for unity, as Jean Quandt's study, *From the Small Town to
the Great Community,* makes clear. Quandt demonstrates the dedication
of Progressive intellectuals to offset the individual isolation and fragmentation of life in urban, industrial America and to restore a sense of
community, purpose, and shared value; she points out that they saw in

80. Morton G. White, *Social Thought in America: The Revolt Against
Formalism* (New York, 1949), 28–29, 46. In *The Lost Science of Man*, Becker locates the central problem of the emergent discipline of sociology in efforts to
make the "indignant ethical man" compatible with the "detached scientist" and
thus to end the glaring disproportion between science and ethics. See pp. 20, 22,
81. George H. Haines IV and Frederick H. Jackson, "A Neglected Landmark
in the History of Ideas," *Mississippi Valley Historical Review,* XXXIV (September, 1947), 201–20. The authors point out that, in fact, the contributors to the
congress delved into their own fields of specialization, giving lip service only to
the grand theme of unity.

the restoration of the unity of knowledge a means to this end. Their commitment to the new scholarship was not a random pursuit of truth for its own sake; they firmly believed that free inquiry would reveal the essential unity of knowledge and the oneness of man, nature, and society. Using Dewey as a prime example of this point of view, Quandt shows how he opposed the split between the cultural and the useful and the overspecialization of knowledge. Knowledge was power, according to Dewey; therefore its expansion certainly was not to be halted. But it was to be tied to action and available for use rather than compartmentalized and separated from the totality of experience.[82] The "new" theorists became the ideologists of Progressivism; they provided the intellectual foundation for attacks on laissez-faire capitalism and contributed to the prevailing faith in knowledge as an instrument of social change.[83] As individuals, they participated in reform movements of all sorts, exulting in action to such an extent that "active participation in politics, economics, and social reform became a professorial hallmark."[84]

According to Hofstadter, the Progressive era was a high-water mark of rapprochement between the intellectual and American society. The new complexity of government and administration that was a consequence of the need to control the economy, he argues, resulted in a widely acknowledged dependence on expertise. The interests of democracy itself led to an abatement of the suspicion of the expert that had originated in the democratic ethos of Jacksonian America. In the Progressive era, Hofstadter affirms, "partly as expert, partly as social critic, the intellectual now came back to a central position such as he had not held in American politics for a century." The ferment in ideas, although it did not bring a social revolution, created a widespread confidence among intellectuals that the gulf between the world of thought and the world of action finally had been bridged, affecting the morale even of those scholars whose work was far removed from the bustle of everyday

82. Jean B. Quandt, *From the Small Town to the Great Community: The Social Thought of Progressive Intellectuals* (New Brunswick, 1970), especially Chap. 8. The book includes an intellectual who did not reject the idealist view; Josiah Royce plays a large part in the study.

83. Sidney Fine, *Laissez-Faire and the General Welfare State* (Ann Arbor, 1956), 169–288, and White, *Social Thought in America.*

84. Herbst, *German Historical School,* 162.

life. Hofstadter concludes that "the most abstracted of scholars could derive a sense of importance from belonging to a learned community which the larger world was compelled to consult in its quest for adequate means of social control."[85] Higham, noting the relative decline in status of humanistic scholars during the early years of the twentieth century, considers Hofstadter's characterization "too simple [a] picture." Although the new type of professor, the practical man, the expert, was winning public approval, he argues, "the humanistic scholar more often felt elbowed aside" and by the time of World War I was being dramatized as a self-denigrator in the new academic novels and had become the prime butt of popular jokes about absentmindedness.[86]

The differences between Hofstadter and Higham suggest some of the difficulties in dealing with the subject of the academic intellectual's status in American society. In their social origins, the World War I generation of professors still represented a fairly homogeneous group. Existing evidence suggests that the chief breeding ground for the first and second generations of professional university scholars (those reaching maturity between the 1870s and the First World War), as for their pre-professional predecessors, still was the New England Protestant middle class.[87] But there was no single professorial "class" in America, no cultural elite with recognized social status and authority, no equivalent of the German "mandarinate."[88] Writing in 1906, William Graham Sumner pointed to the ambivalence of American attitudes toward intellect. On the one hand, he noted, Americans laud education and the multiplication of educational institutions; on the other hand they reserve their admiration for the "common man," with his supposedly superior store of native wisdom.[89] Merle Curti has dubbed this simultaneous faith in the

85. Richard Hofstadter, *Anti-Intellectualism in American Life* (New York, 1963), 198, 205.
86. Higham *et al.*, *History*, 65n, 65. Higham attributes this status decline in large part to social and professional changes attendant on the breakup of the aristocracy of culture.
87. Metzger, "Expansion and Profession," 54n.
88. See Veysey, *American University*, 301, and Shryock, "Academic Profession," 33. A penetrating portrait of the "mandarinate" in Germany may be found in Fritz K. Ringer, *The Decline of the German Mandarins: The German Academic Community, 1890–1933* (Cambridge, Mass., 1969).
89. William Graham Sumner, *Folkways* (Boston, 1906), 205–206.

rational and suspicion of the life of reason, which he sees continuing to our own time, an "American paradox."[90] Without probing the question of the sources of the paradox, a clue to the status of professors during the time of this study—the period of America's involvement in the First World War—may be found in Shryock's observation that the prestige of professors has risen during periods of involvement by them in the affairs of the "real" world. If professorial prestige periodically has risen, he argues, it is "not because Americans have ceased to prize action above thought, but rather that more academicians have qualified for recognition by becoming men of action."[91] Academicians in large numbers became "men of action" during United States involvement in the First World War. There is every indication that they were well aware of the correlation between their "usefulness" and their legitimacy in the eyes of American society.

In this respect and in many others, the response of American professors to the challenge of World War I provides a valuable test case for the subjects covered in this chapter and can be understood only in reference to them. When the war came upon America, the modern university in this country only recently had been established and lacked a clear identity and sense of purpose. It drew heavily on English and particularly on German influences but derived its special character and claim to legitimacy from a commitment to the ideal of service. Within the university the position of the faculty was insecure; its dual professional-employee status created tensions that could and did lead to confrontations and conflict. The scholarly disciplines themselves were in a rudimentary state and were seeking to define their character and limits. Professional consciousness too was rudimentary; the AAUP had just been founded in 1915 and commanded neither widespread support in the profession nor influence in the infrastructure of university politics. The social status of the newly professionalized professoriate was uncertain, reflecting the ambivalence of American society to the life of the mind. The challenge of war both exposed and sharpened many of the tensions, contradic-

90. Curti, *American Paradox*. The theme is treated in greater depth in his essay "Intellectuals and Other People."
91. Shryock, "Academic Profession," 53.

tions, and uncertainties in the academic community. Furthermore, it confronted professors with a challenge to their loyalties. They found that loyalties that could be maintained simultaneously during normal times—to one's country, institution, professional standards and ideals, to the cause of peace, and to friends and colleagues—suddenly came into conflict in the crucible of war, and choices were forced on the basis of priorities that were not necessarily acknowledged or even recognized. The challenge of war brought into sharp focus questions concerning the uses of knowledge and the uses of the university in modern America.

II

Neutrality
Years

BY THE TIME American professors were confronted with the challenge of war, the European conflict already was almost three years old. In the period between the war's outbreak and American intervention, opinion took shape among American professors, forming the basis for their eventual view that it was necessary or desirable for America to enter the war. Although the full spectrum of opinion from pro-Germanism to neutrality to support for the Allies was represented on the campus, the greatest weight was on one side. In that American professors overwhelmingly sympathized with the Allies, they mirrored the sentiment of the American public. One element of their attitude toward the belligerents, however, was unique and partook of the professors' previous professional experience. Although critical from the start of German objectives and methods in the war, many American professors could join the chorus of condemnation of Germany, particularly when the chorus had a vulgar ring, only after confronting the role that Germany had played in their professional lives. The confrontation proved to be complicated and painful, adding a personal dimension to these professors' anti-German sentiment. A review of the climate of opinion on the American campus during the neutrality years is essential to the subject of the American professors' eventual support of the war.

Writing to a friend in Canada, the University of Minnesota political scientist Cephas D. Allin recounted an "amusing" feature of the 1915 American Historical Association convention. Two men of known pro-Ally sentiment were scheduled to appear on a panel to discuss the issues of the war. The program committee, in an effort at impartiality, "put on a man of German extraction to represent what they expected to be the German side of the question, but unfortunately, the man chosen was Lingelbach of Pennsylvania . . . and Lingelbach was more anti-German than any of the rest."[1] The program committee could have found acknowledged spokesmen for the German cause or at least individuals who publicly expressed sympathy for Germany's position, although in some instances to recruit members of social science disciplines other than history would have been necessary. The committee could, for example, have called on John W. Burgess, retired from Columbia University where he had used the German model to build the first graduate faculty of political science in an American university and who, after successfully negotiating (along with Nicholas Murray Butler) the German-American exchange professorships, had served as the first Roosevelt Professor at the University of Berlin in 1906–1907. Burgess seems to have been the only scholar who fully met the expectation of the founders of the German University League that intellectual and professional indebtedness to Germany would lead American professors naturally to sympathize with German aims in the war.[2]

In 1915 Burgess published an analysis of the war that was essentially the same as the position of the German spokesmen for the Central Powers.[3] He described Germany as being in the vanguard of civilization, a

1. Cephas D. Allin to George M. Jones, January 15, 1916, in Department of Political Science Correspondence, University of Minnesota Archives, hereinafter cited as Minnesota Department of Political Science Correspondence. "Lingelbach gave the best paper in the whole convention," Allin concluded, "and I felt very proud of him indeed."
2. For Burgess' role in the founding of the faculty of political science and his profound indebtedness to German mentors, see R. Gordon Hoxie, "John W. Burgess, American Scholar: Book 1, the Founding of the Faculty of Political Science" (Ph. D. dissertation, Columbia University, 1950).
3. John W. Burgess, *The European War of 1914: Its Causes, Purposes, and Probable Results* (Chicago, 1915). For a detailed exposition of the German view see William W. Whitelock (trans.), *Modern Germany in Relation to the Great War* (New York, 1916).

peace-loving, democratic nation whose overseas policy was the pursuit of commerce, not territorial expansion. He believed that, far from having initiated the conflict, the German nation was the victim of Allied aggression. Burgess attributed the war exclusively to Allied imperialism: Russian desire to expand into the Balkans, French desire "to make conquest of Elsass-Lothringen," and British determination to crush Germany's political, industrial, and commercial power. In response, Germany was fighting to secure the freedom of the seas and to contain the threat from the barbarian East. The war was the agency, Burgess proclaimed, by which mankind would choose subjugation under the hegemony of the degenerate British Empire or free development under the authority of the progressive Central Powers. For this reason and because, historically, German "militarism" always had come to America's aid whereas British navalism had been America's chief enemy, Burgess believed that it was in the direct interest of the United States for victory to go to Germany and its allies.[4]

Burgess went even further than the kaiser's government to defend the German cause when he tried to demonstrate that the German Empire never was pledged to uphold Belgian neutrality.[5] Burgess' views and the way he supported them were regarded with great disfavor by fellow scholars. Harvard's Albert Bushnell Hart, professor of government, called Burgess a "doddering old idiot" and observed, "I do not know of another man in the whole lot [of Americans who had participated in the exchange professorships] who has been so affected by his residence in

4. Burgess publicly protested American trade, particularly in munitions, with and loans to the Allies not only as unneutral and therefore contrary to international law but as portending the "denationalization" of America—its splitting up into component ethnic parts. See numerous memoranda and petitions to public officials and letters to the press in New York City, Rhode Island, and Washington, D.C. in John W. Burgess Papers, Special Collections, Columbia University Library.

5. Burgess, *The European War of 1914*, Chap. 6. Burgess elaborated on and refined his arguments in *America's Relation to the Great War* (Chicago, 1916). After American intervention in the war, both books were withdrawn from circulation by mutual agreement between Burgess and the publisher. See John W. Burgess to Henry Cabot Lodge, September 20, 1918, in Burgess Papers.

Berlin as to come to the defense of Germany."[6] Only a little bit more charitable, Guy Stanton Ford, professor of history at the University of Minnesota, wrote that Burgess' book *The European War of 1914* "has been regarded by friends of Professor Burgess as more the evidence of his senility than of his intelligence or patriotic motives."[7]

Burgess' books are unique examples of public, fully developed, and unreserved commitment to the German cause by an American scholar. But other men expressed themselves briefly in print in a way to suggest at least sympathy for Germany's position. The historians William M. Sloane of Columbia, William R. Shepherd of Columbia, and Preserved Smith, who had no institutional affiliation at the time, all spoke disparagingly of America's overwhelmingly pro-Ally sentiment. Sloane reminded Americans of their own history of expansion by compulsion and conquest, and Smith was indignant at Britain's moral outrage over German behavior in Belgium, which, on the basis of Britain's imperial record, he considered to be rank hypocrisy.[8] The University of Pennsylvania economist Simon N. Patten challenged the charge that Germany was the aggressor nation. He saw the war as the "inevitable" expression of the underlying reality that "Germany stands for the rising economic interests of Central Europe, while the Allies arrayed against her represent the various forms of race feeling dominant in the smaller states." Between the two there was one choice, for "the race patriot is a nuisance, a menace, a bar to progress," whereas the Central Powers, representing the economic future of the continent, are "the standard bearers of progress." Within the context of this interpretation, he viewed moral outrage

6. Albert Bushnell Hart to Frank Taussig, April 6, 1915, in Albert Bushnell Hart Papers, Houghton Library, Harvard University. Burgess appeared to Hart to be "an example of the American perverted by too close contact with Germany and German ideas.... Burgess absorbed the formal, analytic side of his German teaching and lost sight of the actualities which are at the bottom of government." Hart to F. E. Chadwick, October 18, 1915, in Hart Papers.

7. Guy Stanton Ford to George Creel, February 15, 1918, in U.S. Committee on Public Information Papers, National Archives, cited hereinafter as CPI Papers.

8. William M. Sloane, "Fair Play and Neutrality," *Vital Issue*, I (1914), 8–9; New York *Times*, September 20, 1914, Sec. 4, p. 1, November 11, 1915, p. 5; Preserved Smith, letters to the editor, *Nation*, XCIX (November 5, 1914), 548, *Nation*, C (February 11, 1915), 168–69, and *Nation* CIV (March 1, 1917), 238.

against the violation of Belgian neutrality as an inappropriate response. "Every nation in periods of growth has disregarded the rights of its weaker neighbors. . . . Growth [always] has meant a centralization which eliminates the weak to the advantage of the strong," Patten remarked.[9]

From the perspective of cultural relativism Franz Boas, the German-born Columbia University anthropologist, tried to balance the scales of public opinion that were weighted so heavily against Germany. He pointed out to Americans that, in condemning the ideals and political and social system of the German nation, they unjustifiably were elevating their own way of life to the status of universal truth. "The American . . . is inclined to consider American standards of thought and action as absolute standards; and the more idealistic his nature, the more strongly he wishes to 'raise' every one to his own standards. . . . He claims that the form of his own Government is the best, not for himself only, but also for the rest of mankind; that his interpretation of ethics, of religion, of standards of living, is right. Therefore, he is inclined to assume the role of a dispenser of happiness to mankind." Boas cautioned Americans to remember that "nations have distinctive individualities, which are expressed in their modes of life, thought, and feeling." With obvious reference to American antipathy toward German statism, he pleaded for recognition that a thickly settled country sometimes must restrict individual freedom of action in the interest of community welfare.[10] Boas' letters to his family during August, 1914, are a private expression of anguish over "false patriotism" in all countries. "That one cherishes one's own way of life is a natural thing," he acknowledged. "But does one need to nourish the thought that it is the best of all, that everything which is different is not good but useless, that it is right to despise the people of other nations?" Regarding the causes of the war itself, Boas declared that "Ger-

---

9. Simon N. Patten, letters to the editor, *New Republic,* I (November 14, 1914), 21–22, and *New Republic,* I (November 28, 1914), 22. By 1917 Patten had changed his views sufficiently to enable him to support American intervention in the war. See Daniel M. Fox, *The Discovery of Abundance: Simon N. Patten and the Transformation of Social Theory* (Ithaca, 1967), 124.

10. New York *Times,* January 8, 1916, p. 8.

man arrogance, French lust for revenge, English envy, lust for power—
these are behind the whole thing."[11]

Boas was consistent in his view that it was unwarranted to interfere in
the internal affairs of another state, even when that view was at the expense of his own political preferences. He was invited to join the Society
of the Friends of the German Republic, an organization of Americans
of German birth or descent, whose purpose was "to aid the German
people to establish a Government responsible to the people," *i.e.*, to encourage the overthrow of the kaiser's government. Boas declined the invitation on the grounds that it was "impudent and futile for citizens of
one State to arrogate to themselves the right to interfere in any way with
the political affairs of another State." After the November, 1918, revolution in Germany, Boas asked to join the society for the same reason that
he previously had refused the proffered membership—to guarantee the
security of German democracy from outside interference: "German
democracy has been born, and my hearty wishes go out to it. It is no
longer a question of interfering in Germany, but of preventing improper
interference on the part of our own country. There is grave danger that
German democracy may appear too free to American conservatism. . . .
I wish to join your society provided you can assure me that your en-
deavors will be directed towards the prevention of interference with the
free development of Germany." Boas was told that under these conditions he was not welcome as a member.[12]

11. Franz Boas to his son Ernst, August 6, 1914, to his wife, August 7, 1914,
and to his son Heinrich, August 15, 1914, all in Ronald P. Rohner (ed.), *The
Ethnography of Franz Boas* (Chicago, 1969), 271–75. Boas said he could not
"warm up for either side. If the war was unavoidable, the brutal actions of Germany could be explained by her emergency. But I cannot forgive them the breach
of their contract with Belgium."
12. Franz Boas to J. Koettgen, September 25, 1917, Boas to the President of
the American Friends of German Democracy, November 19, 1918, and Franz
Sigel to Boas, November 22, 1918, all sent by Boas to the *Nation*, where the
letters were published in CVII (December 7, 1918), 704. By contrast, Burgess'
affection for Germany did not survive the collapse of the kaiser's government.
Asked by Boas to join an association to promote intellectual cooperation between
America and the German republic, Burgess replied: "I am not sure that any close
intellectual relation with Germany under its present regime is desirable for our
country. The Germany of Ebert and Barth and Scheidemann and Liebknecht is

Despite these evidences of outright pro-Germanism, sympathy for Germany, and attempts at impartiality, the preponderance of opinion on the American campus was hostile to Germany and in favor of the Allies. For example, in response to a suggestion in 1915 that Harvard employ a stranded German professor, the historian Archibald Cary Coolidge replied that he did "not think that Harvard, or pretty much any American university would be a pleasant place for a German professor to teach or reside in, as long as the war lasts. The atmosphere is too overcharged." Guy Stanton Ford recalled that, although professors' sentiment during the neutrality years generally "partook of the attitude of the region [where their institution was located]," it was "more [pro-Allied] than anything else." And the Yale economist Henry W. Farnam reported in late 1914 that he had "not yet met a single acquaintance, whether in academic or business circles who does not desire the success of the allies in the war."[13]

Pro-Ally sentiment among professors was comprised of two complementary elements: an identification of American interests—political, economic, cultural, and strategic—with those of Great Britain and a view of Germany as the aggressor nation, whose political system and world political ambitions represented a threat to those interests and to world peace. The first of these elements rarely was expressed separately; usually it appeared with a critique of German ambitions and conduct. The Yale historian George B. Adams is an exception. He was convinced that American interests lay in close cooperation with Great Britain, and he interpreted the war largely in that light. Indeed, in 1898 he had looked forward to war with Spain as a means of drawing the United

---

not the Germany I knew and respected, but it is the Germany which, in my day, was regarded as little less dangerous to our Western Civilization than the present Bolshevism of Russia." John W. Burgess to Franz Boas, undated, in Burgess Papers.

13. Archibald Cary Coolidge to Walter Lichtenstein, June 26, 1915, in Archibald Cary Coolidge Papers, Harvard University Archives; "Memoir of Guy Stanton Ford" (Oral History Collection, Special Collections, Columbia University Library, 1955), II, 367; Henry W. Farnam to Gilbert Parker, October 28, 1914, in Henry W. Farnam Papers, Historical Manuscripts Collection, Yale University Library. See also Clarence Alvord to Albert Beveridge, September 10, 1915, in Albert Beveridge Papers, Library of Congress, and Paul Elmer More, "The Philosophy of the War," *Unpopular Review*, III (January–March, 1915), 14.

States and Britain together. He had written, "It is one of my fondest
hopes to see a cordial agreement btwn Eng. & the U. S. at least upon
general questions of policy.... I should my self regard a war with
Spain, or with almost any other country, as worth all it might cost if it
should result in bringing our two nations into some kind of a union
upon a policy of mutual support and defense." When war came he had
hoped for an incident that would require British assistance to solidify
the new friendship between the two countries. "One such act, downright
and unmistakable, would be worth reams of kind words, important as
they are, in putting a complete and final end to the past."[14]

During the neutrality years, Adams frequently expressed the opinion
that American ideals and interests were at stake in the war and that
these would justify, indeed necessitate, intervention to forestall German
victory. He wrote: "We are now so spread upon the map of the world,
other interests besides those of mere territory so link us with all those
quarters of the globe in which there still remains the question of empire,
that it is of vital importance to us what sort of power it is which exercises world empire in close contact with our interests and our possessions." Because German concepts of empire were based on "conquest
and exploitation" and because empire for the British meant "duty and
obligation," he concluded that "our interests and our possessions are secure alongside a British empire" and that "in time of stress we should
find in the British navy that means of protection for our outlying lands
which we have failed to provide for ourselves."[15] From a larger frame of
reference Adams argued: "When England falls the doom of the United
States is sounded. All our interests, those of language, commerce, civilization, and government, are common with her. History will declare that
England holds no interest in this war that we have not held with her."[16]
In a similar vein, although primarily concerned with German violation
of international law, the Johns Hopkins philosopher Arthur O. Lovejoy
observed that, "in spite of England's many past sins against the light,

14. George B. Adams to Hugh E. Egerton, March 16, 1898, and Adams to
Egerton, June 26, 1898, in George Burton Adams Papers, Historical Manuscripts
Collection, Yale University Library.
15. Chicago *Daily News,* August 22, 1916, clipping *ibid.*
16. New York *Times,* March 10, 1917, p. 2.

any serious weakening of the British Empire would be an incalculable and irreparable loss to the material and the higher moral interests of the United States, and to the cause of free government throughout the world."[17]

Advocacy of an Anglo-American entente did not necessarily imply the kind of concrete alliance that Adams seems to have meant. For example, Richard T. Ely, professor of economics at the University of Wisconsin, also welcomed the opportunity to cement the friendship of England and America, but he had in mind an intangible alliance. Confined to private expressions of opinion by President Charles R. Van Hise's admonition against faculty members discussing the war within the university community or taking public stands on its issues, Ely wrote numerous letters to British friends emphasizing the affinities of the English-speaking peoples and urging that the ties be strengthened after the war.[18] Ely believed that "it is in the interest of Americans, as well as of English people, that we should get closer together." Reminding his English friends of the influence on the United States exercised by German universities, he advocated a modification of the British university system to attract American students and "to bring together the higher education of England and America." He expressed the hope "that it may be possible to make plans to bring together more closely the English speaking people of the world after the war." Although he believed that America could "never belong to the British Empire as a political entity," he wanted "to see above the British Empire an intellectual and spiritual Empire which shall take us in also." Ely urged that, in order to counteract any possible influence of German propaganda in the United States, "there should be those in this country whose business it would be to give enlightenment and bestir themselves in behalf of the allies." He explained, "My idea would be that England should send a number of

17. Arthur O. Lovejoy, letter to the editor, New Republic, X (February 17, 1917), 75.
18. For the Van Hise statement see faculty minutes, September 28, 1914, pp. 191–92, in Faculty Documents, University of Wisconsin Archives, hereinafter cited as Wisconsin Faculty Documents. Because of the large German-American population in the state and because the war aroused emotion-charged "race feeling," Van Hise viewed it as a divisive subject akin to partisan politics, which the university was forbidden by law to engage in.

strong men to this country to watch over her interests and to advance them as occasion may offer."[19]

Ely defended American neutrality as the most effective way of aiding the Allies' war effort. He was not convinced, he said, that in its present state of military unpreparedness the United States could do any more than it was doing for the Allies. Furthermore, he pointed out, "England and the Allies derive the greatest benefits from American neutrality," particularly in food and war supplies, and therefore should help to maintain the status quo.[20] This was a refreshingly frank defense of neutrality in terms of its implications, rather than on technical and legal grounds. In reply to charges that the sale of munitions to the Allies was unneutral, American scholars more typically argued that arms shipments reflected not government policy but British control of the seas and that withholding them from the Allies would be an unneutral action.[21] This position may be technically correct, but it is not insignificant that neutrality under the conditions of British control of the seas accorded so conveniently and well with American inclination to support the Allies. It would have been unthinkable for the United States to have pursued a policy of neutrality that really damaged the Allied cause and significantly aided the Central Powers.

Professors were engrossed more frequently in discussions of German ideals and interests than of Anglo-American affinities, reflecting their view that Germany was responsible for bringing on the war and, under its present political system, represented a perpetual threat to world peace. Shortly after the war began, the noted German professor Georg Simmel wrote to his fellow sociologist Albion W. Small of the University of Chicago to complain that the world was believing lies about Germany. Challenging the basis of Simmel's complaint, Small rejoined that nine out of ten American professors were, like himself, not sympathetic to Germany's claim of being the injured party. American evaluation of

19. Richard T. Ely to R. H. Rew, January 28, 1915, November 10, 1914, Ely to Horace Plunkett, December 22, December 23, 1915, and Ely to C. F. Bastable, April 23, 1915, all in Ely Papers.

20. Ely to E. Williams, January 28, 1915, Ely to Rew, January 28, 1915, *ibid.*

21. See, for example, Arthur O. Lovejoy, letter to the editor, *New Republic,* IV (September 11, 1915), 156–57, and Munroe Smith, "American Diplomacy in the European War," *Political Science Quarterly,* XXXI (December, 1916), 513–18.

the claims of the belligerents, he explained, rested neither on sensational atrocity stories nor on any naïve conclusions from "the Belgian incident" that Germany's political morality was lower than that of England or France. It was clear to all, Small continued, that militarism was behind the war; and, although he acknowledged the presence of militarism in all the warring nations, he insisted that "nobody knows better than the Germans that they have nowhere more startlingly exemplified their racial superiority of *thoroughness* than in their preparedness for war and in their theories about war." He concluded, *"Germany has done more than all the rest of the world put together in the way of elaborating and publishing this militaristic ideal."*[22]

Small's statistical estimate of professorial sentiment was impressionistic, but the written evidence supports his conclusion that there was not much discernible sympathy for German ambitions and conduct among the ranks of American professors. From the private correspondence and the publicistic and scholarly writings of professors, a picture emerges of Germany, bent on challenging British naval, commercial, and colonial supremacy, seizing the opportunity presented by the 1914 diplomatic crisis to do so, and engaging in outlaw tactics under dubious justifications of "might makes right" and military necessity. Germany was portrayed as a militaristic autocracy, which unless defeated would be a perpetual threat not only to peace but to "civilization," *i.e.,* Anglo-American culture, ideals of government, and principles of law and ethics.

In random comments professors expressed the view that Germany was chiefly responsible for precipitating the war and was a peculiarly dangerous and contemptible adversary. For example, immediately after the war began, the University of Chicago historian William E. Dodd branded Germany the aggressor and called the kaiser "a menace to mankind."[23] Similarly, the historian Frank J. Mather of Princeton declared

22. Albion W. Small, "Germany and American Opinion," *Sociological Review,* VIII (April, 1915), 106–11. Small's letter to Simmel was written on October 29, 1914. At that time Small hoped the war would end in a stalemate so that militarism everywhere would be discredited and abolished.

23. William E. Dodd to W. L. Chenery, August 22, 1914, in William E. Dodd Papers, Library of Congress.

that the Allied war effort was "merely . . . a gigantic and most difficult police enterprise against a power which has wantonly broken the peace of Europe."[24] Dodd's colleague, Andrew C. McLaughlin, charged that "Little Will has made a fearful blunder. Not only was the whole diplomatic strategy stupid to the verge of criminality, but his continual insistence on the right & glory of might has done more than any other one thing to make a vast war come."[25] Protesting against the German conduct of war, the University of Illinois political scientist James W. Garner characterized the destruction of the University of Louvain as the most heinous military crime "since the burning of the library of Alexandria."[26] The University of Michigan historian Claude H. Van Tyne portrayed the Allied war effort as a fight to save "the cause of democracy" and ridiculed the kaiser as "International 'Bugaboo Bill.' "[27] On the heels of American intervention, Ely characterized the war as a "fight for civilization and human liberty against barbarism."[28]

In analytical treatments of German political, diplomatic, and military history, professors spelled out the view of German war guilt in greater detail. Adams devoted numerous letters to the editor, articles, interviews, and speeches to publicize his opinion that the war was caused by Germany's quest for world empire and determination to oust England by force from its position of colonial supremacy. He portrayed the war further as the challenge of German autocracy, a "highly centralized paternalism which regulates the minutest concerns of the citizen and makes him responsible in all details of life to a mechanical bureaucracy," to Anglo-Saxon democracy, "free individualism and local independence," and insisted that "the character of civilization itself" was at stake in the war's outcome.[29] Bernadotte Schmitt, historian at Western Reserve University, provided a detailed elaboration of this point of view in a lengthy book. He, too, portrayed the war as a German challenge to

24. New York *Times,* October 9, 1914, p. 8.
25. Andrew C. McLaughlin to William E. Dodd, September 10, 1914, in Dodd Papers.
26. James W. Garner, letter to the editor, *Nation,* XCIX (October 8, 1914), 431.
27. New York *Times,* September 6, 1916, p. 8, October 20, 1916, p. 8.
28. Richard Ely to Mrs. H. K. W. Bent, August 26, 1917, in Ely Papers.
29. Chicago *Daily News,* August 22, 1916, clipping in Adams Papers.

British naval, commercial, and colonial supremacy and as the challenge of a statist, bureaucratic, and militaristic autocracy to the dominant influence of a culture that championed individual liberty, peaceful compromise, and generosity to the vanquished. He concluded, "We are permitted to hope that British stubbornness, British credit, British valor will yet . . . prevail against the forces of militarism and absolutism, and that the German *débacle* . . . is as inevitable as the fall of the first French empire."[30]

Even when denunciation was absent, Germany was still held responsible for the outbreak of the war. For example, although the Yale historian Charles Seymour, unlike Adams and Schmitt, refused to pass judgment on Germany's right to claim "a place in the sun," his interpretation of German ambitions and actions was not unlike theirs. "The moral right of the German nation to . . . [predominant] political influence . . . can hardly be determined; the Germans sincerely believed that they, as well as the nations first in the field, had a right to world empire, and, if they were capable of seizing it, to supreme world empire. It was because political primacy on the continent seemed the essential basis of Germany's world empire that she was determined to give the law to Europe in 1914 either by diplomacy or by war."[31] Similarly, Munroe Smith, political scientist at Columbia University, also disclaiming any intention to condemn the Central Powers, located the war's source in the triumph of militarism at Berlin and Vienna and in the departure by German militarists from the cardinal principles of Bismarckian diplomacy, which stressed the value of the defensive position and the danger of preferring a policy aiming at power and prestige to one designed to promote national interest.[32]

The force of the issue of Germany's political system in determining lack of sympathy for its position in the war must not be underestimated. Even the pacifist David Starr Jordan, former president and chancellor of

30. Bernadotte Schmitt, *England and Germany, 1740–1914* (Princeton, 1918), 498.
31. Charles Seymour, *The Diplomatic Background of the War, 1870–1914* (New Haven, 1916), 287.
32. Munroe Smith, *Militarism and Statecraft* (New York, 1918). The book is a collection of articles that had begun to appear in print in 1914.

Stanford University, who thought Belgium alone of the nations involved
was without complicity in the war's outbreak, viewed dynastic Germany
as a special threat to world peace. Shortly after the war began he publicly branded Germany a dangerous "anachronism." He wrote, "Her
scientific ideals are of the twentieth century. Her political ideals hark
back to the sixteenth. . . . A great nation which its own people do not
control is a nation without a Government. It is a derelict on the international sea. It is a danger to its neighbors, a greater danger to itself." He
concluded, "Of all the many issues, good or bad, which may come from
this war, none is more important than this, that the German people
should take possess[ion] of Germany."[33]

The view that Germany was an inherently warlike autocracy that
must, consequently, be defeated was a characteristic starting point of
professorial opinion about the war; but it did not necessarily lead to uniform conclusions about the nature of the Allies. In 1915 the economist
Thorstein Veblen, at the time a lecturer at the University of Missouri,
published a detailed analysis of Germany's remarkable technical and industrial accomplishments since the late nineteenth century. He attributed Germany's success both to the latecomer's advantage of having
the model of a ready-made industrial system at its disposal (the initial
and persistent technological and cultural costs of innovation falling on
the pioneer nation—England) and to the capacity of the dynastic state to
develop and harness the system for its own interests. The book is important as much for its contribution to Veblen's theory of modern business
enterprise as for its comparison of the dynastic states and the Western
democracies. But Veblen developed at considerable length a picture of
the German political system as a reactionary, essentially feudal autocracy, demanding fealty and subservience from its subjects and relying
on aggression as the best means to counteract the disintegration of discipline in modern life.[34]

33. New York *Times,* September 23, 1914, p. 8. For the evolution of Jordan's
views from pacifist noninterventionism to support of American involvement in the
war, see Edward M. Burns, *David Starr Jordan: Prophet of Freedom* (Stanford,
1953), 23–32, 84–85.
34. Thorstein Veblen, *Imperial Germany and the Industrial Revolution* (Ann
Arbor, 1966), xx, Chap. 3.

This is not to say that Veblen charged Germany with special responsibility for the outbreak of the world war. On the contrary, his argument
was so detached that it lent itself to contradictory interpretations. After
American intervention in the war, the book was both banned under the
Espionage Act by the Post Office Department and recommended as
good propaganda by the government Committee on Public Information
(CPI).[35] It is to a later book, *An Inquiry into the Nature of Peace and
the Terms of Its Perpetuation,* published in April, 1917, that one must
turn for Veblen's preference in the war. Here Veblen argued that the
first condition for the establishment of peace was the defeat of Germany
and its allies, the dynastic powers that depended on war to accomplish
their predatory schemes. However, in arguing for the defeat of Germany, Veblen was far from espousing the cause of the Allies. If he believed that the establishment of world peace depended on the defeat of
the Central Powers, he considered that a virtual revolution in the Allied
nations was essential for the perpetuation of world peace. Veblen traced
the origins of international conflict back to the institution of property
and the principles of business enterprise. He predicted that, unless there
was a relinquishment of "upperclass and pecuniary control," with all its
restrictive practices and neglect of popular well-being, the victorious Allies would return to preservation of the rights of ownership by force.[36]

Veblen's detached indictment of the German system was unusual; the
partisan position of the Columbia University sociologist Franklin H.
Giddings was far more characteristic. Giddings not only denounced Germany as a militarist, absolutist state, but he also interpreted the war as a
conflict between autocracy and democracy. He not only proclaimed that
victory for the Central Powers would mean the vindication and expansion of militarism and autocracy, but he argued, as a corollary, that
democracy and world peace depended on an Allied victory. Like

35. Joseph Dorfman, *Thorstein Veblen and His America* (New York, 1961),
382.
36. Veblen included Japan, one of the Allies, among the atavistic, dynastic
powers. See Thorstein Veblen, *Essays in Our Changing Order,* ed. Leon
Ardzrooni (New York, 1964), 248–66, and Thorstein Veblen, *An Inquiry into the
Nature of Peace and the Terms of Its Perpetuation* (New York, 1945).

Adams, Giddings had applauded the Spanish-American War for leading to a "good understanding and friendly alliance with Great Britain." Originally a member of the Anti-Imperialist League, shortly after the Spanish-American War he declared that, "among the bitterest opponents of all that has been done, none is found who does not rejoice that at last we recognize our kinsmen over sea as our brethren and our co-workers in the tasks of civilization."[37] Although in the early months of the world war Giddings had praised "public socialism" in Germany,[38] he came to see the war as a Manichaean struggle between darkness and light. Calling for total victory for the Allies, he described the conflict as the "last stand of the massed and organized forces of despotism against liberty, enlightenment and progress" and declared, "If it is won by the democratic peoples, it is won forever." Should Britain and France be defeated, another war between autocracy and democracy inevitably would ensue. "There can be no enduring peace on this earth until absolutism is destroyed," he concluded.[39] After the United States intervened in the war, Giddings developed his views in *The Responsible State,* in which he feverishly called for the destruction of the Prussian state because it was a "metaphysical monstrosity," abstract, idealized, unrestrained in its exercise of power. "To exorcise this monstrosity and cast it out forever, the civilized world is arrayed against the Hohenzollern in desolating conflict," he declaimed. "Back of all immediate aims lies the ulterior purpose of the allied nations to define the powers and to establish the supremacy of a responsible state, accountable to the conscience of mankind."[40]

Professors found in the conduct of the war further proof that the Ger-

37. Franklin H. Giddings, *Democracy and Empire: With Studies of Their Psychological, Economic, and Moral Foundations* (London, 1900), 285. For Giddings' earlier identity as an antiimperialist see Fred H. Harrington, "The Anti-Imperialist Movement in the United States, 1898–1900," *Mississippi Valley Historical Review,* XXII (September, 1935), 211–30.

38. New York *Times,* October 20, 1914, p. 12, October 25, 1914, Sec. 5, p. 4.

39. Franklin H. Giddings, "The Bases of an Enduring Peace," *International Conciliation,* No. 113 (April, 1917), 14, 16.

40. Franklin H. Giddings, *The Responsible State: A Reexamination of Fundamental Political Doctrines in the Light of World War and the Menace of Anarchism* (Boston, 1918), 7.

man state was a menace. They regarded Germany's actions in Belgium and its use of the submarine against passenger vessels and merchant shipping as illegal and immoral and, consequently, viewed Germany with particular suspicion and hostility. Even Boas found the violation of Belgian neutrality unforgivable; he despaired that it had taken place. "Why did Germany overrun Belgium and thereby lose the sympathy of all the world?" he lamented. "There must have been a reason which we do not know."[41] Wallace Notestein, historian at the University of Minnesota, expressed bitter disappointment at America's passing over the "violation of Belgium and innumerable German atrocities."[42] Lovejoy called for breaking diplomatic relations with Germany over the sinking of non-combatant vessels carrying American passengers and seamen. Munroe Smith observed that the submarine could not function without disregarding considerations of humanity and violating the law and concluded, therefore, that its use against merchant vessels was inadmissible and constituted a form of outlawry.[43] Dodd called the sinking of the *Lusitania* "deliberate international murder" and suggested that "war may be the only way we can defend ourselves against the brutalities of a nation gone mad."[44] One year after the event, at the Carnegie Hall *Lusitania* Memorial Meeting, Giddings described the conflict as a "titanic struggle between two eternally different and irreconcilable ideas or philosophies of right and wrong." He continued, "A line is drawn between one notion of right and another notion of right; between one notion of wrong and another notion of wrong. On one side or the other of that line we must stand . . . we cannot be neutral."[45]

Giddings' words appear tame in comparison with the moral ardor of the Harvard philosopher Josiah Royce. Germany's violation of Belgian neutrality and use of the submarine against noncombatant vessels made a mockery of Royce's ethical universe, and he suffered enormous per-

41. Boas to his wife, August 7, 1914, in Rohner (ed.), *The Ethnography of Franz Boas.*

42. Wallace Notestein, letter to the editor, *Nation,* CIII (August 24, 1916), 174–75.

43. New York *Times,* March 30, 1916, p. 12, August 27, 1916, Sec. 2, p. 1.

44. Unidentified copy, undated, in Dodd Papers.

45. New York *Times,* May 20, 1916, p. 13.

sonal anguish from the tragedy of the war.[46] His ability to keep up with his private and professional obligations, he said, was "very greatly hindered, and at times almost wholly inhibited, by the war, and by its chaos of sorrows and of crimes." He lamented, "The troubles of the war haunt me a great deal, and are a very heavy burden to me as onlooker, unable to counsel and unable to help, but longing for the triumph of the true Humanism, whenever this horror is over, and whenever the Devil has got . . . his due. . . . I often think how sad this would make [William] James, if he had been forced to witness it." He concluded that "the brevity of life has its conveniences."[47] In fact, Royce lived only a year after writing this letter. Those who knew him claimed that the emotional toll taken by the war hastened his death.[48]

Royce's philosophy, largely shaped by his studies at Göttingen and Leipzig universities, was grounded in the concepts of loyalty and community. Individual salvation was to be achieved by loyalty to a cause; potential conflicts between loyalties would be avoided by a transcendent "loyalty to loyalty"; the supreme object of loyalty was the "great community," the oneness of mankind, an ideal that the scientific, technical, and social accomplishments of the nineteenth and twentieth centuries were making realizable.[49] Although there was room in Royce's vision for "rational and genuinely self-conscious" devotion to one's own nation, this rational patriotism was to be integrated and not at odds with the interests of the greater, all-encompassing human community. When Ger-

46. Royce long had been appalled by the inhumanity and irrationality of war and had devoted considerable thought to the possibility of its prevention. In 1914 he published a book entitled *War and Insurance*, which proposed a system of international mutual insurance against various calamities, with war chief among them.

47. John Clendenning (ed.), *The Letters of Josiah Royce* (Chicago, 1970), 632, 635.

48. George H. Palmer, "In Dedication: Josiah Royce," in Clifford Barrett (ed.), *Contemporary Idealism in America* (New York, 1964), 8; *Dictionary of American Biography*, XVI, 210.

49. Josiah Royce, *The Philosophy of Loyalty* (New York, 1908); "The Hope of the Community" (MS in Royce Papers). The published version of "The Hope of the Community," which appeared as an essay in *The Hope of the Great Community* (New York, 1916), was shortened. Sondra Herman's *Eleven Against War: Studies in American Internationalist Thought, 1898–1921* (Stanford, 1969) contains a useful chapter on Royce's ideas of loyalty and community. See also Quandt, *Small Town to Great Community*.

many trampled on Belgium's "sacred dignity" and "drowned the babies on the Lusitania" in overmastering pursuit of its own national triumph, Royce's sacred ideal of community was challenged, and Royce concluded that the war was not a conflict between competing nations but an assault by one nation against all of humanity.[50]

It is only in the light of this view that the passion and partisanship of Royce's noted speech of January 30, 1916, at Tremont Temple can be understood. Royce is reported to have "electrified" the mass meeting in the Boston hall, having become the "inspired vehicle of a righteous indignation."[51] Charging Germany with being the "willful and deliberate enemy of the human race," Royce concluded that it was "impossible for any reasonable man to be in his heart and mind neutral." In ringing tones he called up the image of bleeding Belgium, described the Allied cause as "the cause of mankind," and advocated a course of support for that cause that implied American intervention in the war:

> Let us enthusiastically approve of supplying the enemies of Germany with financial aid and with munitions of war, let us resist with all our moral strength and influence those who would place an embargo upon munitions, let us bear patiently and uncomplainingly the transient restrictions of our commerce which the war entails, let us be ashamed of ourselves that we cannot even now stand beside Belgium, and suffer with her for our duty and for mankind, and while we wait for peace let us do what we can to lift up the hearts that Germany of to-day has wantonly chosen to wound, to betray, and to make desolate. Let us do what we can to bring about at least a rupture of all diplomatic relations between our own republic and those foes of mankind, and let us fearlessly await whatever dangers this our duty as Americans may entail upon us, upon our land and upon our posterity.[52]

The integrity of Royce's ideas makes them valuable examples and il-

50. Royce, "The Hope of the Community," 23, 24, 13, 14–15.
51. *DAB*, XVI, 210; Professor Charles R. Lanman, "Minute on the Life and Services of Professor Josiah Royce," minutes of the faculty of arts and sciences, November 7, 1916, in Faculty Records, X, n.p., Harvard University Archives, hereinafter cited as Harvard Faculty Records.
52. Josiah Royce *The Duties of Americans in the Present War* (N.p., n.d.), 6–7. Angoff found the quiet philosopher's "new and amazing oratorical powers" ironic, at the very least, but to a Harvard colleague the address was "the climax of . . . [Royce's] greatness." Angoff, "The Higher Learning Goes to War" 177, and Lanman, "Minute," in Harvard Faculty Records.

lustrations of the shock experienced by American professors at Germany's actions in Belgium and on the high seas. The German government's justification of the actions on the grounds of military necessity suggested that these actions were not merely horrible incidents in a horrible war, but part of a conscious and deliberate policy of "frightfulness," and that no considerations of law or ethics would restrain Germany in pursuit of its national ambitions. This shock explains how individuals who were horrified at the war's destructiveness and bloodshed could, in apparent contradiction, oppose American efforts to secure a negotiated peace that would bring the carnage to a close. Lovejoy rejected the notion that morality demanded that the United States should try to stop the war. On the contrary, he insisted, morality in long-range terms demanded the defeat of Germany, which alone could guarantee lasting peace. "I sometimes think that the moral indignation of Americans is more intense—and more evanescent—than that of any other people," he said. "Yet I cannot think that we have wholly forgotten, or shall soon forget, the events of August, 1914. And so long as we remember them, the cause of America . . . must be, above all, the cause of Belgium, and of those principles of law, of international good faith, and of the rights of little and peaceful nations, of which Belgium is the tragic symbol."[53]

The German peace initiative of December, 1916, brought forth protests that the interests of humanity demanded a fight to the finish. Adams declared that to end the war before Germany was decisively defeated "would be a crime against humanity." Giddings echoed the charge when he accused American pacifists, who urged a response to the German initiative, of "doing their best to put civilization back a thousand years."[54] Munroe Smith wrote a lengthy protest against American peace moves for a "pro-Ally committee" of which he was a member. Acknowledging the "havoc and horror" of the war, its catastrophic destructiveness and bloodshed, its legacy to the future of "unbearable" burdens, he concluded nevertheless that "a bad peace [one that would

53. Arthur O. Lovejoy, letter to the editor, *New Republic,* IV (September 11, 1915), 156–57.
54. New York *Times,* December 3, 1916, Sec. 7, p. 2, December 19, 1916, p. 10.

permit Germany any advantage] would be a greater evil than this worst of wars. . . . Far better than such a peace is further warfare, to the end that those who have given their lives for national freedom and international justice shall not have died in vain."[55]

That Germany's foremost scholars made themselves the spokesmen of their nation's cause, defending and justifying even its worst excesses, completed the case against the country in the eyes of American professors. The notorious 1914 appeal of leading German savants, "To the Civilized World," became an appropriate symbol for a habit of mind that Veblen characterized as a "distemper of the [German] intellect," that Hart described as an "intemperance and defiance of the ordinary rules of logical thinking . . . [on the part of] the great intellectual leaders of Germany," and that James Harvey Robinson branded "jesuitical."[56] "To the Civilized World" was a protest by ninety-three leading representatives of German arts and sciences against the "lies and calumnies" circulated by Germany's enemies in an effort to stain its honor—specifically, charges of aggression, trespass, and malconduct in conquered territory. The savants offered no factual disproof of the charges, only denial and countercharges. A few examples will suffice to illustrate the document's tone and substance:

> *It is not true* that Germany is guilty of having caused this war. . . . Germany did her utmost to prevent it. . . . Not till a numerical superiority, which had been lying in wait on the frontiers, assailed us did the whole nation rise to a man.

> *It is not true* that we trespassed in neutral Belgium. It has been proved that France and England had resolved on such a trespass, and it has likewise been proved that Belgium had agreed to their doing so. It would have been suicide on our part not to have been beforehand.

> *It is not true* that our troops treated Louvain brutally. Furious inhabitants having treacherously fallen upon them in their quarters, our troops,

55. Munroe Smith, "A Protest," December, 1916, (Typescript in Munroe Smith Papers, Special Collections, Columbia University Library).

56. Thorstein Veblen, "Another German Apologist," *Dial,* LXII (April 19, 1917), 344; Albert Bushnell Hart to Bernhard Dernburg, December 5, 1914, in Hart Papers; and James Harvey Robinson, "War and Thinking," *New Republic,* I (December 19, 1914), 18.

with aching hearts, were obliged to fire a part of the town as punishment.

> *It is not true* that our warfare pays no respect to international laws. . . . Those who have allied themselves with Russians and Servians, and present such a shameful scene to the world as that of inciting Mongolians and Negroes against the white race, have no right whatever to call themselves upholders of civilization.[57]

Among the signatories of the manifesto were Ernst Haeckel, Gerhart Hauptmann, Karl Lamprecht, Max Planck, Wilhelm Wundt, Eduard Meyer, Adolph von Harnack, and Walther Nernst.

The manifesto suggested profound mental corruption and political subservience on the part of German scholars that both disappointed and repelled American professors. To Robinson, the "pitifully feeble" manifesto was "but the sign and seal of the success of German *Kultur* in making all her subjects accept the Kaiser and his decisions in exactly the same unquestioning and dutiful spirit in which the Jesuit accepts the organization of the Roman apostolic church and the decrees of its head."[58] Lovejoy characterized the document as a "scandalous episode in the history of the scholar's profession." His reflections deserve to be quoted at length because of the implications for the future, when American scholars would have their own professionalism tested by the challenge of war. Lovejoy declared:

> We have learned much from German scholars about historical "objectivity" and the niceties of historical criticism; what we receive when we look for an application of these principles to contemporary events, is a clumsy compilation of fictions, irrelevancies, and vulgar appeals to what are apparently conceived to be American prejudices. . . . the incident has in it too much of instruction and warning for Americans of the same profession, to be allowed to pass without notice. In connection with other circumstances it seems, for one thing, to show that the professional class, in the country where it has played the greatest part, has signally failed, at the most critical moment in German history, to perform its proper

57. John Jay Chapman, *Deutschland über Alles or Germany Speaks* (New York, 1914), 37–39.
58. Robinson, "War and Thinking," 18.

function—the function of detached criticism, of cool consideration, of insisting that facts, and all the relevant facts be known and faced.[59]

Lovejoy continued to express concern about the implications for American scholars of the "sad spectacle presented by the German professors since the war began." It is clear, he said, "that the German professorate as a body has been subtly but deeply corrupted, by governmental and court influences. I hope the Assn [AAUP] may in the long run do a good deal to keep us on our guard against our own potential sources of corruption in the profession."[60]

Disapproval of the German manifesto seems to have inspired at least the form of one of the first collective responses by American professors to an episode of the war. In 1916 Professors Paul Fredericq and Henri Pirenne of the University of Ghent were removed to Germany and imprisoned there because of their refusal to cooperate with German attempts to convert Ghent into a Flemish university.[61] Under the leadership of J. Franklin Jameson and Waldo G. Leland of the Carnegie Institution of Washington, with the cooperation of AHA President George Lincoln Burr, ninety-three professors of history at leading American universities petitioned the U.S. secretary of state to request the German government to release the Belgian historians to a neutral country for the war's duration. A lectureship for either Fredericq or Pirenne would be waiting at Cornell University and a lectureship for Pirenne at Princeton University should they choose to come to the United States. The petition stated that had time permitted many more signatures could have been obtained. However, the implication of the appeal of ninety-three historians is too clear for the number to have been accidental. Furthermore, in the confidential covering letter to the signatories the following suggestive sentence appears: "Even if no good is done to the two Belgians, such an impressive showing of our sympathy and our unanimity will do us some

59. Arthur O. Lovejoy, letter to the editor, *Nation*, XCIX (September 24, 1914), 376. See also letter to the editor, *Nation*, XCIX (November 5, 1914), 548, for further discussion by Lovejoy of "the intellectual and moral qualities reasonably to be expected from professional scholars, above all from the leaders of the profession."
60. Arthur O. Lovejoy to William E. Dodd, July 12, 1915, in Dodd Papers.
61. See *History*, n.s., I (July, 1916), 111–12.

good, especially when accompanied by definite offers, of such a generous character, from two universities." Clearly, a comparison with the moral and professional failure of the German ninety-three was intended in the historians' desire to win points for their discipline's reputation for professional solidarity in a humane cause.[62]

The overwhelming lack of sympathy for Germany from American professors struck at least one observer as particularly regrettable and ironic. Writing less than a year after the outbreak of the war, Paul Elmer More accused professors of being especially guilty among Americans of frenzied hostility to Germany and lamented: "A land to whom a few years ago most of our scholars were looking up as to the leader of scientific thought and education generally, they suddenly cast out of the pale of humanity; they mock its culture and deny its civilization."[63] There certainly is substantial evidence of attitudes that fit More's characterization of professional opinion as irrational and indecent. For example, Columbia University's Brander Matthews challenged the Germans' reputation for cultural superiority by pointing to their breaking their word in Belgium, destroying works of art in Louvain, bombing civilian centers, displaying bad manners, and retaining a "barbaric medieval alphabet." Although he accorded recognition in one sentence to German musical distinction, he lengthily denigrated German contributions in painting, sculpture, architecture, belles lettres, and pure and applied science.[64] Frank J. Mather, engaging in a common pastime of comparing the con-

62. See J. Franklin Jameson and Waldo G. Leland to "Dear Colleague," June 7, 1916, and 93 professors of history to the secretary of state, June 7, 1916, both in Carl Russell Fish Papers, State Historical Society of Wisconsin. The government and the scholars worked closely together in the enterprise. Not only did the historians approach the government with the project and convince it to take up the cause, but the government was persuaded to use the historians' petition as the basis of its action—*i.e.*, to send the document itself to Ambassador James W. Gerard in Berlin, who would use it in his approach to the Germans. For their part, the historians followed the government's recommendations for their tactics. There is no record of the project's outcome. Fredericq and Pirenne finally were released in 1918.

63. More, "The Philosophy of the War," 14. It should be noted, however, that More signed the April 17, 1916, "Address to the People of the Allied Nations," which in effect charged Germany with being an enemy of the "highest ideals of civilization." For a report of the text of the address, see New York *Times,* April 7, 1916, p. 5.

64. New York *Times,* September 20, 1914, Sec. 2, p. 14.

cepts of culture and *Kultur,* described the aim of culture as an enlightened and humane individual and the aim of *Kultur* as an enlightened
government, to which the individual is subordinated, and concluded that
"Germany has singularly little culture." He proclaimed: "Germany, as
measured by the production of cultured individuals, takes a very low
place today. . . . In the field of scholarship, Germany is in the main
chiefly laborious, accurate, and small-minded. Her scholarship is related
not to culture, but is a minor expression of *Kultur.*"[65] The Harvard philosopher Ralph Barton Perry spun out a justification for the expression
of passionate hatred against Germany. Where questions of morality are
involved, he explained, passions inevitably are aroused. "In moral matters there is no judging without feeling. Those who judge that in the
present war the cause of the Allies is also the cause of humanity and of
justice will feel as they judge. And in proportion to their concern for
humanity and justice they will feel strongly and deeply. It is unfortunate
that one cannot love humanity and justice without hating inhumanity
and injustice. But there is no escape from moral indignation save in apathy or in sentimentalism."[66] Finally, even the German Ph.D. degree,
long the jewel in the American scholar's professional crown, could be
portrayed as an object of dubious value. Dodd wrote his wife in the first
month of the war: "Germany is the enemy of mankind in this war and I
am almost ashamed that I have my doctorate from such a people."[67]
Later in the war, Yale's President Arthur T. Hadley expressed a similar
sentiment when he said, "I studied in Germany in the later seventies
(though perhaps I should be ashamed to confess it now)."[68]

It would, however, be a mistake to conclude from evidence of this
sort that professors typically experienced an uncomplicated revulsion

65. *Ibid.,* November 8, 1914, Sec. 3, p. 2. For a discussion of the German concept of *Kultur,* misunderstood by Mather and most other professors who commented on the subject, see Ringer, *The Decline of the German Mandarins,* 86–90.
66. Ralph Barton Perry, letter to the editor, *New Republic,* V (December 18,
1915), 172.
67. William E. Dodd to his wife Mattie, August 25, 1914, in Dodd Papers.
68. Arthur T. Hadley to A. G. Shipley, March 18, 1918, in Presidents' Papers,
Historical Manuscripts collection, Yale University Library, hereinafter cited as
Yale Presidents' Papers.

against Germany that led directly to categorical and complete cancella-
tion of past debts. For many of them, the conflict between their professional and personal associations with Germans and their impressions of
German war policy and military conduct produced considerable anguish
and feelings of ambivalence, of which they were fully aware.

Henry Farnam has left a detailed and personal description of the psychological toll exacted by Germany's conduct and the role played
by its scholars in its defense. He had received a doctorate from a German university, had since then maintained a great fondness for Germany's "ways, its scenery, its literature and its people," and came to feel
"as if an old friend had suddenly allowed the baser part of his nature to
get the better of him." When the war broke out, Farnam was on his way
to the University of Berlin to serve as Roosevelt Professor for the
academic year 1914–1915. At first he was disappointed by the cancella-
tion of the assignment and the waste of work and money that had been
invested in preparation for it. But after several weeks of observing the
course of the war he concluded that he no longer desired to go to
Germany for any purpose. "What I had intended to say about our
struggle for higher social ideas would not have been understood," he
wrote. He was, he said, "very much grieved at the violations of treaty
obligations displayed by the German government, and . . . absolutely
astounded not merely at the standards of public ethics displayed by
many of our [scholar] friends, but at the illogical and extreme utterances
to which they have put their names." He regretfully concluded that "we
must face the fact that there is a deep gulf between even the best
Germans whom we know and like personally, and ourselves, in our
views of political ethics."[69]

Confronted with the task of explaining American opinion about the
war to a German colleague and friend, Farnam stepped with caution.
He answered Professor E. W. Drechsler's request for an outline of
American sentiment with reluctance, consulted a group of Yale colleagues about the contents of his reply, and sent the letter to Nicholas

69. Henry W. Farnam to A. Maurice Low, October 9, 1914, to Nicholas
Murray Butler, August 30, 1914, to Gilbert Parker, October 28, 1914, and to
A. S. Hardy, October 17, 1914, all in Farnam Papers.

Murray Butler, head of the exchange program in America, for final approval, both because he suspected that his connection with the Roosevelt Professorship might put him in a semiofficial position and because he wanted to make sure that he would not "impair the friendly academic relations now existing." The letter, written in German, was very long and carefully worded. Farnam took great pains to balance out "emotional" opinions on both sides of the question and to assure Drechsler of the generally high esteem in which Germany was held by Americans and of their admiration for the Germans' dedication to their fatherland and spirit of self-sacrifice in the war. But then, in an equally detailed and circumspect manner, he described the "painful impression" made on Americans by the attack on Belgium and its justification on the grounds that "need knows no commandment"; the "painful" effects on the friends of Germany of the reportedly inhumane treatment of the Belgian civilian population; and the rejection by Americans of Germany's apparent commitment to the "total suppression of England."[70]

As the war progressed, Farnam became more distressed and less patient with the Germans. He was outraged at the sinking of the *Lusitania,* a "wholesale slaughter" that he believed would be "coupled in history with the massacre of St. Bartholomew's day and the Black Hole of Calcutta," and at "the disingenuous arguments by which the German representatives try to fasten the guilt of the action on its victims." Consequently, he wished to dissociate himself from any connection with German culture that officially was approved by the Germans, and he resigned from the board of directors of the Germanistic Society of America. Nevertheless, in anticipation of the possibility of repairing the damage to German-American relations after the war, Farnam withdrew only from the position of officeholder and not from membership in the society. "I am hoping that we may discover that our friends are under the influence of a terrible obsession, and that the attitude of many of them at the present time is not normal," he said. But Farnam's final judgment was more despairing. Offered reimbursement for the expenses incurred in going to Germany as Roosevelt Professor in 1914,

70. Henry W. Farnam to Nicholas Murray Butler, January 27, 1915, and Farnam to E. W. Drechsler, January 26, 1915, both *ibid.*

Farnam submitted an estimate of one thousand dollars, but concluded that the material losses were "small compared with my own psychic damage. The loss of the opportunity to do what I had been hoping might be a useful and rewarding piece of work, the sudden emergence of what seems almost like an opaque wall between the standards of my German friends and my own, the difficulty if not impossibility of ever again having that same feeling of interest and sympathy in German life and history which I have cherished since my boyhood, all belong to the imponderable yet very real losses of the year."[71]

The president of Farnam's university was expressing similar feelings of ambivalence about the Germans. Germany's "barefaced . . . [invasion of Belgium], whose neutrality she had guaranteed," made Arthur T. Hadley an early supporter of the Allies. "If a country that deems it right to repudiate its agreements gets too powerful, it constitutes a danger to all the rest of us; and I should hate to see this sort of treaty breaking crowned with success," he said. Although he was convinced that there was a profound "difference of political ethics between the German-speaking and English-speaking nations," Hadley concluded, "I have so many good friends in Germany that I dislike to put the matter any more strongly than this; and this itself goes very deeply." Hadley's correspondence with German friends was full of expressions of personal sympathy, of acknowledgments that the available evidence was insufficient to draw extreme conclusions, and of commitments to do all he could to secure fair consideration of Germany's position in America. He assured a Munich professor, "I have had too much experience in Germany, and have derived too much profit from that experience, to be willing to have the German nation treated unfairly in my countrymen's thoughts." He was frank to disclose his doubt to German correspondents about their statements of fact and to tell them that he was unconvinced by German justifications of the Belgian invasion. But he urged his Munich friend to supply him with a copy of the documents with which the German gov-

71. Henry W. Farnam to Nicholas Murray Butler, May 12, 1915, May 14, 1915, and May 27, 1915, all *ibid*. Farnam's conclusions about the implications of German conduct for America made him an early and active advocate of military preparedness.

ernment claimed to prove the unneutrality of Belgium and promised to make them publicly available in the Yale University Library.[72]

Finally, Hadley felt constrained by his past association with Heinrich von Treitschke, as pupil and friend, and by the "great debt of gratitude to him for the intellectual stimulus which he gave, and for the help which he rendered in judging ethical questions from more different points of view than I could have enjoyed without him" to correct popular misconceptions about the great German historian in America. Consequently, he wrote an article in which he tried to demonstrate the error of the common tendency to attribute German nationalism to Treitschke's influence, to link the views of Treitschke with those of Friedrich von Bernhardi and Nietzsche, and to confuse Treitschke's faith in Germany and military virtues with a glorification of Germany and militarism. But Hadley betrayed the ambivalence of his feelings when he confessed that his "sense of the fitness of things" prompted him to donate the money he received for the article to a Belgian relief committee, making Treitschke "contribute to Belgian relief in spite of himself."[73]

If Albert Bushnell Hart did not feel ambivalent about Germany, he certainly made a serious effort to separate his emotional response to German conduct from his intellectual judgment that the war's origins and issues were enormously complex. Like so many of his fellow professors, Hart had been trained in Germany and held a German doctorate. Like Farnam, he was to have been exchange professor in Berlin for the academic year 1914–1915 and had found the appointment postponed by the war's outbreak. Immediately after the war began, he wrote a book whose tone would characterize his public writings on the issues almost until the United States intervened. In the preface to *The War in Europe,* Hart declared that the volume was free from prejudice, because his friendships included men from all the belligerent nations. His book, he said, was not intended to be an argument, for on many questions the

72. Arthur T. Hadley to E. P. Howe, August 31, 1915, to G. R. Parkin, September 25, 1914, to Friedrich von der Leyen, November 9, 1914, to Friedrich Schmidt, September 22, 1914, to Julius Peterson, January 18, 1915, and to von der Leyen, March 17, 1915, all in Yale Presidents' Papers.
73. Arthur T. Hadley to Friedrich Schmidt, November 28, 1914, and Hadley to Lady Osler, December 23, 1914, both *ibid.*; Arthur T. Hadley, "The Political Teachings of Treitschke," *Yale Review,* n.s., IV (January, 1915), 235–46.

evidence was not yet available and on others there were honest differences of opinion. His purpose was "to treat the subject fairly and impartially," he said.[74] He expressed sympathy for all the peoples involved, partiality only to the United States.

Although Hart made it plain that he considered the invasion of Belgium unjustifiable, he interpreted the war as a product of long-standing racial animosities and conflicts of interest and, consequently, unavoidable. The only argument in *The War in Europe* was that in the modern world the safety of American democracy depended on military and naval preparedness.[75] In his numerous public statements on the war, Hart continued to place the long-standing ethnic animosities and conflicts of interest among the belligerents in historical perspective and to analyze their ambitions and conduct in the context of their historical development and current needs. He was unconcerned with whether the belligerents' behavior lived up to popularly defined standards of honor, morality, and civilization; he was very much concerned with the effect of that behavior on American rights and property. Consequently, he protested as much against British as against German maritime assaults on American neutrality.[76] As a consequence of his impartial approach to the war, Hart was not an advocate of victory for the Allies and he welcomed President Woodrow Wilson's efforts to secure a negotiated peace.[77]

74. Albert Bushnell Hart, *The War in Europe: Its Causes and Results* (New York and London, 1914), vi.

75. Hart was an active advocate of preparedness and universal military service. He was chairman of the Committee on Patriotism Through Education of the National Security League, a preparedness organization founded in 1914. For his activities in this role see the Hart Papers. In addition, he spoke and wrote frequently in favor of redefining and clarifying the Monroe Doctrine to strengthen it against any European challenger. See, for instance, his *The Monroe Doctrine: An Interpretation* (Boston, 1916).

76. See articles by Hart in the New York *Times*, August 2, 1914, Sec. 5, p. 1, October 18, 1914, Sec. 5, p. 4, December 27, 1914, Sec. 5, p. 1, March 21, 1915, Sec. 5, p. 4, November 14, 1915, Sec. 4, p. 1, February 20, 1916, Sec. 5, pp. 1, 3, March 12, 1916, Sec. 6, pp. 1, 2, May 14, 1916, Sec. 5, pp. 1, 3, and October 22, 1916, Sec. 5, pp. 6, 7. Compare Hart's attitude with Royce's plea that America bear British restraints on her commerce "patiently and uncomplainingly." Royce, *The Duties of Americans in the Present War*, 7.

77. *Ibid.* January 28, 1917, Sec. 5, pp. 1, 2. Although Hart applauded Wilson's "peace without victory" address, he revealed perspicacious awareness of the difficulty of applying its principles in a world where great powers, the United States among them, held dominion over other peoples.

Hart's private papers add another dimension to the picture. On the one hand, they confirm the impression of his lack of commitment to either side and demonstrate an initial desire to see the case for Germany fairly presented to Americans. In October, 1914, he wrote a letter to Dr. Heinrich Albert, representative of the German government in America, arguing that, "as a former German student, doctor of a German university, and accustomed for years to say that the Germans were the best people on the continent," he was in a position to judge that "the cause of the Germans has been presented to the American public in a clumsy and unconvincing manner." He insisted that "what the Germans ... need very much, is a straightforward, brief, and convincing statement upon the charges brought against them by their adversaries, some of which can without doub[t] be weakened or destroyed by a statement of facts." He suggested clarifying the following issues: the actual status of Alsace-Lorraine since 1871; the relation between the German government and people; the nature of the German military system; the German view of the invasion of Belgium; the character of the German regime in conquered territory; the military situation that led to the destruction in Louvain and Reims; and such broader prewar issues as the effect of British sea power on German trade, German policy in the Balkans, and the potential consequences of Slav nationalism for Germany. The letter indicated a sincere concern that American lack of sympathy for Germany stemmed in part at least from Germany's ineffectual defense of actions that might prove to be defensible on other grounds.[78]

However, one month later, Hart composed a letter to Bernhard Dernburg, German propaganda chief in America, which reveals that he had concluded that Germany indeed was guilty of atrocious conduct and which expressed amazement, shock, and fury "at the kind of arguments that are poured in upon innocent Americans." Acknowledging his "debt of gratitude" to the country in which he had received his professional education and his Ph.D degree, he demonstrated that he was forced to conclude that the invasion of Belgium, the drastic treatment of Belgian noncombatants, the destruction of Belgian and French cities without military advantage, and the Germans' apparent dedication to the use of

78. Albert Bushnell Hart to Heinrich Albert, October 5, 1914, in Hart Papers.

force suggested that the defeat of Germany was desirable for America as well as for the rest of the world. "What prevents Germany from treating the United States like Belgium, except the present and rather unconvincing fact, that it is not to the interest of Germany to do so?" he asked. "What if that ever becomes her interest? What is going to relieve mankind from the doctrine of force heaped on force if Germany when at war feels it necessary to pursue the methods of Attila?" But it would appear that Hart thought better of his sentiments and tone, for on top of the letter he wrote, "Not sent."[79] When he returned in print to the subject of Belgium, he presented a legal rather than an emotional challenge to Germany's defense of the invasion, arguing generously that "the greatness, the power, the moral strength of Germany, its acknowledged intellectual and commercial strength were all reasons for holding back from a step which brought little military advantage and desperately wounded the warmest friends of Germany in other lands."[80]

Finally, although Hart privately reacted with horror to the *Lusitania* sinking, in public he continued dispassionately to discuss the legal and practical complexities of the use of the submarine as a new weapon of war and to protest equally the British and German infringement on American neutral rights.[81] He refused to permit his humanitarian objections to submarine warfare to affect his perspective on the Germans as a people or to lead him into association with anti-German organizations. Hart wrote, agreeing with a friend, that the Fryatt case (the German execution of the captain of a British merchant vessel for attempting to ram an approaching German submarine) was "simple murder of a noncombattant." He continued, "Nevertheless, I do not feel inclined to go into any organization which is distinct[ly] Anti-German any more than I would enter one which is . . . distinct[ly] Anti-English. There are lots of good Germans, and Germany has got to be recognized at the end of

79. Albert Bushnell Hart to Bernhard Dernburg, December 5, 1914, *ibid.*

80. New York *Times*, December 27, 1914, Sec. 5, p. 1.

81. See Albert Bushnell Hart, "Cogent Facts Bearing on the Lusitania Horror" (MS in Hart Papers), and Hart's articles in New York *Times*, November 14, 1915, Sec. 4, p. 1, February 20, 1916, Sec. 5, pp. 1, 3, March 12, 1916, Sec. 6, pp. 1, 2, May 14, 1916, Sec. 5, pp. 1, 3, October 22, 1916, Sec. 5, pp. 6, 7.

the war as a living sister nation. There is no use trying to put 65 million people to the ban."[82]

Considering the effort and the success with which Hart avoided having his judgment affected by his feelings, it is all the more regrettable that, after American intervention in the war, he not only reversed his opinions but tampered with the truth about his previous posture in so doing. Convinced of the need to take up arms by the challenge to American sovereignty posed by the resumption of unrestricted submarine warfare ("a child may be trampled down by a madman; but not the United States of America!"),[83] Hart became a thoroughly committed propagandist for the American cause, chiefly through the National Security League. Ironically, the objectivity of his preintervention writings cast a temporary shadow over his patriotism shortly after the war ended.

The War in Europe and Hart's other early publicistic writings on the conflict apparently were taken by German representatives as evidence of sympathy with the Central Powers, for Hart's name was found on a list of pro-Germans, probably composed in 1915, in the intercepted diary of a German spy. The list was made public shortly after the armistice, in testimony before a subcommittee of the Senate Judiciary Committee investigating German propaganda in America. Requesting and receiving the opportunity to clear his name before the subcommittee, Hart minimized the value of his German education ("I thought I got a good deal more out of the time I spent in Paris than out of what I spent in Germany") and insisted that he had held Germany responsible for the outbreak of the war from the beginning.[84] When the pro-German charge first was made public, Hart told the press that *The War in Europe* "sets forth the responsibility of the Germans for the war, which I then and ever since have believed was the deliberate work of that power, in con-

82. Albert Bushnell Hart to William Roscoe Thayer, September 26, 1916, in William Roscoe Thayer Papers, Houghton Library, Harvard University.
83. New York *Times,* February 18, 1917, Sec. 5, pp. 8, 9.
84. Hart's testimony may be found in U.S. Senate, *Brewing and Liquor Interests and German Propaganda: Hearings Before a Subcommittee on the Judiciary* (Washington, D. C., 1919), 65th Cong., 2nd and 3rd Sess., Pt. 2, pp. 1621–38. In addition to his training in Germany, Hart had spent, he said, "some time in an institution in Paris."

nection with Austro-Hungary."[85] Reviewing the book for the Senate sub-committee, he apologized for its fairness, calling it "a good deal too neutral." He continued, "I must say it is a colorless book, and I wish now that there had been a little more paint in it." In spite of the written evidence to the contrary, he assured the subcommittee: "If I had known what I knew six months after that book was written, it never would have been written in that tone."[86] Subsequently, Hart adopted the attitude he previously had warned against—he put the entire German nation to the ban and went so far as to make the gratuitous and unworthy demand of his German-American friend and colleague, Professor Kuno Francke, that he prove his loyalty to his adopted country by denouncing publicly Germany's conduct in the war and holding the entire German people responsible for complicity in it.[87]

The dynamics of the response of American scholars to the German nation at war was more complicated than Paul Elmer More's characterization of the response as irrational and indecent would suggest. To be sure, the level of the American scholars' discourse about Germany frequently was astonishingly low. But for many of them to take up the popular vulgar characterizations of the enemy required first a period of intense inner conflict, which suggests that their extreme reactions against Germany took place less in spite of than because of long-standing personal and professional associations with and debts to the German nation. Disappointment, more than distemper, is suggested in Farnam's lament that it seemed "as if an old friend had suddenly allowed the baser part of his nature to get the better of him" and in Hart's observation that the destruction in Louvain was "what you would expect from Albanians but not from Germans."[88] The description left by his son of the war's impact

85. Statement for the Associated Press, December 6, 1918, in Hart Papers.
86. Senate, *Brewing and Liquor Interests and German Propaganda*, 1624, 1625, 1636. See also Hart's account of the episode, "The Trail of the German: From the Reminiscences of Albert Bushnell Hart," December 20, 1918 (MS in Hart Papers).
87. See Albert Bushnell Hart to Kuno Francke, January 30, 1919, Francke to Hart, February 3, 1919, and Hart to Francke, February 12, 1919, all in Hart Papers.
88. Henry W. Farnam to A. Maurice Low, October 9, 1914, in Farnam Papers, and Hart to Dernburg, December 5, 1914, in Hart Papers.

on the German-trained archaeologist James Henry Breasted perfectly illustrates this conflict:

> [Breasted] looked on helplessly while the forces he had observed as a
> student began to engulf the old academic Germany which had trained
> him and been the first to recognize and reward his subsequent labors. He
> was shocked to find his loyalty to these old German academic associa-
> tions and friendships condemned as pro-Germanism by colleagues whose
> dispassionate, peace-time detachment had given way to hysterical bitter-
> ness and hatred; and was humiliated to find that his own powers of cool
> reasoning were themselves no longer immune to such corrosive influ-
> ences. . . . It seemed to him that he was watching the preposterous, futile
> destruction of everything upon which his life had been built—the human
> relationships, the idealistic values, the fine freedom of roving minds in
> the unboundaried world of scholarship. Never before in his darkest mo-
> ments had he suffered such anguish of mind.

But gradually Breasted virtually brought to a halt his wide correspondence with German colleagues. And after America intervened in the
war, he made a poignant gesture of capitulation to the "corrosive influences" when he gave his enlisted son the little German dictionary he had
used as a student, rebound and inscribed with the words *Dictionary of
the Enemy's Language.*[89]

By the time the United States intervened in the war, professors had
well-established attitudes about the belligerents and the conflict. They
identified with the objectives of the Allied cause, largely through their
identification with England; they viewed Germany with suspicion and
revulsion and, consequently, were susceptible to the absolutist, moralistic interpretation of the war as a contest between good and evil. For
many of them, this conclusion was reached only after a painful personal
struggle that required a renunciation of past debts and associations. This
renunciation amounted to a denial of part of themselves and suggests
that behind the eagerness of these individuals to serve the cause were elements of an expiation for their indebtedness to German training and
scholarship and of a quest to "belong" in American society.

89. Charles Breasted, *Pioneer to the Past: The Story of James Henry
Breasted* (New York, 1945), 227, 235. Subsequently, Breasted wrote propaganda
for the National Security League, one of the most hyperbolic and irresponsible of
the wartime patriotic organizations.

III

On the
Bandwagon

PRO-ALLY SENTIMENT on the American campus, as among the population at large, did not necessarily imply interventionism during the neutrality years but, when the decision to intervene in the war was made by the president and Congress, it had the widespread support of college professors. This is not surprising. In time of war, loyalty to the nation commonly assumes precedence over other loyalties, even to the cause of peace, and only the exceptional individual sets himself against the national purpose. Not to join with the call for victory, when the life of the nation is threatened and its blood and treasure are committed to the battlefield, is an invitation to charges of lack of patriotism, if not of treason. Even for the committed opponent of war to resist the force of mass suggestion, to set himself apart from popular beliefs and passions, to become an Ishmael, requires indomitable courage and conviction. The moving accounts of terrible isolation, loneliness, and fear suffered by resisters to the First World War both in America and abroad are cogent illustrations of the perils of pacifism in wartime. That the national cause gained support from the major religious denominations and from prominent pacifists and socialists in all the belligerent nations during the war indicates that it is less remarkable to support than to oppose a war once it has begun.[1]

1. Julian Bell (ed.), *We Did Not Fight: 1914–18 Experiences of War Resist-*

This is not to suggest that the cause was supported in the American academic community with reluctance. The contrary, in fact, was true. Professors were so enthusiastic about intervention that the editors of the *New Republic* in all seriousness could characterize the American cause as a thinking man's war. A week after intervention in an editorial entitled "Who Willed American Participation?" they argued that the influence of the disinterested intellectual, particularly the college professor, had brought America into the conflict. "College professors headed by a President who had himself been a college professor contributed more effectively to the decision in favor of war than did the farmers, the business men or the politicians," they stated. Consequently, in the eyes of the editors the war assumed the appearance of a disinterested crusade in behalf of ideas, not of interests. This oversimplification no doubt was a product of wishful thinking, but the portrait of the academic community's attitude contained more than a kernel of truth. As a group, American professors were among the most enthusiastic supporters of the cause.[2]

At bottom, the decision to support the war was a political one; intervention appeared to be a necessary or desirable response to the German challenge. Professors held many varieties of opinion why joining the fight against the Central Powers was necessary or desirable, and all of them did not come to the conclusion at the same time. Some advocated intervention in advance of the declaration of war; others supported the fact when it appeared certain or was accomplished.

---

ers (London, 1935); Bertrand Russell, *Why Men Fight* (New York, 1916), 4; and Jane Addams, *Peace and Bread in Time of War* (New York, 1922), Chaps. 6, 7. For American religious, pacifist, and socialist support of the war, see Abrams, *Preachers Present Arms*; Merle Curti, *Peace or War: The American Struggle, 1636–1936* (New York, 1936), 254–55; A. C. F. Beales, *The History of Peace* (New York, 1931), 290–92; and David A. Shannon, *The Socialist Party of America* (New York, 1955), Chap. 5. James Weinstein, *The Decline of American Socialism* (New York, 1967), Chap. 3, and Charles Chatfield, *For Peace and Justice* (Knoxville, 1971), Pt. 1, are good sources for the ideas and activities of socialists and pacifists who continued to oppose American intervention in the war.

2. *New Republic,* X (April 14, 1917), 308. There were, of course, individual professors who did not share this enthusiasm, who viewed American entry into the war as mistaken and unjustifiable. Franz Boas was one of them. See New York *Times,* April 9, 1917, p. 3.

One of the clearest sources of early interventionism was a commitment to Anglo-American unity. Desire to enter the war seemed to follow logically from the view of the identity of British and American ideals and interests. The case of George B. Adams illustrates not only this logic, but the extent to which a committed Anglophile would go to accomplish the realization of his aims. It will be recalled that Adams' belief in America's identity of interest with Britain led him to argue from the war's outset for American intervention to forestall German victory. It is not at all surprising to find Adams condemning Wilson's diplomatic response to the resumption of unlimited submarine warfare in February, 1917, and virtually itching for war. He said, "I feel as if we are in the most ridiculous and disgraceful position that we have been in since the war began." Wilson, he complained, "will endure almost anything before he will himself begin war." Immediately after intervention, Adams expressed the hope that "one thing that . . . may result from the present situation is some sort of permanent alliance, or at least some common understanding in regard to international policy between us and England."[3]

Adams thought the main obstacle to such an "understanding" was a mistaken view among Americans that the British Empire was committed to "ideals of conquest and domination,"[4] and he embarked on a campaign to improve American popular opinion about England. Publicly, he urged Britain to grant true internal independence to the English-speaking commonwealths and recommended an American alliance with the empire reformed along these lines.[5] Behind the scenes, Adams and a number of other Anglophiles, including the attorney Charles P. Howland, officers of the Rockefeller Foundation General Education Board,

3. George B. Adams to George Crump, March 4, 1917, in Adams Papers; Adams to J. Franklin Jameson, May 1, 1917, in National Board for Historical Service Papers, Library of Congress, hereinafter cited as NBHS Papers.
4. Adams to Jameson, May 1, 1917, in NBHS Papers.
5. The *Nation* published Adams' argument for reform of the British Empire. See George B. Adams, "The British Empire and a League of Peace," *Nation*, CVI (April 4, 1918), 392–94. But the journal, not wanting to give the appearance of endorsing an alliance scheme, turned down the article's second installment, in which Adams urged an Anglo-American alliance as the basis of future arrangements for world peace. See H. R. Mussey to George B. Adams, November 15, 1918, in Adams Papers. Adams printed the piece at his own expense.

the scholar George Louis Beer, and Professors James T. Shotwell of
Columbia and Dana C. Munro of Princeton, established a semisecret organization to promote an Anglo-American "understanding" through a
subtle propaganda campaign in the United States, in cooperation with a
similar group in England. Adams' recommendation of tactics to overcome obstacles in the campaign suggests that he was not burdened with
an ivory-tower squeamishness about practical political manipulation:

> I believe it would be wise to arrange to have the organization begin
> somewhere in the west ... so that in the plan the Atlantic seaboard
> should seem to follow and not lead. . . . The East often instructs the
> West and leads it on to its better opinion, but ... the East can decide
> nothing by itself. I feel certain also that about this particular matter
> there will be more slowness and reluctance among the masses in the
> West than in the East, and that the first impulse when an actual prop-
> aganda is started will be to look upon it with suspicion. If the movement
> can seem to originate in the West itself, and the West appear to be in the
> lead, I am sure a good deal will be gained. This plan may very likely call
> for something like a self-denying ordinance on the part of those who
> have been so long interested in the project, but I think they will be the
> last to object.[6]

Adams recognized that, because of popular suspicion of Britain, neither an Englishman nor an American, who would be looked upon as
merely an "Anglo-maniac," could speak in behalf of the British Empire
in America. He therefore proposed a plan to bring the South African
general Jan Smuts to the United States to popularize the Commonwealth
of Nations. When his committee decided that President Wilson's approval was necessary before contacting Smuts, Adams was not pleased
because he feared refusal. He reluctantly acquiesced in the decision, but
suggested that Howland use a less-than-candid approach to the president. He advised Howland to "put the emphasis on the purpose of the
plan to persuade the American people to take a more decided part in
the settlement after the war than we have usually been willing to take in
European affairs. . . . [The President] would be more attracted to the

6. See the many letters between George B. Adams and George Louis Beer
and between Adams and Charles P. Howland, from 1916 to 1919, and Adams to
Beer, ca. January 12, 1918, all in Adams Papers.

plan, if that part of the purpose is put forward than if the bringing about of a better understanding with England is emphasized, though of course, the two things are really one." In spite of careful tactical maneuvering, the plan was squelched by the White House.[7] The White House also squelched an "Anglo-American educational campaign" initiated by the British government (with the cooperation of U.S. Ambassador Walter Hines Page) and the General Education Board, which would have sent such prominent representatives of American higher education as Chicago's President Harry Pratt Judson, Wisconsin's President Charles R. Van Hise, and William Howard Taft, then on the Yale faculty, to speak in England about the United States and the war.[8] Both schemes had a conspiratorial air, marked by the exchange of confidential communications and oblique references to subjects that were better not discussed in writing.

Franklin H. Giddings provides another example of early interventionism in which dedication to the unity of the English-speaking world was one of the themes. Giddings was an active member of the American Rights Committee, which promoted prowar sentiment in America; he denounced American neutrality at least a year before intervention.[9] He greeted the resumption of submarine warfare with the observation that it simply brought America "face to face with the situation which clearheaded men have foreseen for two years, which the muddleheads have been unable to comprehend, and which the creatures whose only interest in life is to fatten on the sufferings of their fellow-men have denied." His proposals for congressional response to the situation clearly implied preparation for war. When Wilson secured the arming of merchant ships, Giddings applauded the action, and he attacked the group of pacifists that gathered in Washington for a last-ditch appeal against war as a "mob . . . made up of morally obtuse women and their consorts." He

7. George B. Adams to Charles P. Howland, June 10, 1918, Howland to E. M. House, June 24, 1918, House to Howland, June 24 [*sic*], 1918, Howland to House, June 29, 1918, and House to Howland, July 27, 1918, all *ibid*.

8. See the lengthy correspondence about the project in Presidents' Papers, University of Chicago Archives, hereinafter cited as Chicago Presidents' Papers.

9. See, for example, Giddings' address at the Carnegie Hall *Lusitania* Memorial Meeting, New York *Times*, May 20, 1916, p. 3.

concluded, "I hope this will be their last indecent exposure in public."[10] After the war was over, Giddings counted among its gains that preponderant world power was secured for the English-speaking peoples. Recognizing the necessity of preponderant power, he said, "We rejoice that preponderance today is with those peoples who first among the nations have been democratic, who practically have shown that they care for justice, whose faces are set against militarism, and who cherish the continuing culture of historic civilization."[11] The theme of Anglo-American amity would gain academic spokesmen during the war and was expressed repeatedly in calls to revise the American historiography of the Revolution and subsequent Anglo-American relations, particularly in school texts.[12]

Commitment to Anglo-American harmony and hegemony was but one route to war support. By early 1917 many professors began to be convinced that German "militarism" and "autocracy" represented both an immediate and a prospective threat to American national interests, peace, and security. The Harvard historian Frederick Jackson Turner was among them. Turner had been projecting for many years a large role in the world for American commerce and influence. In 1898, when Adams sent one of his early efforts in behalf of improved relations with England (a privately printed book entitled *Why Americans Dislike England*), Turner, at the time on the faculty of the University of Wisconsin, wrote to assure Adams that he was not "an anti-Englishman." He went on to explain, "The only fears I have in regard to England grow out of her vast commercial interests and the inevitable rivalries that will arise between us and her when we follow the destiny which our position,

10. *Ibid.*, February 2, 1917, p. 9, February 27, 1917, p. 2, March 30, 1917, p. 4.
11. Franklin H. Giddings, "What the War Was Worth," *Independent,* XCIX (July 5, 1919), 17. Cf. Adams, who listed "world leadership of Anglo-Saxons" among "gains from the war," memo, ca. 1918, in Adams Papers.
12. See, for example, Harry Elmer Barnes, "Anglo-American Relations Reconsidered," *North American Review,* CCVII (May, 1918), 681–94; James T. Shotwell, introduction to Charles Altschul, *The American Revolution in Our School Text Books* (New York, 1917); Robert Livingston Schuyler, "History and Public Opinion," *Educational Review,* LV (March, 1918), 181–90.

our material resources and the historical tendencies of the nation, set us in competition for the trade of the Pacific and South America." Turner ended by defending America's right to "commercial expansion and influence in South America and the Pacific" and declared, "These unexploited countries are our field for commerce, and we are entitled to elbow room and to the Monroe Doctrine."[13]

The growing crisis with Germany in the early months of 1917 appeared to Turner to represent a challenge to American power and influence, and he favored intervention on that account. "If we will not fight for free seas," he argued, "we will not fight to prevent a [German] coaling station in Mexico, or a revolution of the German colony in Brazil, or a German protectorate over Columbia [sic]." He continued, "I have become convinced that only by using this great national stress to strengthen our sinews and harden our tissues and learn our national lesson, shall we hereafter play an independent part in the world's affairs."[14] When the United States entered the war, Turner argued that national interest in the struggle, not cosmopolitan ideals, should be stressed, that it should be pointed out "just how far America has been in the past, and is likely to be in the future, compelled to be a satellite of triumphant and contemptuous Germany, if she does not resist now, for her *own* sake."

> It will be a dangerous thing for America ... to lead the way in discarding the patriotic, nationalistic, aspects of its ideals for democracy; the other nations will hold their own national feeling and aims. . . . Unless we generate ... a center of *American* purpose, we shall be swept into the whirling energies of England, as a mere floating mass of useful material, if indeed we do not become inert and useless *as* material.[15]

Turner did not want to ignore ideals, but he wanted to interpret the war

13. Frederick Jackson Turner to George B. Adams, January 25, 1898, in Adams Papers.
14. Ray Allen Billington and Walter Muir Whitehill (eds.), *"Dear Lady": The Letters of Frederick Jackson Turner and Alice Forbes Perkins Hooper, 1910–1932* (San Marino, 1970), 236.
15. Frederick Jackson Turner to Waldo G. Leland, June 19, 1917, in NBHS Papers.

in terms of American national ideals rather than ideals of an internationalist, cosmopolitan character. His enthusiasm for the cause was increased by his view of Germany as a threat to "civilization."[16]

Many professors shared the view that German militarism and
autocracy represented a threat sufficient to bring America into the war.
The Columbia political scientist Charles A. Beard was not satisfied with
arming merchant vessels as a response to the resumption of submarine
warfare. He called for "more drastic action" and said, "I have thought
for some months that this country should definitely align itself with the
Allies and help eliminate Prussianism from the earth."[17] In various
textbooks on which he collaborated during and immediately after the
war, Beard portrayed the conflict as a struggle against a ruthless military
dictatorship that made freedom and peace impossible for people everywhere in the world and pointed out that America had to contribute
to the defeat of Germany to avoid being threatened in the future.[18]
Compared with Beard, Andrew C. McLaughlin was a reluctant convert
to the cause, but ultimately he supported it on the same grounds. Although he had accorded German militarism a large role in the outbreak
of the war, he was skeptical of the ambitions of the Allies and came to
support American intervention slowly. Once the United States was in the
war, McLaughlin expressed the view that Germany's clear intention to
dominate the world made intervention necessary. "German victory appeared to mean the success of ruthlessness or conquest by military preparation; it meant the enthronement of might; and it meant that we
must henceforward live in a world of struggle—we and our children af-

16. Turner declared, "We are fighting for the historic ideals of the United
States, for the continued existence of the type of society in which we believe, be-
cause we have proved it good, for the things which drew European exiles to our
shores, and which inspired the hopes of the pioneers." Frederick Jackson Turner,
The Frontier in American History (New York, 1962), 335; Billington and White-
hill (eds.), *"Dear Lady,"* 246n.
    17. New York *Times,* February 17, 1917, p. 2.
    18. See Frederick A. Ogg and Charles A. Beard, *National Governments and the
World War* (New York, 1919); Charles A. Beard and William C. Bagley, *The
History of the American People* (New York, 1918), Chap. 23; and James Harvey
Robinson and Charles A. Beard, *Outlines of European History: Part II, From the
Seventeenth Century to the War of 1914* (Boston, 1918), Preface, Supplement
on the War.

ter us,"[19] he explained. Similarly, Arthur O. Lovejoy was convinced that, unless America and its allies "cut the claws of the Prussian eagle," Germany would be a "perpetual menace" to the world. Germany's irresponsible government, policy of aggression, and preponderant military power threatened a "legacy of woe" for future generations.[20]

If the negative appeal of the dangers of German victory seemed insufficient to justify American intervention, the war could be interpreted as offering the prospect of a new international order and profound social change at home and abroad. The Columbia philosopher John Dewey was the most influential exponent of this point of view. He arrived at it slowly and, to antiwar former allies who could not and would not travel the route with him, his ultimate support of the war on optimistic grounds betrayed the poverty of pragmatism, a failure to confront real issues that was, in effect, a philosophical sellout.[21] Because of the influence of Dewey's position, it deserves examination in detail.

Until the decision for war actually was made, it did not appear likely to gain Dewey's support. Not only did his theory of an "empirically idealistic" pragmatism provide a philosophical basis for neutrality between the "idealist" Germans and the "empiricist" English, but his commitment to the solution of problems by the application of intelligence in every way suggested rejection of war as a technique for the resolution of differences among nations.[22] Indeed, on the very eve of intervention when it was certain that the country soon would be at war, Dewey wrote

19. Andrew C. McLaughlin, "The Great War: From Spectator to Participant," *History Teachers Magazine*, VIII (June, 1917), 185.

20. New York *Times*, December 3, 1917, p. 12. For other expressions of the view that American intervention was a necessary response to German militarism and autocracy, see Albion W. Small, "Americans and the World Crisis," *American Journal of Sociology*, XXIII (September, 1917), 145–73, and the following publications of the National Security League: Albert Bushnell Hart and Arthur O. Lovejoy (eds.), *Handbook of the War for Readers, Speakers, and Teachers* (New York, 1918); [Munroe Smith (ed.)], *Out of Their Own Mouths: Utterances of German Rulers, Statesmen, Savants, Publicists, Journalists, Poets, Businessmen, Party Leaders, and Soldiers* (New York, 1917); Claude H. Van Tyne, *Democracy's Educational Problem* (New York, 1918); and Richard T. Ely, *Suggestions for Speakers on the United States and the World War* (New York, 1917).

21. See White, *Social Thought in America*, 172.

22. White's *Social Thought in America* is the best discussion of the subject. See Chaps. 9, 10, 11.

an almost lyrical tribute to America's hesitation to fight for a cause that was not its own.[23] But to have expected Dewey to remain above the battle was to overlook or underestimate clues in his opinions and beliefs, in the light of which his supporting the war was consistent and logical if not necessarily predictable.

In January, 1916, Dewey had attacked the "professional pacifist's" outright condemnation and rejection of force as a "sentimental phantasy" that divorced ends from means, thereby preparing the ground for a theoretical justification of war. In so doing, he attempted first to draw a distinction between force and violence by arguing that "force figures in different roles. Sometimes it is energy; sometimes it is coercion or constraint; sometimes it is violence. . . . The objection to violence is not that it involves the use of force, but that it is a waste of force; that it uses force idly or destructively." He then concluded that it was "intolerable . . . that men should condemn or eulogize force at large, irrespective of its use as a means of getting results. To be interested in ends and to have contempt for the means which alone secure them is the last stage of intellectual demoralization." There was another straw in the wind when Dewey signed the April, 1916, "Address to the People of the Allied Nations," which not only expressed the hope for an Allied victory but also the belief that the Allies were "struggling to preserve the liberties of the world and the highest ideals of civilization."[24] But perhaps most fundamental to Dewey's eventual enlistment in the cause was his association with that wing of Progressivism that saw in democratic collectivism a solution to the economic and social ills of industrial

23. John Dewey, "In a Time of National Hesitation," *Seven Arts*, II (May, 1917), 3–7. Although it was published in May, the article was written before the declaration of war.

24. John Dewey, "Force, Violence, and Law," *New Republic*, V (January 22, 1916), 295, 296. White declares that Dewey's distinction between force and violence was not a philosophical formulation and argues that, in view of the well-defined political meaning of the word *force*, the distinction was a mere verbal trick. See White, *Social Thought in America*, 164, 165. The address declared that the invasion of Belgium was an irremediable crime and that upon the outcome of the war depended the sanctity of treaties, the rights of small nations, and the control of militarism. The names George B. Adams and Franklin H. Giddings appeared among the list of signers. New York *Times*, April 17, 1916, p. 5.

America. Collectivist Progressives like Dewey long had been urging the centralization of power to increase the efficiency of the economic and social order and to rationalize and humanize it in the interest of the common welfare. This orientation, together with his sympathy for the Allies and his view that force could, and sometimes must, be used to attain a desired end, would make it possible for the "empirically idealistic" instrumentalist to accommodate with conviction to the decision for war.

The necessity to defeat Germany seems to have been the least significant element in Dewey's war support; he treated it almost incidentally. Americans viewed the fight against Germany, he said, as "a job to be done, a hard job, but one which had to be done so that it could be done with." In itself, the fight against Germany was a disagreeable task, which "has to be accomplished to abate an international nuisance."[25] More important was Dewey's belief that once war was a certainty it was a fact that had to be faced and that to continue to decry the war with injunctions against the use of force was "moral innocency." In his eyes the "idealistic youth" who refused to accept the fact of war were suffering from "the tendency to dispose of war by bringing it under the commandment against murder, the belief that by *not* doing something, by keeping out of a declaration of war, our responsibilities could be met, a somewhat mushy belief in the existence of disembodied moral forces which require only an atmosphere of feelings to operate so as to bring about what is right, the denial of the efficacy of force, no matter how controlled, to modify disposition; in short, the inveterate habit of separating ends from means and then identifying morals with ends thus emasculated."[26] Finally, the fact of war could be accepted with conviction because the war appeared to offer precisely that opportunity for

25. John Dewey, "What America Will Fight For," *New Republic,* XII (August 18, 1917), 69. In America's and his own time of hesitation, Dewey thought the necessity to defeat Germany presented the least problem. "We but meet a clearly proffered challenge," he wrote; America's profound hesitation to enter the war lay elsewhere. Dewey, "In a Time of National Hesitation," 6.

26. John Dewey, "Conscience and Compulsion," *New Republic,* XI (July 14, 1917), 298.

social control in the interest of social justice for which Dewey long had been arguing.[27]

The concept of social control first was applied to the international sphere and the outcome of the war itself. According to Dewey, America's declaration of war created a "plastic juncture," which could be molded to secure a Wilsonian peace. The fact of war, disagreeable in itself, offered the prospect of a "permanently different" world, the war could be used to establish "a world organization and the beginnings of a public control which crosses nationalistic boundaries and interests." Dewey continued to justify United States participation in the war as an opportunity to consciously affect the world's future by securing an international organization to outlaw war.[28]

But Dewey justified the war as a means of social control in both a more immediate and a more wide-ranging sense. Because war demanded paramount commitment to the national interest and necessitated an unprecedented degree of government planning and economic regulation in that interest, Dewey saw the prospect of permanent socialization, permanent replacement of private and possessive interest by public and social interest, both within and among nations.[29] The war, he believed, inevitably and inexorably was hastening the process of social change, and he did not hesitate to predict its outcome. In an interview with a reporter from the New York *World* a few months after America became a belligerent, Dewey rhapsodized that "this war may easily be the beginning of the end of business." Out of the exigency of war, he said, "we are beginning to produce for use, not for sale, and the capitalist is not a capitalist . . . [in the face of] the war." The capitalist conditions of

27. See the following for demonstration of the war's appeal to Progressives who were committed to social control: Charles Hirschfeld, "Nationalist Progressivism and World War I," *Mid-America*, XLV (July, 1963), 139–56; Quandt, *Small Town to Great Community*, 141–45; and Herman, *Eleven Against War*, 138.

28. John Dewey, "The Future of Pacifism," *New Republic*, XI (July 28, 1917), 359; Dewey, "What America Will Fight For," 69; John Dewey, "Morals and the Conduct of States," *New Republic*, XIV (March 23, 1918), 232–34; and John Dewey, "The Discrediting of Idealism," *New Republic*, XX (October 8, 1919), 235.

29. John Dewey, "What Are We Fighting For?" *Independent*, XCIV (June 22, 1918), 474, 480–83.

manufacture and sale have come under government control, and "there is no reason to believe that the old principle will ever be resumed. . . . Private property . . . has already lost its sanctity. . . . industrial democracy is on the way."[30] Dewey was, of course, correct in recognizing that war overhauls customary standards and practices, but there was no reason to be confident that the "plastic juncture" would be manipulated in the interest of his version of the good society.[31]

An interesting version of the theme of war and change came from the pens of Carl Becker and Charles Beard. They were too skeptical to believe that the war augured domestic and international democracy, yet they were convinced of the necessity to achieve that end. They insisted both that it was an error to portray the war as a struggle for democracy and that the United States must devote itself to turning the war into just such a struggle. Becker's observations on the subject were made in a long letter responding to a Committee on Public Information appeal for suggestions for a Fourth of July address to foreign-born workingmen. He warned that an appeal based on the "common contrast between the horrors of German autocracy and the shining virtues of American and Allied democracy" was bound to fall on deaf ears. In truth, he said, although the United States at present had "a certain political democracy, in industrial and economic organization we have never been so little democratic." This was known best to the foreign-born worker in America who had been "touched by the ideals of socialism" and who came into contact with American institutions "precisely where they are least democratic, in big cities . . . and in connection with great corporations." Becker observed:

You talk to him of our ideals of liberty and he thinks of the shameless

30. Typescript in Columbia University Archives, Low Memorial Library, Columbia University. The interview proceeded with Dewey's prediction of enormous war-engendered changes in the family and the status of women, though in this case he declined to endorse them all.

31. Making a slightly different observation along the same lines, Hirschfeld points out not only that conservative, even reactionary, forces in America were strengthened by the war, but that although many of the precise reforms urged by nationalist Progressives were accomplished, they were ambiguous in their operation. It readily became apparent, he says, that a centralized, planned economy does not necessarily contribute to a democratic order. Hirschfeld, "Nationalist Progressivism and World War I," 155.

exploitation of labor and the corruption in government and of the ridiculous gulf between wealth and poverty. In talking to these men it does
no good to use all these oratorical phrases about American democratic
ideals and institutions. The last thing the average foreign working man,
either in Europe or in this country, wants is to establish American institutions as he knows them—the Capitalist and Bourgeois regime is
precisely what he wants to destroy. To reach the foreign born laborer,
therefore, it is necessary to make him feel that this war is not a Capital-
istic war; that it is the culmination of a generation of Imperialistic reaction, a reaction which is not confined to Germany although there it has
been most pronounced; and that we are in the war, not only to save
France but to save our own soul, not only to safeguard democracy from
German militarism, but against our own backslidings. The war will not
touch this class of men much unless they are convinced that the war is to
result in the real democratization of our industrial as well as of our political life.[32]

Beard was convinced that winning the confidence of the Social Democrats in Germany and the newly empowered revolutionaries in Russia
was necessary in order to bring the war to a successful conclusion. This
could be done, he argued, only by convincing them that the conflict was
not "at bottom or even potentially a capitalist war for colonies, markets,
and concessions." They knew their history too well, he said, to be fooled
by the "pat little phrase 'liberty against autocracy.' " America could
convince them of its sincerity in waging a war for democracy only by
repudiating the imperialist ambitions of its allies and rectifying its own
shortcomings at home, particularly in the area of social and industrial
democracy. "The world of democracy for which they are willing to die
in the Russian trenches or risk their lives in bursting the bonds of
Kaiserism is not the world of Milner, Cecil, Maxse, and Balfour. . . . The
kingdom of heaven for Kerensky and Liebknecht is not described in
Lochner v. New York."[33] Becker and Beard looked forward to a new
world after the war, but they had considerably less faith than some of
their fellow professors that the new world was already in the making.

The commitment to Anglo-American community of interest, the
belief in the necessity to crush "Prussianism," and the conviction that

32. Carl Becker to Samuel B. Harding, May 23, 1918, in CPI Papers.
33. Charles Beard, "The Perils of Diplomacy," *New Republic,* XI (June 2,
1917), 137.

the war would bring about a new order at home and abroad all served to win the support of professors for American intervention. But in order to understand the particular quality of the professors' support—not only the level of their enthusiasm but the role they played as servants of the cause—it is necessary to look beyond their political views and to consider the response to the war of the institutions within which they worked and which commanded their loyalty and the apparent implications of the war for their disciplines and their professional self-image.

When the United States entered the war, the institutions of higher learning donated their intellectual and physical resources to the war effort almost without reservation. Beyond the expectation that their students would help fill the government's military manpower needs, which had been true in previous wars, the leaders of higher education assumed that the university as an institution had a special contribution to make to the cause. The ground for this assumption had been prepared when the service ideal was articulated during the years of the emergence of the modern university and implemented during the Progressive era. Given the infusion of the American university with the ideal of social service and the past response by its professors to calls on their expertise by municipal, state, and federal agencies, it is not remarkable that in a national emergency the universities assumed they had a public role to perform. Furthermore, the character of World War I as a technological, total war determined that the institutions of higher learning, which were a primary source of the research facilities and personnel and the trained men needed to wage such a war, would be called upon by the government for particular kinds of service.

The initiative for mobilizing the colleges and universities as a resource for the national defense was assumed by the institutions themselves when diplomatic relations with Germany were broken. In February, 1917, the Intercollegiate Intelligence Bureau, under the sponsorship and chairmanship of Dean William McClellan of the University of Pennsylvania Wharton School of Finance and Commerce, was established "to assist the government in getting college students and alumni who desire to enlist [in government service] and placing them where their specialized training will count." The headquarters of the bureau were in Washington, with branches at about two hundred universities, colleges, and technical and agricultural schools across the country.[34]

Within individual institutions, plans were formulated to assist the government in the event of war. For example, at Columbia University early in February the mechanical engineering and electrical engineering departments placed themselves entirely at the disposal of the Navy Department. On February 6 a general assembly was held at Columbia "to voice the University's loyalty to the President in the crisis attending the breach in diplomatic relations with Germany."[35] As a result of the assembly, Columbia "went definitely on record as desiring to place itself at the services of the City, State and Nation in whatever way it could be of the greatest use at the present time," and a special committee was appointed "to consider and to institute ways and means by which the University and its members may render public service to the nation, the state and the city should occasion therefore arise because of the existing international situation." The women at Columbia requested and secured the establishment of the University Committee on Women's Work as part of the mobilization of the university for war. On March 5 the Columbia trustees pledged the "loyal support of the University to the Government of the United States in all measures of national defense."[36]

34. Telegram, William McClellan to N. M. Butler, February 6, 1917, and McClellan to Butler, February 8, 1917, and enclosure, both in Columbia University Archives. Charles F. Thwing, *The American Colleges and Universities in the Great War, 1914–1919: A History,* (New York, 1920), 24–25.

35. Frank D. Fackenthal to R. S. Griffen, February 8, 1917, Josephus Daniels to N. M. Butler, February 9, 1917, and W. S. Slichter to Griffen, February 14, 1917, all in Columbia University Archives; *Columbia University Annual Reports, 1918* (New York, 1918), 463–64.

36. Frank D. Fackenthal to John Purroy Mitchell, February 6, 1917, N. M. Butler to "Dear Sir" [the various appointees to the special committee], February 7, 1917, Virginia Gildersleeve to Butler, February 12, 1917, Butler to Gildersleeve, February 15, 1917, and Gildersleeve to Fackenthal, February 23, 1917, John B. Pine, clerk of the board of trustees, to the President of the United States, March 6, 1917, all in Columbia University Archives. The propriety of placing the resources of the university at the disposal of the state before war had been declared and on the basis of the sentiments of a public meeting was questioned in at least one quarter. Assistant Professor of Economics Henry R. Mussey complained that "the University by the stand to which it was officially committed at the meeting of February 6, and the further steps that are apparently being taken to commit it irrevocably to a position of unquestioning support of whatever mea-

Similar measures were undertaken at other campuses. At Harvard the Committee on Military Affairs was appointed on February 12 "to organize and correlate all the University plans for military preparedness" and within the month was reported to be "actively at work to the end that the facilities at Harvard may be used to the fullest advantage in the event of war."[37] On February 15 the faculty of the College of the City of New York passed a resolution that the school "should take whatever steps may be necessary to co-operate with other colleges and universities in placing at the service of the National Government the physical and intellectual resources of these institutions."[38] In the middle of March, fifty scientists at the University of Chicago asked President Judson to recommend to the trustees "that they offer the scientific laboratories and equipment of the University to the federal government for use in case of war" and expressed their willingness to volunteer their personal services to the government to perform any duties for which they were qualified. Shortly thereafter, a petition was sent to President Wilson, Secretary of War Newton D. Baker, and the Illinois senators and representatives expressing the support of 153 University of Chicago faculty members and administrators for preparedness and plans for "military, industrial or scientific service in case of war."[39]

One month after intervention, the commissioner for engineering and education of the Council of National Defense called a meeting of both

---

sures the 'constituted authorites' may ultimately decide upon, is, in advance of the actual outbreak of hostilities, abdicating its function of serving as a center for sober and thoughtful discussion." Henry R. Mussey to E. R. A. Seligman, February 15, 1917, in E. R. A. Seligman Collection, Special Collections, Columbia University Library.

37. Roger Pierce, memorandum of preparedness, March 23, 1917, in Lowell Papers.

38. Quoted in S. Willis Rudy, *The College of the City of New York: A History, 1847–1947* (New York, 1949), 349.

39. Judson Herrick to Harry Pratt Judson and accompanying letter from fifty professors of science, March 16, 1917, and memorial of members of the faculties and officers of administration of the University of Chicago, ca. March 21, 1917, both in Chicago Presidents' Papers. See also the report of a telegram sent by University of Wisconsin faculty members in February to President Wilson and the Wisconsin members of Congress, in Carl Russell Fish report on university activities in the war, September 5, 1918, in Fish Papers, and memorial of President Hadley and 190 members of the Yale faculty to President Wilson, in Henry W. Farnam to "Sir" [Wilson], March 20, 1917, in Farnam Papers.

the officers of the principal national associations of colleges and universities and the heads of a number of institutions of higher learning.
About 150 representatives of higher education met in Washington on
May 5 and, among other things, set up a committee of presidents and
deans as a university section of the Committee on Engineering and Education, to apprise educators of the government's needs and to arouse
national leaders to the importance of colleges and universities for war
service. But the committee was ineffective and, in the absence of any
coordination, "war activities ramified at once in scores of different direc-
tions."[40] The government had begun to call upon the physical plant,
manpower, and expertise of the institutions of higher learning. In the
face of a serious depletion of students and faculty members for war service and of confusing, overlapping, and often contradictory instructions
to the colleges and universities from different government departments
and officers, the university community itself met in January, 1918, and
established the Emergency Council on Education to centralize and coor-
dinate the war service of higher education.[41] In February, 1918, the government finally established the War Department Committee on Education and Special Training to serve as the official link between itself
and the colleges and universities.

Writing from the perspective of the exigencies of national defense,
critics have emphasized the enormous cost to the war effort of the many
months of delay in formulating a "rational policy for the conservation

40. Parke R. Kolbe, *The Colleges in War Time and After* (New York, 1919),
46, 49; Samuel P. Capen, "The Effect of the World War, 1914–18, on American
Colleges and Universities," *Educational Record*, XXI, (January, 1940), 43. Harvard's President Lowell resigned from the committee because he found the meetings "not productive of great good." A. Lawrence Lowell to University of Kansas
Chancellor Frank Strong, November 27, 1917, in Lowell Papers.

41. See, especially, "The Origin of the Movement and the Reasons for It" and
"The Emergency Council on Education," ca. January, 1918, both in Lowell Papers. The presidents of Harvard, Princeton, and Yale suspected that the council
would only add to the proliferating number of organizations, so they resisted its
establishment. But once the council was organized, they supported it. John G.
Hibben to A. Lawrence Lowell, January 3, 1918, and Lowell to Hibben, January
7, 1918, both in Lowell Papers; Arthur T. Hadley to Hibben, January 4, 1918, in
Yale Presidents' Papers. The Emergency Council on Education shortly changed
its name to American Council on Education.

and effective use of scientific personnel and equipment."[42] There is, of course, another facet to the problem, and that concerns the exigent situation created by the crisis of war within the institutions of higher learning themselves. The integrity of the colleges and universities as centers for higher learning was threatened seriously by the combined pressure of calls on their resources and their own overwhelming inclination to serve the cause.

From the start, university spokesmen took the position that their purpose was primarily, even exclusively, to aid the war effort to the maximum of their capacity. The May 5 meeting of college and university representatives in Washington adopted a unanimous resolution whose preamble stated: "In the supreme crisis that confronts the Nation the colleges and universities of America have the single-minded thought and desire to summon to the country's service every resource at their command, to offer to the Nation their full strength without reservation, and to consecrate their every power to the high task of securing for all mankind those ideas and ideals that gave them birth and out of which have grown their most precious traditions."[43] In particular, the resolution affirmed readiness to change courses of study and the academic calendar in accordance with national needs, requested the formulation and publication of plans for close cooperation between the government and the universities, and further requested information about the government's methods of war prosecution so that the universities could mobilize their own forces more effectively.[44] In its first public statement the Emergency Council on Education announced that its object was "to place the resources of the educational institutions of our country more completely at the disposal of the national government and its departments." John G. Hibben, Arthur T. Hadley, and A. Lawrence Lowell opposed the

42. Capen, "The Effect of the World War, 1914–18, on American Colleges and Universities," 40; see also "Education and the Last World War," *Educational Record,* XXI (July, 1940), 427–29; Roland Haynes, "The Colleges in the Preparedness Program, 1917–18 and 1940," *Educational Record,* XXI (October, 1940), 489–96; and Paul V. McNutt, *Civilian Morale and the Colleges,* American Council on Education Studies, Ser. 1, Vol. V, No. 13 (Washington, D.C., 1941), 8.
43. Quoted in Kolbe, *Colleges in War Time,* 27.
44. Thwing, *The American Colleges and Universities,* 26.

formation of the council because they thought it would hinder the universities' war service. Lowell suspected that the council would "draw off energy that could be better devoted to the primary object of assisting the Government." At Harvard, he said, "we are in no perplexity about what we had better do to assist the Government . . . we are continually receiving calls from the Government which we are doing our utmost to meet; and . . . all our professors are working to the full extent of their powers."[45] No words better convey the image of the university consecrated in service to the cause than Columbia University President Nicholas Murray Butler's assurance to the secretary of war that, "if by any act of ours or by the service of any one, or all, of our great army of students and teachers we can strengthen the hands of the government at this critical hour in the world's history, we regard it as only a privilege and an honor to be permitted to do so."[46]

There is no lack of testimony to the immediate and enduring disruption of the campus caused by intervention. The situation at Yale will serve as an example. Immediately after the United States entered the war, Hadley wrote:

> Have placed laboratories at disposal of Government, organized research committee for National Defense Council, and promised leave of absence to instructors needed by Government. Have organized four year course for training reserve artillery officers, aviation unit already in service, naval training unit, and motor boat patrol for Long Island sound. Will graduate at once any senior called to service of the Government. Have formed Emergency War Council, consisting of President, Secretary, Treasurer, Deans of College and Scientific School, and Military Science professor, with authority to deal with any situation which may arise without waiting for approval of faculty.[47]

To another correspondent Hadley described conditions at Yale: "You can hardly appreciate the degree of excitement here and the number of

45. "The Emergency Council on Education," January, 1918, A. Lawrence Lowell to William L. Bryan, January 7, 1918, John G. Hibben to Lowell, January 3, 1918, and Arthur T. Hadley to Herman V. Ames, February 13, 1918, all in Lowell Papers.

46. Nicholas Murray Butler to Newton D. Baker, September 24, 1917, in Columbia University Archives.

47. Arthur T. Hadley to J. S. Nollen, April 12, 1917, in Yale Presidents' Papers.

readjustments that have to be made almost daily, both in our educational mechanism and in our relations to the state." By the fall semester Hadley reported, "We are beginning our college year short forty professors and more than a thousand students." By the spring semester the number of faculty members on leave of absence for war work was up to seventy, with fifty more on at least part-time leave. Hadley concluded, "Those of us who are left have to work pretty hard and do some things that we are not used to doing."[48]

On college campuses everywhere, policies had to be devised hastily concerning the granting of academic credit and degrees to students who left for military service without completing the academic year and concerning the conditions upon which faculty members were to be released for war service. The equivalency of military training with academic training had to be calculated; as students were recruited to work on farms, calculations also had to be made of the educational value of agricultural labor.[49] Even the women's colleges, which did not suffer the loss of students to military service, reported a considerable impact of the war on the atmosphere, organization, and activities of the campus.[50]

Indeed, the face of higher education was changed for the period of the war. Clearly, the new face was not the same in every kind of in-

48. Arthur T. Hadley to M. H. Robinson, April 14, 1917, Hadley to W. M. Blair, Sept. 25, 1917, and Hadley to Evarts Tracy, March 8, 1918, *ibid.* A more detailed description of the impact of student and faculty losses and of the economic consequences of the war on the campuses will be found in Chap. VI herein.

49. Martin W. Fain, secretary to the president of the University of Cincinnati, to the secretary of the University of Wisconsin, September 27, 1917, and Charles R. Van Hise to University of Cincinnati President Charles W. Dabney, October 2, 1917, both in Presidents' Papers, University of Wisconsin Archives, hereinafter cited as Wisconsin Presidents' Papers; A. Lawrence Lowell to State University of Iowa President Walter A. Jessup, January 29, 1918, in Lowell Papers; Arthur T. Hadley to University of Rochester President Rush Rhees, October 26, 1917, in Yale Presidents' Papers; Report of the Committee on Credit for War Service at the University of Chicago, March 16, 1918, in Divinity School Correspondence, University of Chicago Archives, hereinafter cited as Chicago Divinity School Correspondence; and Harry Pratt Judson to Clark University President G. Stanley Hall, May 27, 1918, in Chicago Presidents' Papers. A good summary of the various provisions made can be found in Kolbe, *Colleges in War Time*, 34, 122–23, 132–33.

50. Marian Churchill White, *A History of Barnard College* (New York, 1954), Chap. 9, and Kolbe, *Colleges in War Time*, 216–20.

stitution. Agricultural colleges performed experimental and practical work of a very particular sort; scientific and technical institutes made contributions of a kind different from women's colleges; large university centers had different resources and more complicated problems of adjustment than small, isolated colleges. But the overall picture is one of reorganizing college work to serve the interests of the government at war. The reorganization may be seen in the donation of the physical plant to the government (including laboratories, shops, and other teaching facilities); the establishment of special military courses of study; the introduction or increased prominence of military training on the campus; the adjustment of the curriculum in accordance with war-related needs and interests; the establishment of war committees that recruited faculty for on-campus and off-campus publicistic work, managed war fund drives on campus, and served as liaison between the campus and local and national patriotic societies; and the granting of leaves of absence to administrators and faculty for military and nonmilitary war service. The greatest reorganization of all took place under the Students' Army Training Corps program, which in the fall of 1918 turned the American campuses into military training camps for the War Department. This program is treated separately in Chapter VI.[51]

Beyond the general influence of the service ideal, the readiness of university communities to reorganize their purpose so thoroughly in the face of the challenge of war had several sources. Hints of competitive patriotism appear here and there in the record. When diplomatic re-

51. See "Report of Committee U on Patriotic Service," *American Association of University Professors Bulletin*, V (March, 1919), 30–31, for a summary of evidence that substantial donations of faculty and facilities for war service took place at institutions of every type, in every area of the country. College catalogues are an excellent source of information about special courses, lecture series, and general campus war work. See, for example, "Cornell's Work During the War," *Register of Cornell University, 1918–1919*, X (January 1, 1919), 169–72, and "War Activities of the University," *Bulletin of the University of Wisconsin, 1917–18* (Madison, 1918), 59–61. Curriculum changes are summarized in Kolbe, *Colleges in War Time*, 106–16, 207–29. For examples of university war publications see *Facts About the War*, compiled or written by members of the faculty of the University of Minnesota (Minneapolis, 1917); *War Book of the University of Wisconsin: Papers on the Causes and Issues of the War*, by members of the faculty (Madison, 1918); Walter B. Pitkin and Roscoe C. E. Brown (eds.), *Columbia War Papers* (New York, 1917); and *The World Peril: America's Interest in the War*, by members of the faculty of Princeton University (Princeton, 1917).

lations with Germany were broken, the *Columbia Alumni News* proclaimed that "Columbia, of the universities of the land, has always been among the first to offer herself to the public service when need arises. The time for service has again arrived and the need is great. Columbia will heed the call."[52] After war was declared, Professor James T. Shotwell wired a colleague at Columbia to make every effort to secure attendance for a lecture there by Guy Stanton Ford, to counteract the "impression growing in Washington that eastern universities are not as active as middle west." On the occasion of the publication of the Minnesota faculty war book, *Facts About the War,* Cephas D. Allin exulted that "Minnesota has 'effected a scoop' on most of the other universities of the country."[53]

Outside criticism and pressure to which institutions were subject were further factors influencing their response to the war. The University of Wisconsin provides a particularly good example, because both political and ethnic factors in the state put the university on the defensive frequently during the war. Since the early years of the century, the university had been caught in the struggle between Progressive and conservative forces in the state; identified with Progressive elements, the university's fate seemed to depend on the vicissitudes of political changes in the state capital. The university also was subject to the influence of the press, which shaped public attitudes toward its program.[54] Once the country was at war the University of Wisconsin became particularly prone to attacks from its political and journalistic critics. Its vulnerability was increased by the defensive character of patriotism in the state, resulting from the presence of large numbers of German-Americans in Wisconsin and the opposition of Robert M. La Follette, Wisconsin's senior senator, to the war. Two episodes occurring during the academic

52. "Editorial," *Columbia Alumni News*, VIII (February 9, 1917), 462.
53. James T. Shotwell to J. C. Egbert, July 29, 1917, Shotwell to D. S. Muzzey, July 29, 1917, both in CPI Papers; Cephas D. Allin to William Anderson, July 20, 1917, in Minnesota Department of Political Science Correspondence. Allin later welcomed the opportunity for Minnesota to profit from the difficulties created for other universities by the war. "We have the opportunity of a life time now to strengthen the teaching forces at the University, because the eastern institutions have been so badly hit by the war," he observed. Allin to Guy Stanton Ford, February 4, 1918, in CPI Papers.
54. Curti and Carstensen, *The University of Wisconsin*, II, 34, 71–72, 8.

year 1917–1918 reveal the particular sensitivity of the university to negative reflections on its patriotism.

When Assistant Secretary of Agriculture Carl Vrooman spoke at the University of Wisconsin in November, 1917, something in the student response led him publicly to voice the suspicion that the university was insufficiently militant, that it was "guided by a milk and water patriotism, a kind of platonic patriotism." The charge immediately was picked up by the Wisconsin press. One paper declared it an insult to the state that the question of the university's loyalty needed to be raised. "Wisconsin's place in the union is already enough questioned," it charged. "The university, a state institution, should not contribute to the country's doubt." Van Hise felt impelled to protest Vrooman's attack, and he wrote President Wilson eight typewritten pages of defense against the accusation, describing in detail the wholehearted and total mobilization of the university community in support of the war. Copies of the letters to Wilson were sent to the secretary of war, to Vrooman, and to the regents and visitors of the university. Clearly, Van Hise viewed the situation as serious, for he directed Professor John R. Commons in the preparation of a lengthy document in praise of his own patriotic activities and leadership.[55]

The situation was to be repeated in the spring, when Princeton Professor Robert McNutt McElroy, chairman of the National Security League Committee on Patriotism Through Education, publicly accused the University of Wisconsin of being unpatriotic and of harboring traitors.[56] Had the university been confident of the security of its position, its spokesmen could have issued a brief dismissal of the clearly

55. Summary of Vrooman address, *Wisconsin State Journal*, November 22, 1917, Milwaukee *Journal*, November 23, 1917, December 5, 1917, Charles R. Van Hise to President Woodrow Wilson, November 27, 1917, Richard Lloyd-Jones to President Woodrow Wilson, December 1, 1917—in which Lloyd-Jones, chairman of the university Board of Visitors and editor of the influential *Wisconsin State Journal,* repudiated Van Hise's defense to Wilson and supported Vrooman's charge against the University—and folder "Commons (Defense of Van Hise's Wartime Activities)," all in Wisconsin Presidents' Papers.

56. The circumstances surrounding McElroy's charge are described in Curti and Carstensen, *The University of Wisconsin*, II, 117–18.

outrageous and irresponsible charges. Instead, they embarked on an elaborate and protracted campaign of self-justification that included publication of a pamphlet, passage of a faculty resolution, and communications to United States congressmen, to the University of Wisconsin faculty, regents, and alumni, to the Princeton faculty, to leading national newspapers and magazines, and to the members of the Wisconsin state legislature. Van Hise wrote two letters of protest to Princeton President Hibben, and the university still was arguing its case in early 1919, at a congressional investigation of the activities of the National Security League.[57]

An obverse to the problem of outside suspicion of universities was the prospect offered by the war for institutions of higher learning to win public confidence and support by demonstrating their usefulness to the cause. This prospect was spelled out explicitly by Shotwell in a letter urging the collection of documents relating to the war contributions of American universities. "In view of the need of stiffening the public conscience in support of education, some good use might be made of this material," he argued. Shotwell referred specifically to the campaign by university representatives then being waged in Washington to secure tax exemption for donations to institutions of higher learning.[58] "But I am also thinking," he continued, "of the hard times after the war when we shall have to justify ourselves continually in order to receive adequate support." Similar sentiments were voiced by Albert Bushnell Hart when he recommended that something be done "to put the various institutions of learning throughout the country, public and private, into some kind of combination of understanding and effort [in behalf of service in the impending war]. This is the opportunity of the public state universities

57. John B. Winslow, Charles R. Van Hise, and E. A. Birge, *Report Upon the Statements of Professor Robert McNutt McElroy and the Executive Committee of the National Security League Relating to the University of Wisconsin* (N. p., n.d. [1918]); Document 90, Minutes of special university faculty meeting, April 24, 1918, in Wisconsin Faculty Documents.

58. For this campaign see Arthur T. Hadley to George P. McLean, May 25, 1918, in Yale Presidents' Papers; Samuel McCune Lindsay to Dear Mr. President [Judson], June 29, 1917, in Chicago Presidents' Papers; and Lindsay to My dear President [Van Hise], July 19, 1917, in Wisconsin Presidents' Papers.

and other institutions of higher learning to show that they are worth
while."[59] After the armistice, Parke R. Kolbe recounted that with the
outbreak of the war "the universities saw the horizon of their pre-war
opportunities for useful cooperation infinitely widened, and their whole
activity suddenly elevated from the plane of every-day education to that
of national defense. . . . the college, the only source of supply [of
trained men], had acquired in time of war an importance far beyond its
peace-time status."[60] As president of the Municipal University of Akron
and as special collaborator in the United States Bureau of Education,
Kolbe was in a position to make the observation with authority.

The response of professors to the challenge of war cannot be divorced
from the response of the institutions within which they worked and
which commanded their loyalty. The influence of the universities' spirit
of dedication to and actual mobilization for the cause and their desire to
prove their patriotism and demonstrate their value acted in both subtle
and direct ways on professors. To begin with, in the crisis of war the
professors' sense of familial loyalty and obligation to their institution
and its members was heightened. Frederick J. E. Woodbridge has left an
excellent description of the sensitizing effect of the war crisis on a
professor's identification with his own university community. Dean of
graduate faculties at Columbia, Woodbridge was visiting professor of
philosophy at the University of California in the spring semester of the
1916–1917 academic year. When the diplomatic crisis preceding intervention was at its height he wrote Professor E. R. A. Seligman, who was
acting dean in his place: "These are really homesick days for me. In the
anxiety that has come upon the land, I feel a little deserted and desert-
ing to be away from the rest of you and not share with you day by day
the new responsibility. The pleasure of being a member of the faculty of
this university hardly dispels a feeling of isolation. So I am writing not
so much because I have anything to say, but because I must have con-

    59. James T. Shotwell to Nicholas Murray Butler, July 13, 1917, in James T.
Shotwell Papers, Special Collections, Columbia University Library; Albert Bushnell Hart to Ralph Easley, March 13, 1917, in Hart Papers.
    60. Kolbe, Colleges in War Time, 21, 23.

tact with Columbia."[61] Given this kind of identification, the individual professor was likely to be highly susceptible to the communal patriotism that was expressed in the wartime spirit of dedication on the American campus and the ready mobilization of its resources.

There were more concrete institutional influences at work on individual professors to encourage them to join the campus crusade. When an appeal for participation in campus war activities came from the office of the president or from official campus war organizations, it did not need the force of compulsion to be effective. At Wisconsin, Chairman Carl Russell Fish of the War Work Fund Campaign Committee notified the faculty that the university considered a fund drive for the YMCA and YWCA so important that all university activities were being canceled for a two-hour convocation. Fish told his colleagues:

> It is absolutely necessary in order to obtain our object, that the faculty shall be known to stand behind it individually. All members of the faculty are urged therefore to attend the University Loyalty meeting. . . . They are also requested to sit together in order that their presence may be obvious. A section of seats will be specially reserved for them and it is as inevitable that the failure to fill this section will have an unfortunate effect as it is that if filled it will go far to insuring the success of the movement.[62]

At the University of Chicago, a typical fund appeal to the faculty began as follows: "President Judson has asked the same committee that solicited funds for the Y. M. C. A. war work to bring to the attention of faculty members the needs of the Red Cross." Faculty subscriptions to the Third Liberty Loan Campaign were made easy by the university's arrangement to purchase bonds for the professors and deduct the cost from their salaries.[63] The United War Work Campaign Committee sponsored a plan for faculty speakers to use five minutes of class time to appeal for funds from the students and to take collections on the spot.

61. F. J. E. Woodbridge to E. R. A. Seligman, February 21, 1917, in Seligman Collection.

62. Carl Russell Fish to the members of the faculty, November 19, 1917, in Fish Papers.

63. Elliot P. Downing to faculty members, May 23, 1917, and printed announcement of the bond purchase plan, over the signature of President Judson, spring, 1918, both in Chicago Divinity School Correspondence.

At least one individual found this a "wholly unseemly and undesirable method of raising money" and refused to "be a party to it." But the committee easily recruited a staff of about fifty faculty speakers, which it armed with suggested speech material and subscription cards, to implement the plan throughout the university.[64]

In addition to the influence of the institutional context, the noticeably stimulating effect of the experience of being at war on the academic profession and on particular disciplines must be counted among the factors that kept up the enthusiasm of professors for the cause. Professors themselves drew attention to the vitalizing effect that contribution to the cause had on their disciplines and admonished their colleagues to consolidate the gains of new strength and enhanced reputation for the future.

Contributions to the war effort were most notable and noticeable in the sciences, and scientists were quick to draw the conclusion that they would reap a large reward from the new public awareness of the potentialities of science. It was the opinion of J. S. Ames, professor of physics at Johns Hopkins, that in peacetime, when commercial development was most important, "the university . . . [scientist] is at a great disadvantage. He rarely knows what problem is to be solved. . . . To-day, in order to meet the insistent demands of the war, the whole process is changed. . . . For the first time in the history of science men who are devoting their lives to it have an immediate opportunity of proving their worth to their country. It is a wonderful moment; and the universities of this country are seizing it. The stimulus to scientific work is simply enormous; and the growth of our knowledge is astounding."[65] After the war was over, Robert A. Millikan, the University of Chicago physicist who played a major role with the National Research Council in mobilizing the scientific community, observed that "the world has been waked up by the war to a new appreciation of what science can do." Because political and industrial leaders now recognized the potentialities of science,

64. E. D. Burton to F. R. Mecham, November 1, 1918; Mecham to Burton, November 5, 1918; Burton to Mecham, November 1, 1918, all in E. D. Burton Papers, University of Chicago Archives.
65. J. S. Ames, "The Trained Man of Science in the War," *Science,* n.s., XLVIII (October 25, 1918), 403.

he said, there were new opportunities in every branch of science in America, new opportunities for science as a field of study and as a career, and vast new opportunities for scientists in industry.[66] The various scientific disciplines had their spokesmen who were proud to point out their special contributions to the war effort and who urged that their newly acknowledged usefulness be capitalized upon to strengthen the discipline for the future.[67]

The psychological discipline, in particular, was presented with a unique opportunity by the war. Upon intervention, Robert M. Yerkes of Yale announced that if the war lasted for as long as a year psychologists would have the opportunity to render important service. "For after all, the human factors in the war are as important as are the mechanical and it can not be doubted that brains and not brawn will decide the great conflict," he said. The Committee on Psychology was established by the National Research Council to organize and supervise psychological research and service and got a prompt and hearty response from the membership of the American Psychological Association. The association itself set up twelve committees to deal with aspects of the relationship of psychology to war.[68]

The war worked what one psychologist termed "a miracle" for a particular branch of the discipline, the field of mental testing.[69] Yerkes helped establish a testing program in the army, to determine mental and emotional capabilities and defects among recruits and to measure their abilities in various skills and occupations. The objective was to establish the army's personnel work on a scientific basis. The program not only

66. Robert A. Millikan, "The New Opportunity in Science," *Science,* n.s., L (September 26, 1919), 289–96.
67. See, for example, George T. Moore, "Botanical Participation in War Work," *Science,* n.s., XLIX (March 21, 1919), 269–74; John M. Coulter, "The Botanical Opportunity," *Science,* n.s., XLIX (April 18, 1919), 363–67; L. O. Howard, "Entymology and the War," *Scientific Monthly,* VIII (February, 1919), 109–17; E. H. Johnson, "The Newer Demands on Physics and Physics Teachers Due to the War," *Science,* n.s., XLVIII (August 2, 1918), 101–108; and Charles L. Parsons, "The American Chemist in Warfare," *Science,* n.s., XLVIII (October 18, 1918), 377–86.
68. Robert M. Yerkes, "Psychology and National Service," *Science,* n.s., XLVI (August 3, 1917), 101–103.
69. "The Measurement and Utilization of Brain Power in the Army," *Science,* n.s., XLIX (March 14, 1919), 259.

gave psychologists the opportunity to render important service to the cause; it also gave them the chance to try new testing techniques on a vast number and variety of subjects. The military men accepted the program reluctantly, suspected that the psychologists were using the army as a laboratory for their own purposes, criticized their results, and abandoned testing with the war's end. But the program had established the practical value of psychological testing and made it respectable; after the war it enjoyed a new and permanent vogue in education and industry.[70]

Not only scientists but humanists and social scientists as well sensed in the war situation an opportunity to win confidence in their disciplines, to stimulate interest in them, and to accomplish necessary reorganization and reform. A committee of romance language teachers from institutions in every part of the country sent a circular to their colleagues announcing that America's entrance into the war presented them with special duties and opportunities. The war, they said, had increased interest and enrollments in French, which must be guided, developed, satisfied, and made permanent. The war had presented the opportunity to accomplish changes in purposes and methods of instruction; chiefly the war had established "the rights" of spoken French alongside those of written French. Similar opportunities and responsibilities were pointed out in the fields of Italian and Spanish. Further, the professors were advised to seize the opportunity to "more definitely set before advanced students the teaching of the Romance languages as a worthy career." The circular continued with recommended avenues of war service, including language instruction in the YMCA (for which "only men of genuine Christian character and experience" were eligible) and public speaking and translation in cooperation with state councils of defense

70. Daniel J. Kevles, "Testing the Army's Intelligence: Psychologists and the Military in World War I," *Journal of American History*, LV (December, 1968), 565–81. See also G. Stanley Hall, *The Life and Confessions of a Psychologist* (New York, 1923), 348. Hall asserted that the army program had demonstrated the "vast economic importance of assaying human nature as a chief factor in production" and had given the science of psychology a popularity and usefulness it never before had enjoyed. However, of the new field of industrial psychology, applied to advertising, salesmanship, and personnel work, he warned, "It must not be forgotten that all this work has added very little, if anything, to our real knowledge of man."

and municipal citizens' war boards.[71] Charles Beard announced that the war had thrown political science, economics, social economy, and sociology into the "crucible of circumstance" from which they would emerge vitalized and clearly relevant to problems of the contemporary world; Turner observed that war patriotism had aroused an interest in history, which "shouldn't be forgotten by us"; and Dewey declared that the war experience had demonstrated the efficacy of an instrumentalist approach to social problems and would result in a permanent revolution in the social sciences.[72]

In a postwar novel in which the identity of his own University of Chicago was thinly disguised, Robert Herrick made the observation that the war had a "rejuvenating" effect on the president and the faculty, by providing them with an opportunity to feel important through making a contribution to the "real" world. He wrote:

> [This was so] with the scholar Richard Caxton, with the scientist Dexter and his pneumonia serum, the physicist who was teaching young men how to adapt artillery fire to the weather, to Maxwell who was engaged in calculating the cubic contents of ships and how to pack away in each boat the maximum load, to Mallory who was putting into practise those theories of testing human adaptabilities hitherto worked out in laboratories with the aid of questionnaires. To all these and many more the war had given a sense of reality to their work, to their lives.

To the novel's protagonist, who was returning to the university seeking asylum from the human futility he had witnessed in war-torn Europe, it seemed "odd" that "his fellows were escaping from it into what seemed to them reality!"[73] Upon returning from the direct experience of combat service, the protagonist in George Boas' autobiographical novel *Never Go Back* found academic life (at the University of California) lacking in

71. "To Teachers of the Romance Languages in the United States of America," summer, 1917, in Chicago Divinity School Correspondence, and "To Teachers of French in the United States of America," June 8, 1917, in Chicago Presidents' Papers.

72. Charles Beard, "Political Science in the Crucible," *New Republic*, XIII (November 17, 1917), Supplement, 3–4; Billington and Whitehill (eds.), *"Dear Lady,"* 255; John Dewey, "A New Social Science," *New Republic*, XIV (April 6, 1918), 292–94.

73. Robert Herrick, *Chimes* (New York, 1926), 266.

vitality, full of clichés, and out of touch with the mass of humanity.[74] Both Herrick and Boas touched an important theme in the response of many American professors to the war: The war was seized as an opportunity for participation and experience in the world outside campus walls in a way that suggests that these professors felt the university was out of touch with "real life" and lacking, consequently, in real value. Those who were "left behind" on the campus repeatedly expressed frustration, uselessness, and isolation from reality.[75]

This response is most apparent in the many expressions of longing for direct military experience. Ralph Barton Perry, the Harvard philosopher, told a meeting at the University of California that "it is inglorious not to be *there*, as near the front, as *directly* taking part [in the fighting], as possible." Perry went on, "The luckiest, most enviable and most admirable man of all just now is *the fighting man*, who is dealing the blow." Those who had to remain on the campus were consoled with the assurance that universities, too, had a contribution to make to the cause, in the areas of morale, efficiency, and wisdom. The recognition of this contribution "may help you, as it helps me, to be a bit more reconciled to the relatively inglorious part that some of us are compelled to take," Perry persuaded. "And it may help us to put more heart and conviction into our tame academic pursuits."[76] Bernadotte Schmitt seized the opportunity to work for the Committee on Public Information as a second choice, having been "denied the privilege of active service." He said he was "most anxious to get into the army," but, since he was underweight and would not be accepted by the fighting branches, he was looking for intelligence or historical work instead. When the army finally took him he exulted, "I am now a soldier and all literary and historical investigations are indefinitely postponed."[77]

74. George Boas, *Never Go Back* (New York, 1928), 264–65, 281.
75. In this respect, academic intellectuals were sharing in the "anti-intellectualism of the intellectuals" that Christopher Lasch describes in *The New Radicalism in America* (New York, 1965), Chap. 9.
76. Ralph Barton Perry, "The Universities in War Time," *University of California Chronicle*, XX (1918), 239.
77. Bernadotte Schmitt to Guy Stanton Ford, November 5, 1917, and James T. Shotwell to A. A. Young, September 25, 1918, both in Inquiry Archives, National Archives; Schmitt to Ford, July 6, 1918, in CPI Papers.

Archibald Henderson, professor of literature at the University of North Carolina, wrote his friend William E. Dodd: "I keep thinking of the trenches & death & duty & carnage. I am restless, & feel dissatisfied. I wish I could get away to France." And Dodd, who was prevented from serving by a nervous disorder, confided to his diary: The soldiers "are training for the great ordeal in France to fight my battles which somehow I am ashamed to leave to them—feeling the injustice of staying at home when others give their lives for my safety."[78]

Men who were beyond military age despaired of their years. Richard T. Ely felt "unsettled" by not being able to fight. "I am too old to go to war," he lamented. "In the Spanish war of 1898, I was getting ready to go, but it closed too soon." Turner had just had an operation and wrote a friend: "If the surgeon could have cut off *years* enough to let me carry a gun, I should have been really happy."[79] Of himself and his colleagues at Columbia who were too old to fight, Munroe Smith wrote, "At times we seem to ourselves like the old men who sat on the walls of Troy, chirping like locusts, while the noise of battle rolled along the Scamander and the Simois as it has rolled now for four years through the valleys of the Aisne and the Marne."[80]

Second only to combat experience, the urge for participation and experience expressed itself in a desire to do something other than "humdrum," academic work. Some professors felt impelled to do manual labor in the service of the cause. William Stearns Davis, historian at the University of Minnesota, on his way to Boothbay Harbor for the summer, wrote Guy Stanton Ford that he hoped to get a job as a carpenter

78. Archibald Henderson to William E. Dodd, September 22, 1917, in Dodd Papers; Entry for January 1, 1918, in W. Alexander Mabry (ed.), "Professor William E. Dodd's Diary, 1916–1920," *John P. Branch Historical Papers of Randolph-Macon College,* n.s., II (March, 1953).
79. Richard T. Ely to F. B. Garver, July 25, 1917, in Ely Papers; Frederick Jackson Turner to C. H. Hull, June 5, 1917, in NBHS Papers.
80. "The Faculty Service Flag," address by Munroe Smith. 1918, in Smith Papers. See also Frederick P. Keppel, *Some War-Time Lessons* (New York, 1920), 49–50. "One Columbia man well over the draft age, told me frankly that he would gladly give up an important public office he held for the privilege of fighting with his hands, but he could not be tempted by an opportunity to fight with his head. Through this same impulse many and many a man attempted to conceal his special knowledge in order that he might fight in the line," Keppel recalled.

in a shipyard there. Although he would take a typewriter, he said, he was not sure that he would use it. "This is one of the times when I feel decidedly that the pen is NOT mightier that the sword." Carl Russell Fish decided to spend the summer working in a factory. He wrote, "This is the result of an effort to do something quite tangible, and I believe that manual labor is now the prime necessity, and also that there are plenty of people who are willing to save the country by thinking and writing." Dodd suggested that professors buy land in unsettled parts of the country and become farmers during the summer months.[81]

Others voiced a desire to participate in the experience of war by putting their intellectual abilities to public use. Ely expressed enormous regret at being "left out of the war work which has been going on in Washington" and confessed, "It has been painful to my wife, as well as to myself, that I have not had a more active part than I have had in this greatest war in the world's history." Similar sentiments came from James Henry Breasted, who wrote, "I regret to say that we members of the Oriental Department have not yet been able to find enough to do in aiding the War to carry us away from the University."[82] Yale's Charles Seymour was reported to be "restless" and seeking "a definite, active job" in the war effort, and his colleague George B. Adams sought work in the Inquiry, which struck him as being of "much greater practical importance than the somewhat remote results of scholarship." Clarence Alvord of the University of Illinois, seeking some kind of service to perform, summarized the mood of dissatisfaction among academics who were confined to the campus when he wrote, "As I have seen my colleagues one after another go into service of some sort or another, the feeling of my own helplessness has grown more and more acute."[83]

When individual professors described their calendars, jammed up

81. William Stearns Davis to Guy Stanton Ford, June 4, 1917, in CPI Papers; Carl Russell Fish to Charles H. Haskins, June 7, 1918, in Fish Papers; and William Dodd to Waldo Leland, May 19, 1917, in NBHS Papers.

82. Richard T. Ely to Dean David Kinley, November 22, 1918, in Ely Papers; James Henry Breasted to David A. Robertson, December 18, 1917, in Chicago Presidents' Papers.

83. C. H. Haring to Waldo Leland, May 21, 1917, in NBHS Papers; George B. Adams to James T. Shotwell, December 19, 1917, in Inquiry Archives; and Clarence Alvord to J. Franklin Jameson, June 5, 1918, in J. Franklin Jameson Papers, Library of Congress.

with activities, obligations, and commitments, they communicated the sense of purpose and exhilaration derived from activity in the service of the cause. For the profession as a whole, the AAUP Committee U on Patriotic Service summarized the results of a poll among faculty members across the country as follows: "The war, with its consequent changes in academic life, is reported to have had on the whole a stimulating and broadening effect upon the professors' lives and habits."[84] But there is no better expression of the pleasure, pride, and sense of purpose derived from participation than the account of a professor "demobilized" from service in a government agency at the war's end. He confessed to having had a secret and guilty sense of disappointment when the war ended, because for months he had been "having the time of his life." The letdown of professors when their war service was terminated by the armistice "proved the love of doing well something that one could put one's heart in; the love of expending energy with an undivided conscience and with the approval of one's fellows. It was the sudden consciousness of the new comradeship springing from coordinated and enthusiastic effort; above all it was a sense of scope and power most keenly felt when it was about to be lost."[85]

It is not surprising that the almost passionate desire of American professors to share in the great experience of war was couched frequently in terms of service, for the war presented a magnificent opportunity to put the service ideal into practice; the desire to participate and the impulse to serve coincided nicely. But the response of professors to the challenge of war reveals some implications of the service ideal that should be explored. Upon intervention, the AAUP council

84. Carl Russell Fish to Waldo Leland, September 21, 1917, and Fish to E. B. Greene, June 25, 1918, in NBHS Papers; James T. Shotwell to Guy Stanton Ford, June 22, 1917, and Andrew C. McLaughlin to Ford, September 10, 1918, in CPI Papers; "Report of Committee U on Patriotic Service," 32.

85. [Ralph Barton Perry], "The Demobilized Professor, By One of Them," *Atlantic Monthly*, CXXIII (April, 1919), 538–40. A list of Perry's writings in the Perry Papers at Harvard reveals that he was the author of this article. It concludes: "Everyone will tell you that the best days of all were those in which he could just barely keep his head above water, when everything was in arrears, when life was one continuous succession of alarms, emergencies, and crises. . . . It was almost as good as being at the front, because, at any rate, you were too excited or tired to remember that you weren't at the front."

authorized the president to appoint the Committee on Patriotic Service to ascertain areas of active engagement in the war effort for the association, its local branches, and its individual members.[86] It is conceivable that the professors' association might have responded to the challenge by establishing a committee to evaluate the war's probable effect on the primary purpose, standards, and values of the academic profession and to stimulate awareness and discussion among its membership of the very special challenge to professors in the crisis. Even prowar professors might have concluded that the most valuable service they had to offer *as professors* was to maintain the critical intellect and the institution of higher learning as citadels of sanity in the inevitable madness of war, in order to protect and promote the very values and freedoms in whose name the fight was being waged. Instead, they made themselves servants of the state's pursuit of victory and became implicated in all the compromises and concessions unavoidably involved in that pursuit. When Richard T. Ely delivered a patriotic address that deliberately stimulated a mindless revulsion against the Germans as a people and when John R. Commons worked to defeat the socialist Victor Berger's senatorial bid in 1918 by crudely implicating Berger in treason, they donated their intellectual talents in a way that clearly compromised the standards of their profession.[87] On the other hand, when Thorstein Veblen, as a statistical expert for the Food Administration, prepared a report demonstrating that the shortage of farm labor in the Midwest could be met by ending the harassment and persecution of the members of the Industrial Workers of the World (IWW) agricultural division, he was doing the best that could be expected of him as an intellectual expert—he devoted his considerable

86. "Committee U. Patriotic Service," *American Association of University Professors Bulletin*, III (October, 1917), 12–14; Charles H. Haskins (chairman) to the members of the Committee on Patriotic Service, January 7, 1918, in Chicago Divinity School Correspondence; "Preliminary Report of the Committee on Patriotic Service," *American Association of University Professors Bulletin*, IV (January, 1918), 10–12.

87. Richard T. Ely, *The World War and Leadership in a Democracy* (New York, 1918); John R. Commons, "Scheidemann and Berger—The Arch Traitors to Socialism and Democracy," November, 1918, in Ely Papers.

talents to reach an uncompromising solution of a social problem. He also, however, together with his assistant, was fired for his pains.[88]

The manner in which professors embraced the war and war service may be viewed in part as an expression of uncertainty about their social status and role.[89] To be sure, their support of United States intervention in the war was basically a matter of political judgment. Beyond their political enthusiasm for the cause, they were subject to professional influences that helped determine their contributions to the war effort. As individuals they were caught up in their institutions' mobilization for war service and they were conscious of the benefits that would accrue to their disciplines from participation in the prosecution of the war. But there is a strain of professional insecurity beneath their positive commitments to be of service during a time of national crisis. A sense of uncertainty about the role of the university, about the purpose and value of the academic profession, and about belonging in the larger social world is communicated in their expressions of desire to leap into service as fighting soldiers (even as manual workers) and in the restless quest for surrogate service by those who were left behind. The quest for purpose and "reality" outside campus walls suggests a view of the university itself and of the academic profession as lacking in purpose and unreal. In this respect the professors' response to the war may be seen as an attempted escape from alienation. The attempt had a professional price, however, which must be considered. The remainder of this work will explore the consequences and implications of professors becoming servants of the state in their role as public propagandists, in their response to wartime threats to academic freedom, and in their cooperation with the military assault on the autonomy of the campus.

88. Veblen, *Essays in Our Changing Order*, 319–36. For the firing of Veblen and his assistant, Isador Lubin, see Isador Lubin, "Recollections of Veblen," in Carlton C. Qualey (ed.), *Thorstein Veblen* (New York, 1968), 142.

89. Randolph Bourne also viewed the war support of American professors as an attempted escape from uncertainty, but he thought the intellectuals—college professors, socialists, and literary figures—embraced intervention as an escape from uncertainty about the war itself. See his "The War and the Intellectuals," *Seven Arts*, II (June, 1917), 142–43.

IV

Scholars in
the Service of
the State

WHEN THE GERMAN SAVANTS issued their appeal "To the Civilized World" in 1914, American scholars accused them of prostituting the function of their profession. Arthur Lovejoy, it will be recalled, characterized the manifesto's issuance as a "scandalous episode in the history of the scholar's profession," seeing in the episode both a lesson and a warning to professors in America. To Lovejoy, the function of scholars at all times was the "function of detached criticism, of cool consideration, of insisting that facts, and all the relevant facts be known and faced."[1] To the Germans who issued the manifesto, the document was not intended to reflect the ideal attributes of the professional scholar; it was intended as "an act of defense" against attacks upon their country's honor.[2] The German savants responded to national crisis not as detached professionals but as committed Germans. And for all their criticism of their German counterparts, when confronted with the challenge of war American scholars, too, responded to the call of citizenship at the expense of the standards of their profession. There were, of

1. Arthur O. Lovejoy, letter to the editor, *Nation*, XCIX (September 24, 4), 376.
2. New York *Times*, June 6, 1916, p. 13. See also David Starr Jordan, letter to the editor, *New Republic*, XXII (February 18, 1920), 356–57, for the results of a 1920 poll of men who signed the manifesto.

course, avenues through which a university scholar could discharge the responsibilities of citizenship without at all calling into question his professional integrity. To name but a few, service in the armed forces, the purchase of war bonds, or work for and contributions to the Red Cross and other charitable war organizations presented no challenge to the scholar's integrity. The problem arose when scholars attempted to merge their professional and patriotic roles and to pretend that intellect could be wedded to the national cause without compromise. This effort to serve the cause as a professional, particularly in behalf of the government, challenged the ideal of the scholar as a disinterested seeker of truth.

The challenge was likely to appear less great for the physical scientist than for the social scientist. To be sure, the former first had to be willing to devote his talents to the purposes of war (which were largely, of course, destructive) and to permit the subject and application of his work to be determined by those purposes. Beyond these considerations, if he worked as a technical expert, the results of his investigations, whether they were an explosive device, an optical range finder, or a lethal gas, would not betray that they were undertaken for the government. Once his work was decided upon, its professional character was not likely to be compromised by the purposes to which it was to be devoted. But overestimating the disinterestedness of professional expertise is easy. Just as the psychiatrist for the prosecution plays a different role from the psychiatrist for the defense in a criminal proceeding, so too is an expert in the service of the government the government's expert, to be retained so long as he serves the government's purpose. The issue is especially acute for social scientists, for in their disciplines questions of fact are not easily divorced from questions of value. That Veblen was fired by the Food Administration because his expert opinion was totally unacceptable to the authorities demonstrates, in a negative way, the unavoidable implication of an expert in the purposes and policy of his sponsor.

American social scientists (and humanists as well) contributed to the war effort by playing many public and professional roles that proved to be incompatible with the standard of detached criticism and insistence upon acknowledging and facing all known facts. Their activities ran the gamut from scholarly expertise to blatant propaganda, from partic- ipation in the House Inquiry, laying the groundwork for American policy at the peace conference, to writing tracts for the superpatriotic National Security League. The complex problems raised by the role of wartime expert and ideologue received inadequate attention at the time; but they come to light clearly in the records of two wartime agencies, the National Board for Historical Service, an organization established by historians for professional service to the cause, and the Division of Civic and Educational Publications of the Committee on Public Information, which relied heavily on the talents of professors to produce official war propaganda.[3]

On April 29, 1917, J. Franklin Jameson, head of the Department of Historical Research of the Carnegie Institution of Washington and man- aging editor of the *American Historical Review,* convened a meeting of seventeen historians "to consider the problem of what they and their fel- lows can do for the country in time of war." After meeting for two days the historians established the National Board for Historical Service (NBHS), which was "to bring into useful operation, in the present emer- gency, the intelligence and skill of the historical workers of the country."[4] The actual achievements of the NBHS are only of passing

3. For the work of the Inquiry see Lawrence E. Gelfand, *The Inquiry: American Preparation for Peace, 1917–1919* (New Haven, 1963). Gelfand makes it clear that the "expert" work of Inquiry scholars frequently expressed the political preference of the author. "Many reports show an extreme bias, a par- tisanship which flowed from the author's commitment to some special solution at the peace conference" (p. 225). For the National Security League, see Robert D. Ward, "The Origins and Activities of the National Security League," *Mississippi Valley Historical Review,* XLVII (June, 1960), 51–65. Lovejoy's own wartime ac- tivities included writing propaganda for the National Security League, as well as working for the Maryland State Council of Defense and the Military Morale Sec- tion of the War Department. George T. Blakey, *Historians on the Homefront: American Propagandists for the Great War* (Lexington, Ky., 1970), describes the contributions of historians to the National Security League, the National Board for Historical Service, and the Committee on Public Information. He provides sound criticism of the historians' propagandistic work, but his extremely narrow focus does not lead him to analyze or even to speculate about the reasons for the historians' conduct or its larger implications.

4. Andrew C. McLaughlin, "Historians and the War," *Dial,* LXII (May 17, 1917), 427. The conferees were Henry Bourne (Western Reserve), Edmund Bur- nett (Carnegie Institution), Victor S. Clark (Carnegie Institution), George M.

historical interest. The organization's importance lies in the kind of commitments elicited from the scholars who served it and in its exposure of the contradictions between the scholars' public and professional roles.

Historians were the only social scientists prepared to establish an organized professional body for patriotic service. Guy Stanton Ford, chief academic factotum of the government's propaganda agency and a founder of the NBHS, tried to interest the American Economic Association (AEA) and the Political Science Association (PSA) in establishing similar groups for their disciplines. But the council of the AEA, it was reported, "decided that it was not best to do anything as an organization," having been "influenced to no little degree by the constitutional provision prohibiting the Association from going on record in controverted matters." And the secretary-treasurer of the PSA reported that the political scientists decided to take "no official action. Correspondence indicates group enthusiastic for voluntary organization with historians without committing association."[5]

To be sure, the NBHS was not part of the American Historical Association and the AHA itself, as an organization, did not take an official position on the war. The association and its journal, however, did reflect a commitment to professional contribution to the cause. Jameson felt that a "historical review ought in war time and in times immediately after the conclusion of war to have some immediate purposes to subserve,"

Dutcher (Wesleyan), Guy Stanton Ford (Minnesota, CPI), Charles D. Hazen (Columbia), Charles H. Hull (Cornell), Gaillard Hunt (Library of Congress), J. Franklin Jameson, H. Barrett Learned (Department of Justice), Waldo G. Leland (Carnegie Institution, AHA), Albert E. McKinley (*History Teachers Magazine*), Andrew C. McLaughlin (Chicago), Thomas Walker Page (Virginia), Frederic L. Paxson (Wisconsin), James T. Shotwell (Columbia), and Frederick Jackson Turner (Harvard). The original NBHS was composed of Clark, Robert D. W. Connor (North Carolina History Commission), Carl Russell Fish, Hazen, Hull, Hunt, Leland, Shotwell, and Turner. Later additions included Carl Becker, Archibald Cary Coolidge (Harvard), William E. Dodd, Evarts B. Greene (Illinois), Dana C. Munro, and Wallace Notestein (Minnesota), among others. Ultimately, the Board comprised nineteen historians. It was financed by the Carnegie Institution.

5. Guy Stanton Ford to John R. Commons, May 19, 1917, and Ford to Chester Lloyd-Jones, May 19, 1917, both in CPI Papers; W. F. Willcox to Charles Hull, June 4, 1917, in NBHS Papers; telegram from Lloyd-Jones to George Creel, June, 1917, in CPI Papers.

and he reported that he and his staff "have tried to have a lot of articles that would help to clarify public intelligence for purposes of the present day." Jameson said that he was particularly interested in "printing articles which illuminate the relations between Great Britain and the United States," because "the two nations ought henceforth to be drawn more closely together than ever before." He did not believe in distorting the history of their past relations, he insisted, only in promoting "fuller knowledge of the English point of view."[6] The program committee for the AHA 1917 annual meeting was careful to keep the conflict from intruding unduly into the proceedings. But Waldo G. Leland, secretary of the association, characterized the larger purposes of the meeting as follows: "A national historical society with no thoughts above the level of antiquarianism might better not convene in such days as these, but a national historical society with the right spirit could not hold an annual meeting without sending its members home heartened to the performance of every patriotic duty, nor without extending in some measure throughout the nation the inspiring and clarifying influence of sound historical thinking and right patriotic feeling."[7]

There was lively discussion within the executive council about the propriety of holding the annual meeting in 1918, with AHA President William Roscoe Thayer vigorously in opposition on the grounds that a meeting would contravene the government's admonition against "unnecessary travel" and would cost many thousands of dollars that could otherwise be contributed "towards winning the war." The council voted to hold the meeting; both Jameson and Evarts B. Greene defended the decision to Thayer on patriotic grounds, arguing that the meeting would strengthen the patriotic determination of historians and contribute to national solidarity.[8] On the general subject of the war and the historical

6. J. Franklin Jameson to Ephraim D. Adams, December 17, 1918, in Jameson Papers.

7. Waldo G. Leland, "The Meeting of the American Historical Association at Philadelphia," *American Historical Review*, XXIII (April, 1918), 506.

8. William Roscoe Thayer to Evarts B. Greene, May 25, 1918, in American Historical Association Papers, Library of Congress; Thayer to J. Franklin Jameson, August 14, 1918, and Jameson to Thayer, August 21, 1918, both in Jameson Papers; Greene to Thayer, September 2, 1918, Thayer Papers. The 1918 annual meeting did not take place, after all, because of the influenza epidemic.

profession the council was moved to pass only one minor resolution.[9]

The AHA may have been technically uncommitted on the war and the NBHS may have been technically a voluntary and unofficial organization, but there was more than an incidental relationship between the two. Not only was the initiative for the founding of the board taken by AHA council member and *American Historical Review* editor Jameson, but the secretary of the AHA, Waldo Leland, held the secretarial office in the NBHS. Herman V. Ames indicated that the AHA was in constant touch with the NBHS through Jameson and Leland and had declared its willingness to cooperate with the board in any way possible.[10] Furthermore, the NBHS was given the pages of the *History Teachers Magazine,* whose financing and editorial advisory board came from the AHA, as a regular outlet for its communications. By June, 1918, the magazine's masthead bore the legend: "Edited in Cooperation with the National Board for Historical Service and under the Supervision of a Committee of the American Historical Association." The historians' patriotic organization had the confidence and cooperation of the historians' professional association.

There are several possible explanations why historians proved especially anxious and ready to devote themselves as professionals to public service. One of them was a desire to rescue history from the implication of irrelevancy it might appear to have because of its association with the past. In connection with the founding of the NBHS, fears were expressed that the historian, because he was concerned with the past, would appear particularly useless in the national emergency. Jameson commented that whereas "the public and the authorities are abundantly aware of the usefulness of what . . . [the scientist] is doing . . . both are

---

AHA President Thayer had been a committed partisan of the Allied cause long before intervention, and he wrote several heated tracts on the war. He was a representative of the old tradition of gentlemanly scholarship; he neither had advanced professional training nor an academic post.

9. William T. Hutchinson, "The American Historian in Wartime," *Mississippi Valley Historical Review,* XXIX (September, 1942), 166.

10. Herman V. Ames to J. H. Breasted, May 23, 1917, in Herman V. Ames Papers, University of Pennsylvania Archives. Other overlapping officers of the AHA and NBHS included Turner, McLaughlin, Dodd, and Greene.

prone to regard the historian as occupied only with the dates and details of remote transactions having no relation to the fateful exigencies of the present day." And McLaughlin described the impulse behind the establishment of the NBHS in the following terms: "At first sight it may not appear very evident that men whose labors are devoted to past events can be of much service in a task like that now confronting us. But at the very least the government ought to be informed that there is a large number of trained men anxious and willing to do anything which their training fits them for."[11]

In fact, far from themselves believing that history might be irrelevant to the present crisis, historians were certain that they, in particular, had a public role to play during the war. This is not surprising. Historical study traditionally had been associated broadly with education for citizenship. As Higham demonstrates, scientific historians always had assumed that history had a "utilitarian" function in promoting civic education and political responsibility. With the advent of the new history, this utilitarianism became self-conscious and deliberate and led, above all, to the demand for contemporary relevance.[12] It is understandable that historians, in general, felt called upon to play a public educative role during the war and that new historians, in particular, felt called upon to relate the subject of history specifically to the present crisis. The NBHS provided an outlet for these impulses.

The organization emerged from a series of discussions among Jameson, Leland, Shotwell, and Turner, who were concerned that the "store of competence and patriotic good will" of the nation's historians might run to waste or lie untouched when, instead, their expertise could be "systematically drawn upon to meet actual needs, felt or unfelt, of the government or the public." The "useful tasks" of professional "public service in wartime" proposed by the NBHS founders fell into two general categories: providing historical expertise for the federal and state governments and their various branches and informing and enlightening

11. J. Franklin Jameson, "Historical Scholars in War-Time," *American Historical Review*, XXII (July, 1917), 831; McLaughlin, "Historians and the War."
12. Andrew C. McLaughlin *et al.*, *The Study of History in Schools: Report to the American Historical Association by the Committee of Seven* (New York, 1899), 18–21; Higham *et al.*, *History*, 112.

public opinion about the war's causes and implications.[13] The NBHS had a further objective, as well, which combined professional and patriotic considerations—to revise the high school history curriculum to make it relevant to the war and the problems of the contemporary world. Immediately after the organization was established, Carl Russell Fish sent out a circular that opened with the declaration: "The teaching of history in the country is at a crisis as important in its degree as that which confronts the country." The crisis, he continued, presented the profession with an "opportunity for the greatest usefulness and for a corresponding increase in public estimation." He warned that "if it does not rise to this national emergency the sound teaching of history will receive a set-back from which it will not recover in this generation." To meet the crisis, the NBHS, in cooperation with the U.S. Bureau of Education, proposed a program to "adjust" the teaching of history in the high schools to the national wartime emergency.[14]

In its various activities the NBHS was designed to demonstrate that history was more than a lifeless and irrelevant catalog of past events and that historians had a vital professional contribution to make to the cause. The spokesmen for the organization, announcing its purposes to their colleagues in the profession, emphatically denied that its objectives in any way implied departure from professional canons of objectivity, impartiality, and "truthfulness." Shortly after the organization was founded it was announced that "the board intends to keep strictly within the lines of what is proper to historical students as such. To propagate any set of opinions, to advocate any course of policy, to swerve in any way from historical impartiality, is not part of its program."[15] Charles H. Hull explained to a colleague: "Our concern is that the craft do its part. What that may be we do not undertake to say. We have no orthodoxy. We make no propaganda. We would not exercise a censorship of opinion if we could. Our simple notion . . . is that history men know,

13. J. Franklin Jameson to George M. Dutcher, Max Farrand, Guy Stanton Ford *et al.,* April 20, 1917, in NBHS Papers; McLaughlin, "Historians and the War"; "National Board Organized," *History Teachers Magazine,* VIII (June, 1917), 200–201.

14. See circular, ca. May 3, 1917, in NBHS Papers.

15. *American Historical Review,* XXII (July, 1917), 919.

and some of them are able to tell, the facts on which . . . an informed
public opinion must rest concerning America's participation in the war,
and the way out for ourselves and the world."[16]

The disclaimer against propaganda was met with skepticism in some
quarters of the profession, not only because the board's objective of enlightening public opinion inevitably raised the "fear that history and *ex
parte* propaganda will be mixed," but because some historians thought
that the effort to relate history to present-day needs itself was a form of
propaganda, just as threatening to the integrity of history as was special
pleading in behalf of the cause. W. S. Ferguson, chairman of the history
department at Harvard, reported: "There is existent here a disposition to
believe that the historian should, first and foremost, hold down his own
job, and a certain fear lest a teacher of History be led too frequently to
teach not his own subject, but the present war. As you know, some of
us here do not believe that all History is but an interpretation of the
present situation." Ferguson also indicated that the implications of edu-
cating the public were somewhat distasteful to the Harvard historians.
"The strongest dissentients are in this part indubitably the Irish," he said.
"Now you know the situation here well enough to be aware that Harvard
men are not particularly well pleased to do missionary work among
them." He reported a sentiment within the department that it would be
"unwise" to "cooperate with the Boston Press or public meetings."[17]

The reservations about the NBHS communicated by Ferguson were
echoed elsewhere. Frederic L. Paxson, himself a founder of the board
and one of its committee members, wrote, "I am unaware of any partic-

16. Charles Hull to H. W. Hulme, June 5, 1917, in NBHS Papers.
17. Frederick Jackson Turner to J. Franklin Jameson, May 20, 1917, in
Jameson Papers; W. S. Ferguson to Waldo Leland, May 24, 1917, in History Department Correspondence, 1916–1920, Harvard University Archives, hereinafter
cited as Harvard History Department correspondence. Cf. the attitude of Claude
H. Van Tyne, who spoke actively in behalf of the National Security League. "I
have had the interesting experience," he recounted, "of talking to miscellaneous
crowds in public squares where my academic position . . . is the least of my
charms. It is an experience for one who leads our sheltered academic life to get
out and talk to 'hoboes' and people of every nationality who don't care anything
for our aristotle [*sic*] reputation. . . . I wonder," he mused, "how many of our be-
loved colleagues would stand up under such a test." Claude H. Van Tyne to W.
A. Frayer, April 18, 1918, in Claude H. Van Tyne Papers, Bentley Historical
Library, Michigan Historical Collections, University of Michigan.

ular crisis involving history teaching as such at this time, and entailing general revision of purpose, method, or material in our history teaching." He spelled out his trepidation: "I am distinctly afraid of the efforts which I know to be making in some quarters to use the war as a means of breaking down the teaching of history as history, in order to adopt the teaching of history as economics, or political economy, or something else. We have to be pretty circumspect . . . in order to avoid doing as much damage as good." The NBHS clearly was identified with the new history, particularly by its critics. Fish reported to Hull that several Wisconsin men "are afraid that the 'Robinson-Columbia' school of history has run us off our feet. . . . All the American history men are solid for our whole program, but [C. G.] Sellery and [William L.] Westermann fear of 'There is a Crisis' letter." Hull replied, "Sellery and Westermann are not the only people who have been more or less excited by your 'This is a Crisis' letter. I imagine that it had more to do with the Robinson-Columbia feeling than anything that Robinson has personally done here, for he has done nothing." Westermann agreed to serve on an NBHS committee in order, he said, "to try to put the damper upon possible tendencies . . . to pervert historical teaching and the meaning of history." All explanations notwithstanding, he remained convinced that the only "crisis" was in the work of the NBHS members. "If they permit themselves to suggest to secondary teachers that they should make analogies and draw lessons from the past to stimulate patriotism or to explain the present war, they will have done a serious wrong."[18]

In spite of some reservations about and opposition to the purposes of the NBHS, the board's appeal to the nation's historians struck a responsive chord. Historians all over the country wrote that they would do anything and go anywhere the board might ask to help the cause.[19]

18. Frederic L. Paxson to Evarts B. Greene, May 28, 1917, June 6, 1917, Carl Russell Fish to Charles H. Hull, May 31, 1917, Hull to Fish, June 2, 1917, William L. Westermann to R. V. D. Magoffin, July 10, 1917, all in NBHS Papers. Westermann resigned from his committee because of its "potential harm." Although later he was convinced to return, he continued to be unhappy with its purpose of relating ancient history to the world war.
19. One good example of the many unqualified offers of assistance is Carl Becker to Frederick Jackson Turner, May 14, 1917, *ibid.*

Backed by the confidence of its historical brethren, the board was able to undertake a wide variety of activities on many fronts. True to its original objective, the NBHS actively cooperated with government agencies. It performed research for the Committee on Public Information, providing material for publication, established a committee on research that assisted the Inquiry, met a request from the Bureau of Education to study ways of reorganizing the high school history curriculum in the light of the war, and collected and analyzed for the government a file of thirty to forty leading German and Austrian newspapers and periodicals. When it became known that the NBHS was given material withheld from general circulation, it was evident that to describe the organization as unofficial was misleading.[20] The NBHS assisted in shaping public opinion by arranging for speakers on war subjects at summer schools for teachers, at high school commencement exercises, and at army training camps. In addition, the organization prepared a bibliography on war subjects and collections of war prose and poetry for high school teachers and sponsored a prize essay contest for high school teachers on the subject of why America was at war. The board had a seat on the Emergency Council on Education and on the council's Committee on Education for Citizenship. It made the plans and raised the money for McLaughlin to speak on American history and Anglo-American relations at major English universities and arranged for George M. Wrong of the University of Toronto to address American university audiences on Canadian history and institutions. It encouraged historical societies and libraries to collect and preserve source materials on the war. It was a clearinghouse for advice and information about the war and about war service activities for high school and college history teachers.

Did all of this activity amount, as board members repeatedly proclaimed, to an impartial effort to enhance historical understanding of the war? Or was this activity more akin to what Paxson, at a later date and in another context, referred to as "historical engineering, explaining

20. See "Keeping Out German Newspapers," *Nation,* CVI (June 8, 1918), 670–71, and the reply by Victor S. Clark, "German Newspapers," *Nation,* CVI (June 22, 1918), 736.

the issues of the war that we might the better win it"?[21] The question was a complicated one and, because the public pronouncements failed really to confront it, NBHS disclaimers against propagating opinions, advocating policy, and swerving from historical impartiality appear unsatisfactory. From the private correspondence of board members it becomes clear that there were unresolved contradictions between their attitudes about and expectations of the organization and their avowed devotion to a scientific, scholarly pursuit of historical "truth." McLaughlin wanted the NBHS to interpret the war to the American people and to provide "guidance" for the future. Anticipating the meeting to establish the board, he wrote Jameson: "In my judgment the value of the historian now is chiefly in pointing out the route into the future which his various experiences have enabled him to see. In other words, it is time for us to dare to use our historical information for purposes of prophecy and actual guidance." After the board was established, McLaughlin affirmed that "the immediate and imperative task is to let the people know why we are in the war and the issues involved. This rather than strictly historical work is our present urgent function."[22] McLaughlin did not grapple with the problem of the thin line between the approach he urged and propaganda. Turner, on the other hand, granted that the board had to avoid work of a propagandistic nature; he acknowledged that historians "have a trust to keep as the ministers of historic truth." But he advocated portraying a highly selective truth, with the objective of enhancing popular support for the war. He wanted "the craft to set forth those things in our own and the European past, which cast light on present problems; those sufferings of our fathers and mothers which should hearten us for our own; those American hopes and ideals and characteristics which have meant to us a nation worth fighting for." Whereas Turner didn't avoid the issue of professional impartiality versus propaganda, he managed to evade it.[23]

21. Frederic L. Paxson, "The Great Demobilization," *American Historical Review*, XLIV (January, 1939), 237.

22. Andrew C. McLaughlin to J. Franklin Jameson, April 25, 1917, May 4, 1917, both in Jameson Papers.

23. Frederick Jackson Turner to J. Franklin Jameson, May 20, 1917, *ibid.* Ray Allen Billington concludes from Turner's conviction that "the truth would not be sullied if the Board emphasized episodes from the past that would illuminate

A revealing exchange of letters occurred about the selection of the distinguished historian Edward Potts Cheyney to the NBHS Committee on English History, which suggests that in fact the board functioned along the lines of "historical engineering." Arthur L. Cross, the committee chairman, wrote Fish that in spite of his "personal fondness" for Cheyney and "respect for his scholarship" Cheyney's membership on the committee was inadvisable because he was "a pronounced pacifist . . . [and] his views may not be in harmony with the rest of us." Fish responded that Cheyney was placed on the committee only after serious deliberation and assured Cross, "I should hesitate to make him responsible for anything, but I think he can be handled, and his name will certainly give weight."[24] This exchange indicates that despite its claim that the questions behind the outbreak of the war and United States participation in it were matters of fact, the NBHS operated as if the answers were a matter of opinion, preferring the opinion of Cross, for example, to that of Cheyney.

When we turn to material sponsored by the board, particularly the syllabi designed for use in the grammar schools and high schools and the series of articles on the high school history curriculum in the *History Teachers Magazine,* the difference between "historical understanding" and "historical engineering" becomes clear. Toward the end of 1917 the NBHS asked J. Montgomery Gambrill, professor of history at Teachers College, Columbia University, to prepare a syllabus on the war for use by grammar school teachers. Gambrill was convinced that to make grammar school children hate and fear the enemy was less important than to give them some idea of the problems involved in making the world safe for democracy. Accordingly, the syllabus he prepared emphasized that permanent peace would not be secured by military victory alone, but depended on reconciling nationalism with internationalism, providing military and economic security for all countries, and granting

---

present problems and aid the achievement of a just peace" that Turner "was arguing that history should be warped to suit the national purpose, even though still wearing the garb of objectivity." *Frederick Jackson Turner: Historian, Scholar, Teacher* (New York, 1973), 348.

24. Arthur L. Cross to Carl Russell Fish, May 20, 1917, and Fish to Cross, May 22, 1917, both in NBHS Papers.

them equality of opportunity in the world's markets and in the development of undeveloped lands. His fundamental point was that the narrow nationalistic and imperialistic perspective of the major powers had to be replaced with a larger conception of a world order. To develop this point his syllabus treated in considerable detail the origins and growth of nationalism and imperialism and their relationship to the war.

The NBHS found the syllabus unacceptable. Greene rejected it on the grounds that not only did it fail to provide practical suggestions for teachers, but that the "untrained teacher" might be misled by Gambrill's treatment of nationalism and imperialism to underestimate the liberalism of western Europe, the positive values of nationalism, and the nonpredatory aspects of imperialism. The "untrained teacher," in other words, might see only the disastrous effects of unbridled nationalism and imperialism in which all the belligerents had been engaged instead of seeing the war, as it was being portrayed officially, as a conflict between autocracy and liberal democracy. To be sure, Gambrill's syllabus was no example of impartial scholarship; it expressed *his* interpretation of the war. But the syllabus adopted in favor of Gambrill's was certainly not scholarly and impartial; it was designed to stimulate the emotions of school children by emphasizing the patriotic, heroic, and adventurous facets of the war and the evils of the enemy.[25]

For high school teachers and pupils, the NBHS (together with the CPI) actively cooperated with Indiana University history professor Samuel B. Harding in preparing a syllabus that appeared to be an impartial scholarly document but in fact promoted the official interpretation of the war as a struggle between autocracy and democracy. Harding's *The Study of the Great War: A Topical Outline, with Extensive Quotations and Reading References* was printed first as an NBHS supplement in the *History Teachers Magazine,* was placed at the top of an NBHS recommended reading list for teachers, and finally was issued in pamphlet form by the CPI. The syllabus cited over five hundred references to more than one hundred different sources, giving it the ap-

25. For the account of the Gambrill syllabus, see the useful book by Lewis P. Todd, *Wartime Relations of the Federal Government and the Public Schools, 1917–1918* (New York, 1945), 45–63.

pearance of a scholarly document. Upon scrutiny, however, the scholarly apparatus did not pass muster; it was selected carefully to draw up a one-sided indictment of the Central Powers. More than one third of its references were to other official propaganda leaflets of the CPI. Another third were references to the self-justifying diplomatic "colored books" of the belligerents, arranged so as to support the testimony of the Allies. The remainder were references to safe and standard sources. The document's picture of the war was so one-sided—charging Germany with every brutality and crime and portraying the Allies as infinitely patient and kind—as to be indefensible as history. Lewis Todd puts his finger on the distinction between this work and historical scholarship when he observes: "The drawing of an indictment and the preparation of a well-balanced historical interpretation are totally different problems, both in method and intent; the one is for the pleader and the propagandist, the other for the historian. We are dealing here with the historian turned propagandist."[26]

The NBHS series of articles on the high school history curriculum represented propaganda of a different sort. The articles originated in a request to the board by the Bureau of Education to assist in instructing the nation's high school teachers to teach history in relation to the war. Behind this request was the implication that the past could have meaning and vitality only in relation to the needs of the present, as well as the view that history could and should be used to stimulate patriotism. The NBHS met the request by setting up four committees, under the general chairmanship of Evarts B. Greene, to study the problem. The committees corresponded to the four high school history units: ancient history, medieval and modern European history, English history, and American history.[27] Arrangements were made to publish four articles

26. *Ibid.*, 50–52, and Blakey, *Historians on the Homefront*, 117–18.
27. The membership of the committees was as follows: Ancient History: R. V. D. Magoffin (chairman), J. H. Breasted, S. P. R. Chadwick, W. S. Davis, W. S. Ferguson, A. T. Olmstead, W. Westermann; Medieval and Modern Europe: D. C. Munro (chairman), F. M. Anderson, A. I. Andrews, S. B. Harding, D. C. Knowlton, M. McGill; English History: A. L. Cross (chairman), W. J. Chase, E. P. Cheyney, B. E. Hazard, L. M. Larson, W. Notestein; American History: E. B. Greene (chairman), W. L. Fleming, R. A. Maurer, F. L. Paxson, T. S. Smith, J. Sullivan, E. M. Violette.

(one in the subject of each unit) in each month's *History Teachers Magazine* during the school year 1917–1918.

It was this plan to relate all history to the war that drew strong objections from William L. Westermann. More concerned about protecting the integrity of historical studies than anxious to be of use to the cause, he insisted that the NBHS "should tell secondary teachers to do one thing, namely, to teach ancient history *in its own light,* to do it better than they have done it before, and, as far as possible, without reference to present times." After being convinced to withdraw his resignation from the Committee on Ancient History with the promise that articles appearing in the *History Teachers Magazine* would be signed by the author and would not pretend to represent the views of the committee jointly, Westermann contributed an article, "The Roman Empire and the Great War," which warned that any simple analogies between the history of the past and the present must be "either directly false or, at best, illusory."[28]

The publications of the four committees demonstrate that Westermann's fears were justified. Although there were exceptions, the most typical articles were characterized by grossly oversimplified arguments and crudely drawn historical analogies and were perversions of both history and contemporary affairs. The most bizarre distortions were necessary to draw analogies between ancient history and the war.[29] But the facile quest for relevance appeared in treatments of more recent history, as well. For example, in an article "Internal Problems During the Civil War," Fish admonished the history teacher not to fail to "call attention to the present enslavement of ten times as many individuals by Germany as were ever held in the South. Nor to [fail to] call attention to Lincoln's reiterated insistence that the Civil War must end in victory, not compromise. Nor to the fact that Lincoln throughout professed to be fighting for the best interests of the Southern people." James Westfall Thompson obliterated centuries of history when he drew a straight line

28. Westermann to Magoffin, July 10, 1917, in NBHS Papers; William L. Westermann, "The Roman Empire and the Great War," *History Teachers Magazine,* IX (February, 1918), 87.
29. See, for example, William S. Ferguson, "The Crisis of Hellenism," *History Teachers Magazine,* VIII (November, 1917), 290–91.

between medieval and modern Germany: "The present German Empire and the present program of German imperialism is the lineal descendant of the medieval empire both morally and politically. . . . *Germany always has been, and still is, imperialistic and not national, in its political theory, its psychology, its past history and its present policy.* It is not so far a cry as it seems from the hopes, aspirations, ambitions, policies, purposes, psychology of medieval Germany to the Germany of to-day. The age of the Hohenstaufen was 'the Day' of medieval Germany."[30]

The articles on English history are notably free from such clumsy distortions, but they illustrate even better the difference between promoting historical understanding of the war and the use of history to help win it. If the purpose of the articles really had been to demonstrate the relevance of the past to the war, they would have had to deal with the history of British sea power and imperialism and the implications of that history for German commercial and territorial ambitions. Since the purpose of the articles was to enhance popular support for the war, they were devoted to subjects designed to overcome popular suspicion of England. Many of the articles insistently made the point that America's most cherished social and political institutions had their origins in England.[31] Others emphasized that Britain had been influenced to reform its empire and political system in the nineteenth century by the American example, that by the twentieth century England was as liberal and democratic as the United States, and that the consequent affinity of the two nations provided a firm foundation for present and continued common action. There were repeated calls to reassess the history of Anglo-American relations, particularly concerning the American Revolution.[32]

30. Carl Russell Fish, "Internal Problems During the Civil War," *History Teachers Magazine,* IX (April, 1918), 200; James Westfall Thompson, "The Deeper Roots of Pan-Germanism," *Historical Outlook,* IX (October, 1918), 360, 366. *History Teachers Magazine* became *Historical Outlook* in the fall of 1918.

31. The irony of this point of view being disseminated by an organization of which Turner was an officer is inescapable and suggests the extent to which scholarly conviction took a back seat to propagandistic exigencies.

32. See, for example, Charles H. McIlwain, "Medieval England," *History Teachers Magazine,* VIII (October, 1917), 257–58; St. George L. Sioussat, "English Foundations of American Institutional Life," *History Teachers Magazine,* VIII (October, 1917), 260–61; Evarts B. Greene, "The American Revolution and the British Empire," *History Teachers Magazine,* VIII (November, 1917), 292–

There was a deliberate effort in the historical profession during the war to revise the historiography of England, but this revision wasn't simply an instance of healthy periodic reevaluation of regnant historical orthodoxy. For example, Jameson wrote to E. D. Adams that although he was not especially convinced of "British unselfishness . . . that does not matter; if we are in alliance with them in any sense—and I am very glad that we are—it is right to 'play up' all their nobler and better qualities and all the evidence of willingness on their part to act in the interest of the whole world and its future." From the time of its inception, historians appealed to the NBHS to help undo the damage to Anglo-American relations to which nationalistic history in the United States had contributed.[33] The *History Teachers Magazine* series was one effort in this direction; another was the speaking tour arranged for Andrew C. McLaughlin in England. The NBHS initiated the tour, which was jointly sponsored by the AHA, and raised the money to pay for it. Accompanied by AHA treasurer Charles Moore, McLaughlin spent about three months in England lecturing on various aspects of American history and Anglo-American relations, in this case attempting to improve British popular impressions of the United States, especially in the light of three years of American neutrality in the war. McLaughlin was received warmly and seems to have made a favorable impression. The London correspondent of the *Nation*, pointing out the obvious perils of an American presenting the subject of Anglo-American relations to British audiences, reported that "Professor McLaughlin, while leaving no doubt of his thorough-going Americanism, skated over vast expanses of thin ice with the utmost adroitness."[34]

94; R. L. Schuyler, "The Study of English History," *History Teachers Magazine,* IX (February, 1918), 90–91; and Conyers Read, "The Evolution of Democracy in England," *Historical Outlook,* IX (November, 1918), 428–31.

33. Hutchinson, "The American Historian in Wartime," 170–75; J. Franklin Jameson to E. D. Adams, May 3, 1917, in Jameson Papers; W. E. Lingelbach to Waldo G. Leland, May 7, 1917, Lingelbach to Frederick Jackson Turner, May 22, 1917, Amos I. Hershey to James T. Shotwell, August 6, 1917, Claude H. Van Tyne to Evarts B. Greene, May 5, 1918, and William E. Dodd to Leland, November 21, 1918, all in NBHS Papers.

34. Herbert H. Horwill, "Anglo-American Interpreters," *Nation,* CVII (July 20, 1918), 66. The lectures may be found in Andrew C. McLaughlin's *America and Britain* (New York, 1919), Chaps. 1–4.

It is clear that the impulse behind the establishment of the NBHS was to demonstrate the usefulness of history (even, as Fish suggested, to win for the historical profession a "corresponding increase in public estimation") and to be of service to the cause. These were not unworthy objectives. But at the same time the NBHS historians insisted on retaining their reputation in their work for disinterested, objective, professional expertise. Although the two were not necessarily mutually exclusive, there were inherent contradictions between the roles of servants to the cause and professional experts that the NBHS historians neither faced nor acknowledged. The historians offered service to the government in the name of professional expertise. But the professional expertise of historians does not lie in the area of "prophecy" and "guidance," to use McLaughlin's words, or in the area of showing "the way out for ourselves and the world," in Hull's words. When historians played the role of promoting the cause they could not claim legitimacy for their views in the name of professional expertise. The NBHS *was* promoting a point of view about the war, which was the official point of view that the war, in its origins and implications, was a conflict between autocracy and democracy. Edward Potts Cheyney did not share this point of view, and the NBHS historians had grave reservations about his qualifications to serve on one of their committees in spite of his acknowledged expertise in the field of English history. The NBHS historians in fact were serving as prosecutors of the Central Powers and were engaging in a conscious and deliberate campaign to use history to promote Anglo-American harmony. To have claimed legitimacy for these purposes in the name of disinterested professional expertise gave their efforts a ring of disingenuousness. The confusion between their objectives of promoting the cause and preserving "historical impartiality" was picked up by Samuel B. Harding. When he received a memorandum reminding the members of the high school curriculum committees that their object must not be the "inculcation of particular views," he objected that this seemed to urge history teachers to be "neutral." He insisted, "Surely nothing should be said in our bulletin which under the guise of instilling precepts of scientific poise and restraint would countenance the notion that it is the function of the history teacher to refrain in this crisis from uttering emphatically his conclusions as to the responsibility for this world calamity. . . . In the present emergency it seems clear to me that if the teacher cannot conscientiously and wholeheartedly lend his influence to supporting the war with Germany, during the continuance of the war he ought at least to keep silent." Greene, chairman of the four curriculum committees, replied that the difference between the position of Harding and the authors of the memorandum merely was "a matter of emphasis."[35] The NBHS wanted to have its cake and eat it too, to serve as the promoter of the American cause and be acknowledged as the exemplar of impartial historical scholarship.

The same devotion to the ideal of service and the sense of responsibility for guiding public opinion that led historians to establish, sanction, and cooperate with the NBHS also led historians and other social scientists to volunteer for work with the Division of Civic and Educational Publications of the Committee on Public Information. To reconcile disavowals of propaganda with the conception and activities of the NBHS was difficult enough; even more difficult was reconciling the contradiction between writing tracts for the government's official "information" agency and the ideal of responsible scholarship. But this is precisely what the CPI scholars tried to do. They either denied that they were producing propaganda at all or drew a distinction between "good" (truthful) and "vicious" (deceitful) propaganda. The scholars' denial and distinction suggest an uneasiness about serving as propagandists; they tried to reconcile propaganda and scholarship so that they could with clear consciences aid the government in its effort to unite the public behind the war.

The "fight for public opinion," to use Guy Stanton Ford's words, is an integral element of modern war. A student of propaganda in warfare insists that "no modern army can wage a war without the persistent support of the whole country." The interdependence of the civilian and military fronts in total, technological war, he explains, means that the

---

35. Harding's remarks are quoted in Dana C. Munro to Evarts B. Greene, July 13, 1917, and Greene's reply is in Greene to Munro, July 17, 1917, both in NBHS Papers.

"morale of the nation itself becomes of *military* importance."[36] In 1917, mind mobilization appeared particularly necessary in the United States, not only because of the country's isolationist tradition and heterogeneous population, but because Wilson had made a virtue of neutrality from the distant European conflict, in thought as well as in action, for almost three years. An overriding conviction of the necessity to fight was absent in America in the spring of 1917, and the president, himself partly responsible for the confusion and apathy that followed intervention, was bound to set up machinery to deal with the problem of public opinion.[37]

The CPI was established by executive order on April 13, 1917. Membership included the secretaries of war, state, and the navy in addition to the chairman George Creel, but the CPI so clearly was Creel's bailiwick that it became known popularly as the Creel Committee. The original purpose was to act as the government news agency, and control of the press was one of the CPI's important functions. Under the direction of the ambitious and energetic Creel, the committee proliferated into a complex propaganda organization that flooded the channels of communication in the United States and abroad with the official American interpretation of the war.[38]

Creel's career in journalism and politics in Colorado had long since earned him the reputation of a crusader. He was an ardent supporter of the war, which he viewed in Wilsonian terms as a struggle between democracy and autocracy. A Wilson supporter since 1911, he had worked actively in the 1912 and 1916 election campaigns and had proven to be

36. Guy Stanton Ford, "The Fight for Public Opinion," *Minnesota History Bulletin,* III (February, 1919), 3–26; Hans Speier, "Morale and Propaganda," in Daniel Lerner (ed.), *Propaganda in War and Crisis* (New York, 1951), 6.
37. Todd, *Wartime Relations,* 14.
38. George Creel wrote accounts of the CPI in *How We Advertised America* (New York, 1920) and in his autobiography, *Rebel at Large: Recollections of Fifty Crowded Years* (New York, 1947). James R. Mock and Cedric Larson's *Words That Won the War: The Story of the Committee on Public Information, 1917–1919* (Princeton, 1939) remains the most informative study of the organization; deficient in analysis or criticism, it is useful mainly for its detailed description of the CPI. Sydney Stahl Weinberg's "Wartime Propaganda in a Democracy: America's Twentieth-Century Information Agencies" (Ph.D. dissertation, Columbia University, 1969), Chap. I, is a good source for Wilson and Creel's propaganda objectives.

absolutely loyal to the president. These attributes made him a logical choice to head the administration's propaganda agency. If there was a shadow side in Creel's extreme partisanship, egotism, impulsiveness, and indiscretion, which earned him the suspicion of the nation's press and the hostility of Congress (especially its Republican members), his usefulness was not diminished in Wilson's eyes. Despite repeated attacks by Congress, which at one point expressed its dissatisfaction with the CPI by cutting its appropriation, Wilson gave Creel complete support and assured both the continued existence of the agency and Creel's tenure as its head.[39]

Creel fully justified the confidence of his chief. Operating in the infant field of propaganda, without benefit of precedent or experience and before the great advances had been made in the media of communications, he established an agency that was at once the most centralized and the most far-flung of all the belligerents' propaganda organizations, as well as the most efficient.[40] Adopting a positive conception of his role, Creel eschewed the path of censorship in favor of selling the war to Americans by inundating them with words and images that portrayed the cause as a great crusade for democracy. An American couldn't step on a streetcar, go to the store, open a magazine or a newspaper, go to church, or attend a movie without being exposed to the CPI's message.[41] To give but one example, by the end of the war there were 75,000 Four-Minute Men alone, who gave brief hortatory talks about the conflict wherever Americans gathered communally, particularly in movie theaters. On the basis of the estimated national theater

39. Mock and Larson, *Words That Won the War*, 61. In Chap. 3 Mock and Larson describe Creel's temperamental vagaries and difficulties with the press and Congress.
40. Speier, "Morale and Propaganda," 7, 9.
41. A list of divisions in the CPI indicates the scope of its operations. Domestic Section: Division of News; Official Bulletin; Foreign Language Newspaper Division; Division of Civic and Educational Publications; Picture Division; Film Division; Bureau of War Expositions; Bureau of State Fair Exhibits; Industrial Relations; Labor Publications Divsion; Service Bureau; Pictorial Publicity; Bureau of Cartoons; Advertising; Four-Minute Men; Speaking Division; Syndicate Features; Women's War Work; Work with the Foreign-Born. Foreign Section: Wireless and Cable Service; Foreign Press Bureau; Foreign Film Division.

and movie audience in the fall of 1918, it is judged that the Four-Minute Men "must have reached several million [Americans] daily."[42]

That Creel did not conceive of the CPI as a censorship organization—he was fond of repeating that from the start he had told Wilson that the need was for *"expression* not *suppression"*—does not mean that Americans had the opportunity to choose between divergent views of the war. Creel was correct in pointing out that wartime press censorship was "voluntary" in America, since the press agreed to censor itself according to guidelines provided by the government, but the results were the same as if he had had a strict press censorship law to rely on. The Espionage Act served as the "big stick behind the 'voluntary' censorship of the press" and "gave teeth to the CPI" in its press supervision.[43] After studying the German wartime press for the NBHS, Victor S. Clark concluded that the "voluntary co-operation of the newspaper publishers of America resulted in a more effective standardization of the information and arguments presented to the American people, than existed under the nominally strict military control exercised in Germany."[44] Nor did Creel's preference for "expression" over "suppression" fail to silence points of view contrary to the official interpretation of the war in areas other than press opinion. If American public opinion during the war was, as one historian has described it, a "mental debauch,"[45] then Creel's hyperbolic propaganda barrage, which made one point of view alone about the war legitimate, must take a good part of the blame.

Shortly after Creel's appointment to the CPI he established the Division of Civic and Educational Cooperation to produce literature to supplement the president's pronouncements on the war and to serve as a liaison between the CPI and the nation's educational institutions and civic organizations. Seeking a chairman for the division, he turned for advice to the NBHS. Shotwell referred him to Guy Stanton Ford, who recently had written an open letter to the nation's high school principals

42. Mock and Larson, *Words That Won the War,* 118, 123, 125.
43. Creel, *Rebel at Large,* 157; Mock and Larson, *Words That Won the War,* 11, 42.
44. Victor S. Clark, "The German Press and the War," *Historical Outlook,* X (November, 1919), 427.
45. Henry F. May, *The End of American Innocence* (New York, 1959), 387.

urging them to use the coming commencement exercises to inspire patriotism. Aside from the appeal this letter must have had for Creel, if he were intending to call on the resources of the academic community for the work of the division, Ford had obvious qualifications for the job of its head. Professor of European history, head of the history department, and dean of the graduate school at the University of Minnesota, Ford was a mature and respected scholar (he was forty-four years old in 1917) who had invaluable contacts in the historical profession and throughout the academic community. He had done graduate work in Berlin, had written a doctoral dissertation "Hanover and Prussia," was at work on a biography of Baron Karl vom und zum Stein, and knew German history well. Probably most important of all, he was highly enthusiastic about heading the division.[46]

If Ford had any doubts about occupying a key position in the government propaganda agency there is no evidence of them. On the contrary, from the time of his tenure with the CPI to the end of his long life he justified his activities on the grounds that he adhered to the highest standards of truthfulness, accuracy, and scholarly integrity in directing the division. In 1918, when he defended the CPI before a subcommittee of the House Committee on Appropriations, Ford pointed with pride to the factual accuracy of the material produced by the division he headed. Addressing the Minnesota Historical Society barely a month after the CPI was disbanded, Ford averred: "While doing . . . this national task I have been able to maintain the same standards that I have set for myself both as a member of the history department of the University of Minnesota and as a member of this society." In making assignments to scholars, he recounted, "I said very simply and directly that I wanted the pamphlets to be as accurate as scholarship could make them; that I wanted them to be the kind of work which they would not

---

46. Mock and Larson, *Words That Won the War*, 158–59. Ford wrote the letter to the high school principals for the signature of the commissioner of education, who decided to send it out over Ford's own name. For Ford's background and qualifications see the introduction by George E. Vincent to the *Festschrift* in Ford's honor, *On and Off the Campus* (Minneapolis, 1938), 3–34. Ford's enormous enthusiasm for his job shines through the records of his division.

be ashamed to own 20 years after the war."[47] When he dictated his reminiscences thirty-five years later Ford repeated the theme. "We tried never to compromise good historical workmanship. It's on the record that I said to my contributors, 'Don't do anything that you'll be ashamed of twenty years from now.'" He carefully avoided stirring up hatred for the German people, he said, forbidding the use of the word *Hun,* which "slipped by . . . only once in the long list of publications." Defining propaganda as the "distortion of the facts to bring about the object that the particular distorter seeks," Ford insisted that neither he nor Creel countenanced work of that sort. They operated under the premise, he said, that "truth . . . [is] the best propaganda." Looking back on the experience he concluded: "I left the committee at the end of the war with the feeling that I would never regret or renege on anything that I did then. I never have, and have never had a real occasion to do so."[48]

Before measuring Ford's evaluation of his division against its performance, it is necessary to explore the issue of propaganda, for one clue to the relationship of scholars to the CPI may be found in the superficiality of Ford and Creel's definition of propaganda as lies. The subject of propaganda is enormously complex, and there is a sizable literature, largely by political scientists, sociologists, and psychologists, on its meaning, character, purposes, and effectiveness. It is possible, without entering into the complexities and the differences among the interpreters, to characterize propaganda as an instrument of warfare. Wartime propaganda has the triple objectives of strengthening the martial spirit at home, influencing public opinion in neutral countries, and demoralizing the enemy. On the home front the propagandist's key objec-

47. U.S. House of Representatives, *Sundry Civil Bill 1919: Hearing before Subcommittee on House Committee on Appropriations* (Washington, D.C., 1918), 65th Cong., 2nd Sess., Pt. 3, p. 105. Ford, the Fight for Public Opinion," 3, 24–25.

48. "Memoir of Guy Stanton Ford," II, 382–83, 388, 387, III, 419. Cf. Creel's statement that the word *propaganda* "in the German hands has come to be associated with lies, secrecies and shameful corruptions. Our work is educational and informative, for we have such confidence in our case that we feel that no more than a fair presentation of its facts is needed to win the verdict." Address to the City Editor's Association, Columbus, Ohio, January 19, 1918, in George Creel Papers, Library of Congress.

tive is high morale, manifested in concern for the objectives of the national group and willingness to share in its activities and accept sacrifices and deprivations in its behalf. The most effective way of heightening morale is to convince the population on the one hand that its cause represents absolute justice and on the other hand that the enemy is the personification of evil.[49] Whether by fair means or foul, the objective of wartime propaganda on the home front is clear: to contribute to military victory by boosting domestic morale.

Ford and Creel both acknowledged that mass persuasion was the function of the CPI at home. Justifying the agency to the House subcommittee, Ford declared that upon intervention in the war it became necessary to convince a divided population that the country was engaged in a "life and death struggle." Creel described the CPI to the congressmen as a publicity bureau designed "to bring home the truths of this great war to every man, woman, and child in the United States, so that they might understand that it was a just war, a holy war, and a war in self-defense."[50] So far as the association of scholars with the agency is concerned, for Ford and Creel to concentrate on the high standards of workmanship they expected and claimed to have exacted from their contributors was beside the point. What their academic contributors had to decide was whether joining the administration propaganda agency was compatible with their professional ethics. For under no circumstances would they be able even to pretend, as did the members of the NBHS, that they were acting as objective scholars and were not promoting a point of view about the war. As recruits of the official propaganda agency, they would be expected to promote the administration's point of view. That they might be able to do so by using the techniques of accurate scholarship would not alter the fact that they would be functioning not as scholars but as advertising agents for the government. The im-

49. Harold Lasswell, *Propaganda Technique in the World War* (New York, 1938), 10; Ralph H. Lutz, "Studies of World War Propaganda, 1914–33," *Journal of Modern History*, V (December, 1933), 497; Ernst Kris and Nathan Leites, "Trends in Twentieth-Century Propaganda," in Bernard Berelson and Morris Janowitz (eds.), *Public Opinion and Communication* (Glencoe, Ill., 1953), 279; Speier, "Morale and Propaganda," 15–16.

50. House of Representatives, *Sundry Civil Bill 1919*, 95, 4.

plications of the distinction are revealed fully in the record of the Ford Division.

At the start, it was decided to devote the division primarily to production of promotional literature on the war, so its name was changed from Division of Civic and Educational Cooperation to Division of Civic and Educational Publications. It further was decided that the literature would be produced in the form of pamphlets, to be written mainly by university scholars. Creel explained that the pamphlet form was chosen to spread the message of the CPI because the medium lent itself to the formation of a public opinion that "expresses slow-formed convictions based on facts." The serious-looking pamphlets, with the names of distinguished scholars on their covers, embellished with footnotes and bibliographic references, and introduced by the dean of the University of Minnesota graduate school, did indeed succeed in creating the impression that the government was trying to "inform" the public. Furthermore, the use of pamphlets was an excellent means of reaching millions of people by way of a less ephemeral medium than that provided by the daily press.[51]

The permanent staff of the Ford Division was small. In addition to Ford, it consisted of Samuel B. Harding, who was assistant director, James W. Searson, professor of English and journalism at Kansas State University, who was editorial assistant, and a few secretaries. The division conducted its work with the assistance of more than one hundred social scientists, historians chief among them, who served as "contributors, writers, investigators, translators, advisers, etc.," according to Ford. They came from universities all over the country and included relatively obscure men as well as exemplars of the scholar's profession like Charles Beard, Carl Becker, John R. Commons, Edward S. Corwin,

51. George Creel, "Propaganda and Morale," *American Journal of Sociology,* XLVII (November, 1941), 349. The Ford Division pamphlets were printed and distributed in the millions. It is estimated that more than 75,000,000 pieces of literature were put out. See Mock and Larson, *Words That Won the War,* 159, 160, 164, 171. Even so, because of difficulties with the Government Printing Office, Ford constantly complained that he was not able to keep up with the demand. See, for example, Guy Stanton Ford to Albert Bushnell Hart, September 1, 1917, in CPI Papers.

William E. Dodd, Carl Russell Fish, J. Franklin Jameson, Andrew C. McLaughlin, James T. Shotwell, and Munroe Smith, to name but a few.[52] The files of the Ford Division indicate that there was more academic talent ready and willing to serve the government than could be put to use. Ford complained, "It is almost pathetic to know that one cannot tell . . . [all the university men who offer their services] where they can set themselves effectively at a task."[53]

Considerable evidence supports Ford's contention that in directing his division he avoided the obvious pitfalls of propaganda. On several occasions he turned down requests to print material that he thought was unworthy in tone or content. An article by Gustavus Meyers purporting to demonstrate the "falsity of Germany's 'social progress' claims" was rejected because its argument was not substantiated and its tone was reprehensible. When the director of the CPI Foreign Language Newspaper Division urged Ford to reprint a defamatory indictment of the kaiser, Ford expressed strong opposition to the use of such material. "I should be very reluctant to father anything which sank to the level of vituperation and calling of names, even if these are applied to the present German emperor," he said. Although he knew that material of that sort could be highly effective, he considered it unworthy of a "committee so closely associated with Mr. Wilson's purposes in this war and taking its tone from his attitude on various questions." Similarly, Ford refused to publish a letter allegedly written by the German steel magnate, August Thyssen, describing how the kaiser had to offer bribes, in the form of large estates in Canada and elsewhere, to get German big business to support the war. Ford received numerous requests to print the Thyssen letter. But the original source could not be located, and Ford doubted the letter's authenticity. He went to great lengths to trace the origin of the document, which, to his satisfaction, proved to be a forgery. "The American cause is so thoroughly good and there is so much indisputably genuine that it is unwise to give an opening to our

52. *Sundry Civil Bill 1919*, 100–102. The contributors worked mainly from their own campuses; some of them came to Washington for short periods of time.
53. Guy Stanton Ford to Max Farrand, March 2, 1918, in CPI Papers.

enemies by using material that is open to suspicion," explained Ford.[54]

However, the record does not substantiate Ford's claim that the output of the CPI was "wholly informational and educational."[55] The subject matter of the Ford Division pamphlets was chosen to meet the chief requirement of propaganda: that the Allies' own cause be proven to be absolutely just and that the enemy be personified as evil. Only subjects lending themselves to this kind of treatment were included. In explaining the work of the division, Ford explicitly stated that the pamphlets had two purposes: to demonstrate American aims and objectives in the war and to expose the methods and principles of the enemy, what we were "actually up against when we grappled with this Prussian system as a military and a political and a social and an economic and a philosophic idea of running the world." Creel stated that Ford's original instructions were to set out clearly before the country, on the one hand, why the United States was fighting and what it stood for and, on the other hand, the "form of government that we were opposed to and what character of people we were fighting."[56] The pamphlets were confined to the two general categories of justification of the American cause and indictment of the German system. This principle of selection alone, determined by the objectives of wartime propaganda, made it illusory for Ford to claim that he applied professional standards to the work of his division and avoided stirring up hatred for the enemy.[57]

Correspondence between Ford and a contributor reveals the extent to

54. Samuel B. Harding to Royal Meeker, March 11, 1918, Guy Stanton Ford to George Creel, February 20, 1918, and Ford to J. G. Butler, May 14, 1918, all *ibid.*

55. Ford, "The Fight for Public Opinion," 9.

56. House of Representatives, *Sundry Civil Bill 1919*, 95, 107.

57. The principle of selection that governed the work of the Ford Division is suggested in the pamphlets' titles. See, on the one hand, *America's War Aims and Peace Terms* (Carl Becker), *American Interest in Popular Government Abroad* (Evarts B. Greene), *American and Allied Ideals* (Stuart P. Sherman), *The President's Flag Day Address* (Wallace Notestein), *The War Message and the Facts Behind It* (William Stearns Davis) and, on the other hand, *The Government of Germany* (Charles D. Hazen), *The German War Code* (George W. Scott and James W. Garner), *German War Practices: Part I, Treatment of Civilians, and German War Practices: Part II, German Treatment of Conquered Territory* (Dana C. Munro, George C. Sellery, and August C. Krey), *German Plots and Intrigues* (E. E. Sperry and W. M. West), *Conquest and Kultur* (Wallace Notestein and Elmer E. Stoll), and *The German-Bolshevik Conspiracy* (Edgar Sisson).

which propagandistic principles of selection contradicted "informational and educational" objectives. Ford suggested to James W. Garner, who already had written a CPI pamphlet on the German war code, that he prepare another one on the same subject, but comparing the American and German field regulations in parallel columns to demonstrate their fundamental differences. When Ford examined the American regulations, however, he discovered that the facts did not support the desired conclusion, and he had second thoughts. "The more I look over our own field regulations with the citations from Moltke and other German writers and their utter confusion of necessity and right, the more doubtful I am about the effectiveness of the subject I suggested to you," he wrote Garner.[58] There is no question that to proceed with the original project would have been informative and educational; equally beyond doubt is that Ford could not have been expected to do so.

Contributors to the Ford Division did not always eschew appeals to the passions in their pamphlets or resist the temptation to provoke fear and hatred of the enemy. For example, Stuart P. Sherman's *American and Allied Ideals: An Appeal to Those Who Are Neither Hot Nor Cold,* the reprint of an address prepared for delivery to teachers' associations, was characterized by its own author as having a "distinctly propagandist tone [having been] originally aimed very definitely at teachers of cool temperament,"[59] and Charles P. Tatlock's *Why America Fights Germany* contained a lurid description of an imagined German invasion of American shores. Even when they did resist such temptations, however, the ends toward which their work was directed rendered the most scrupulous means incidental. Wallace Notestein's preparation of *Conquest and Kultur: The Words of the Germans in Their Own Mouths* is a perfect example.

Charged with exposing Pan-Germanism, Notestein was anxious to fulfill the task in a fashion becoming to a scholar. He refused to use existing compilations that he found to be unscholarly, badly translated, or blatantly biased. Many of his selections were excerpted from the original

---

58. Guy Stanton Ford to James W. Garner, June, 7, 1917, June 11, 1917, both in CPI Papers.
59. Stuart P. Sherman to Guy Stanton Ford, January 7, 1918, *ibid.*

sources, which he translated himself.[60] He cited each selection carefully
and identified its author, frequently in great detail. His notes were bal-
anced, fair, and free from editorial comment. The concern behind this
effort was plain from a letter he wrote to his mentor George B. Adams,
to whom he sent the pamphlet for approval. "I hope that you will find it
a careful and fair piece of work," Notestein said. "I have often won-
dered what you would think of this kind of work—propaganda work—
whether a scholar should do it or not. . . . I hope the text and notes are
accurate and painstaking and fair. I have tried hard to make them so.
. . . If you and Professor [George Lincoln] Burr should feel the work
unbecoming a student of theirs, I should regret having done it." For all
Notestein's attention to factual accuracy and other scholarly considerations, the pamphlet (which Adams assured him was a "very useful piece
of work, well done & creditable to you as a scholar"[61]) succeeded only
too well in fulfilling its objective. It drove home the point that expan-
sionism, desire for conquest, worship of power, and love of war were
characteristic of the German people. In the absence, of course, of examples of such sentiment among the Allied population, the impression was
created that these sentiments were characteristic of the Germans alone.
Notestein did not have to use the word *Hun* to draw up his one-sided
indictment; the artful selection of material, scrupulously translated and
edited, was sufficient.

The attempt to portray propaganda as scholarship reached its fullest
expression in the *War Cyclopedia,* a 325-page reference handbook edited by Frederic L. Paxson, Edward S. Corwin, and Samuel B. Harding
and designed to supply Americans who were popularizing the war with
an arsenal of factual information. Dozens of scholars wrote brief articles
on assigned subjects, which were alphabetically arranged and gave the
appearance of factual, encyclopedic coverage of the war's background,
characters, issues, and events.[62] The subjects that were omitted, as well

60. Wallace Notestein to Guy Stanton Ford, September 21, 1917, *ibid.*
61. Wallace Notestein to George B. Adams, November 27, 1917, and Adams
to Notestein, December 4, 1917, both in Adams Papers.
62. For example, Beard was assigned to write articles on "Atrocities," "Belgian

as those included, give some indication of the selectively limited range of the encyclopedia. For example, the *War Cyclopedia* included the Herrero Insurrection but not the Boer War, Karl Liebknecht but not Bertrand Russell. Under the letter *D* one could find "daylight savings" but no entry for Eugene Debs. Furthermore, the contents of the articles made the volume's purposes clear. "Freedom of the press," for example, contained a justification of government censorship, and "business as usual" portrayed American and English businessmen as self-sacrificing patriots.

Sympathy with the purposes of the encyclopedia blunted criticism by professors of its masquerade as a work of scholarship. Becker, for one, was fully aware of the volume's propagandistic crudities, yet he dismissed his own suggestions for improvements as being "perhaps mere hobbies of mine, and . . . not relevant to the purposes of the *Cyclopedia.*"[63] Only Cheyney, a self-proclaimed pacifist who thought American participation in the war was unjustified,[64] objected that the propaganda purposes of the *War Cyclopedia* inevitably conflicted with standards of scholarship. He refused a request to write several articles on the Irish situation because he believed that no reliable material was available for some of the subjects he was assigned and because he knew that, for other subjects, judgments he would in honesty be forced to make would not be printable. He explained: "For instance, to properly characterize Sir Edward Carson [a British leader of the opposition to Irish home rule], his recent policy and present position would, as far as my present knowledge and opinion goes, involve an utter condemnation that I am afraid would appear with ill grace in a semi-official publication

---

Violation," "Frightfulness," *"Notwendigkeit,"* "Blockade," "Declaration of London," and others; McLaughlin was to write about "Edith Cavell," "Blacklist," "Louvain," and "Rheims," among others; and Becker was to prepare pieces on "Scrap of Paper," "Chauvinism," "Poilu," "Tommy," "Boch," and "Italia Irridenta."

63. Carl L. Becker to Guy Stanton Ford, May 13, 1918, in CPI Papers.

64. Edward Potts Cheyney to Miss Hewitt, April 5, 1917, in Edward Potts Cheyney Papers, University of Pennsylvania Archives; Cheyney to J. Franklin Jameson, August 30, 1917, in Jameson Papers.

by an Allied government; while it seems practically impossible . . . to find anything concerning the Irish Convention—it could only be described fairly by some one actually there."[65]

In connection with Ford's claim that the pamphlets were prepared according to the standards of historical professionalism, it should be pointed out that for Ford to prescribe the point of view authors were expected to express in their work was not uncommon. When Becker was asked to write a pamphlet to counteract the "perversions" of the Monroe Doctrine being circulated by the "opposition" in Latin America, he was instructed "to very clearly bring out the joint interest of both North and South America in the Monroe Doctrine as a barrier behind which democracy may develop." For another project Becker was told what material to include.[66] In several instances Ford approached authors because he knew their points of view would be congenial to the audience for which the material was intended. When he considered publishing a popular history of the United States for circulation in Soviet Russia and Latin America, he tried to commission Beard and Willis West, because their "liberal" even "radical" approach "would present the matter from the proper point of view to the Russians or the South Americans." Beard volunteered to give up everything else to devote several months to the job, but he suggested that the book be published by a private firm and then used by the government. Ford was told that Beard "seems to think that a book thus published without the government imprint might be of more value than if issued by the government direct."[67] Beard was aware that the scholarly impartiality of govern-

---

65. Edward Potts Cheyney to Frederic L. Paxson, September 10, 1917, in CPI Papers. Paxson found someone without these scruples who wrote articles that were thoroughly innocuous and in no way portrayed the urgency of the situation in Ireland. The name Edward Carson did not appear.

66. Guy Stanton Ford to Carl L. Becker, June 19, 1919, June 28, 1919, *ibid*. Becker proved to be a hard man to instruct in such a fashion. What he wrote was too indefinite and indirect to serve the purpose. See Ford to Becker, December 24, 1918, *ibid*, in which, for one chapter of a short history of the United States intended for translation and circulation abroad, Becker was told to "see that the Panama Canal gets some attention in view of the interest of South Americans in it and note President Wilson's attitude toward reimbursement to Panama as indicated especially in his last message and in previous utterances."

67. Guy Stanton Ford to Willis West, April 23, 1918, Paul Kennady to Ford, April 1, 1918, both *ibid*. The project never materialized.

ment-commissioned work would be open to question and willing to lend himself to a deception. Although a "radical" approach was sought for publications intended for Soviet Russia and Latin America, the "radical" approach was not sanctioned for publications intended for domestic circulation. When it was suggested that the CPI publish John R. Commons' essay "Why Workingmen Support the War," Ford decided that because the article strongly supported unionization—"some phrasing in the first four pages would lead conservatives and some labor employers to cry 'Bolsheviki'!"—it could not be put out as a government document.[68]

The next to last pamphlet issued by the CPI, *The German-Bolshevik Conspiracy*, probably is the most interesting; its publication was surrounded by controversy, which the CPI tried to put to rest by calling upon the expertise of two reputable scholars, Samuel N. Harper and J. Franklin Jameson. Their role provides the best single illustration of the mental corruption of American scholars during the war.

In the spring of 1918 Edgar Sisson, the CPI's special representative in Russia, returned to the United States with a series of documents, secured at considerable expense, which purported to prove not only that Germany materially had assisted the Bolsheviks in coming to power, but that since the October Revolution the Bolshevik leaders had been paid agents of the German General Staff.[69] The documents were known in Europe and had been viewed with contempt there, even by anti-Bolsheviks, as blatant forgeries. Nevertheless, Sisson was convinced of their authenticity and vital importance. The State Department suspected that the documents were spurious and declined to authorize their publication, but Creel managed to secure Wilson's approval for their pub-

68. Guy Stanton Ford to George Creel, September 30, 1918, *ibid.* At Ford's suggestion the pamphlet was issued under the imprint of the American Alliance for Labor and Democracy, the ostensibly independent organization of prowar labor men, which was financed and controlled by the CPI. For the alliance see Ronald Radosh, *American Labor and United States Foreign Policy* (New York, 1969), Chap. 2, and Frank L. Grubbs, Jr., *The Struggle for Labor Loyalty: Gompers, the AF of L, and the Pacifists* (Durham, 1968).

69. The following description of the early history of the Sisson documents derives mainly from George F. Kennan, "The Sisson Documents," *Journal of Modern History*, XXVIII (June, 1956), 130–54, and Christopher Lasch, *The American Liberals and the Russian Revolution* (New York, 1962), 112–18.

lication by the CPI. They first were released to the press, which issued them serially in September, 1918. They were accepted as genuine by most of the nation's newspapers, primarily because of their implicit endorsement by the government, but undoubtedly also because of their obvious propaganda value. The government endorsement was not accepted by the New York *Evening Post*, which embarked on a systematic campaign to prove that the documents were forged. As part of its campaign the *Post* reprinted a detailed repudiation of the documents, taken from an anti-Bolshevik source, that had been published in Europe months before. The CPI pamphlet already was in the page-proof stage, but the documents' total repudiation by a reputable newspaper could not simply be ignored. Accordingly, Creel asked the NBHS to establish an "authoritative committee" to determine the validity of the criticism before he published the documents.

Attempts to get Archibald Cary Coolidge, Frank Golder, and Robert Lord to serve on the committee failed, because all three were occupied elsewhere in government service. The committee, as finally constituted, consisted of Samuel Harper, professor of Russian language and institutions at the University of Chicago, an outspoken anti-Bolshevik and supporter of the administration's Russian policy, and J. Franklin Jameson, who was an expert in handling manuscript materials but could not read most of the documents because he knew no Russian. Jameson described his position on the committee as that of an "ignorant layman."[70] Harper and Jameson, working from the proof sheets of the CPI pamphlet, deliberated for one week, at the end of which they vouched for the absolute authenticity of the majority of the documents (which were the most questionable ones, because they concerned the period after the Bolsheviks came to power), and withheld judgment on the others without declaring them to be forgeries.

In his introduction to the pamphlet, Sisson wrote: "The documents show that the present heads of the Bolshevik Government—Lenin and Trotsky and their associates—are German agents. . . . They show . . . that the present Bolshevik Government is not a Russian government at

70. Telegram of J. Franklin Jameson to Charles H. Haskins, October 20, 1918, and telegram of Haskins to Jameson, October 20, 1918, both in Inquiry Archives.

all, but a German government acting solely in the interests of Germany and betraying the Russian people ... for the benefit of the Imperial German Government alone." Harper and Jameson refused to comment on these allegations. They confined themselves to the issue of the documents' authenticity and ignored the question of their implications entirely.[71] The CPI printed the documents in late October, with both the introduction by Sisson and the report by Harper and Jameson. The pamphlet received a considerable amount of criticism, chiefly from the *Nation*, but finally was obscured by the armistice. In 1920–1921, the State Department tried to settle, once and for all, the issue of the documents' authenticity, because doubts persisted and the reputation of the government was involved. Although the investigation made some progress, it had to be abandoned because Wilson refused to produce the original documents.

In 1956 George Kennan conclusively proved, on the basis of historical implausibility and internal evidence, that the documents were outright forgeries.[72] His primary concern was to investigate the documents' authenticity; he did not inquire into the motives of those members of the United States government who endorsed the official publication of material that appeared to be patently spurious to so many qualified observers. He did, however, question Harper and Jameson's support of the government decision to publish the Sisson documents. Relying on Harper's autobiography, which was written about 1941 and published posthumously, and on a paragraph in the original manuscript of the autobiography, which did not appear in the published version, Kennan concluded that Harper had not been happy about his role in the affair. Christopher Lasch probed deeper into the Sisson documents controversy and arrived at several conclusions about why members of the American government endorsed the authenticity of documents that had been discredited thoroughly in Europe, with the support of reputable

71. Edgar Sisson (ed.), *The German-Bolshevik Conspiracy* (Washington, D.C., 1918), 3, 29–30.
72. Kennan, "The Sisson Documents," 130–54. Kennan attributes the forgery to a Polish-born Russian journalist, employed by a Russian business firm as part of a campaign against German commercial interests in the Russian Far East. He raises the possibility that Japanese commercial and other interests also may have been involved in the plot.

scholars and the widespread acceptance of the press.[73] Like Kennan, Lasch also relied chiefly on the Harper autobiography and concluded that Harper did not believe in the existence of a German-Bolshevik conspiracy and was "not very happy with his part in the affair."[74] This conclusion was warranted by the sources Kennan and Lasch used. In these sources Harper declared that he and Jameson were under great pressure (from an unidentified government source) not only to verify the documents but to endorse Sisson's interpretation of them, which, he proudly said, they refused to do. Harper pointed out the conflict of interest that arises when a scholar contributes his professional services to a government at war, leaving the distinct impression that he had responded to the call of patriotism at the sacrifice of professional integrity.

Contrary to what Harper says in his memoirs, his correspondence indicates that he did indeed think the documents were genuine and that he was not at all unhappy about his role in the affair. He wholeheartedly approved of the publication of the Sisson documents, which he viewed as a weapon against Bolsheviks at home and abroad. Furthermore, he was perfectly confident about the soundness of his authentication report. The *Nation* thought that the publication of the documents and the Harper-Jameson report cast odium "upon the good name of the Government and the integrity of American historical scholarship." It singled out Harper for special attack, comparing him to a "paid attorney for the anti-Soviet forces in this country." Harper serenely expressed himself as not being worried in the least.[75]

The most telling proof that Harper was sincere in authenticating the documents lies in the record of his gradual disbelief in them. When the State Department agreed to investigate the documents in 1920 (apparently at the urging of Sisson, who was convinced their authenticity would be established),[76] it was reported that Harper was especially inter-

73. A summary of Lasch's argument and my criticism of it may be found in my "Mars and Minerva: World War I and the American Academic Man" (Ph.D. dissertation, Columbia University, 1968), 185–88.

74. Lasch, *The American Liberals and the Russian Revolution*, 115.

75. Samuel N. Harper to Guy Stanton Ford, November 15, 1918, December 9, 1918, both in CPI Papers; "The Sisson Documents," *Nation*, CVII (November 23, 1918), 616–17.

76. Kennan, "The Sisson Documents," 133.

ested "in pushing the investigation . . . as he feels that his own reputation is involved." As the investigation proceeded he confessed, "I do
find myself a bit undecided every now and then." Harper was greatly
distressed when the War Department Military Intelligence Division submitted a report pointing to undeniable evidence of forgery. He wrote,
"MID report . . . is *most* disturbing to me. In view of its sourse [*sic*],
and the categorical statements, it certainly means . . . *doubt* as to the
genuineness of the d . . . documents." He finally expressed great dissatisfaction with Sisson's role in the episode. When Raymond Robins reported to a congressional committee that Sisson had tried to give American
money to Bolsheviks going to Germany, Harper's sense of propriety was
offended. "If S. *did* spend money trying to get Bolsh. theories into Germany, it was a bit 'raw' for him to come out of Russia and blame the
Germans for doing in Russia what he tried to do in Germany. . . . If we
tried to help spread of Bolshevism in Germany by money subsidies,
then I do no[t] see how we can very well criticize Bolsh. for taking assistance from Germans."[77]

In the light of this evidence, Harper's autobiography cannot be taken
at face value. Although Harper may have written the section on the Sisson documents controversy from notes taken in 1918, the autobiography
itself was written more than twenty years later and is not a record of his
feelings at the time. In an attempt at self-justification, Harper in his
autobiography underplayed and misrepresented the documents, describing them as "documents which tended to prove a close relationship
between the Bolshevik leaders and the German general staff in connection with the famous passage across Germany of Lenin and other
leaders in a sealed car."[78] Finally, that Harper thought he could justify
himself by pretending to have unhappily sacrificed standards of scholarship to wartime needs is a revealing indication that he thought to have
heeded the call of patriotism was less damaging to his reputation as a

77. Arthur Bullard to Edgar Sisson, February 20, 1920, Samuel N. Harper to
Allen J. Carter, June 19, 1920, Harper memorandum, attached to letter of Ma-
thew C. Smith to the State Department, January 17, 1921, and Harper to Carter,
undated, all in Edgar Sisson Papers, National Archives.
78. Paul V. Harper (ed.), *The Russia I Believe In: The Memoirs of Samuel
N. Harper* (Chicago, 1945), 111–12.

scholar than really to have believed in the authenticity of forged documents.

It is significant that Harper chose to indict himself for prostituting his professional ethics in the interest of patriotism rather than to confess that his professional judgment was so deficient that he could not detect forgeries. Harper and Jameson's willingness to believe the Sisson documents authentic is most revealing for the purposes of this study, for their credulity calls to mind Lovejoy's charge that the German professoriate gave evidence of having been "subtly but deeply corrupted" when it "signally failed ... to perform its proper function of detached criticism" and appeared really to believe the fictions and irrelevancies it circulated in the name of the cause.[79] All the circumstances surrounding the verification report suggest that Harper and Jameson's professional judgment and ethics had been profoundly corrupted. The two men willingly accepted the job of analyzing the documents under conditions that unavoidably would limit their freedom of judgment. Not only did they know that Creel wanted the documents authenticated and published, but they were given the proof sheets of the CPI pamphlet to work from and were impressed by Creel with the need for a hasty decision.[80] Jameson's presence on the verifying committee under the best of circumstances would have been remarkable. That a self-confessed "ignorant layman" agreed to lend the weight of his name to a report verifying controversial material he could not read does not speak well for Jameson's professional integrity. But Jameson was prepared to believe the documents genuine on the basis of his political convictions alone; that he could not read them appears to have been incidental. He wrote: "The truth is ... that if a certain lot of Americans had not made up their minds to take as favorable a view as possible of Bolshevik action, no one would have thought of doubting the genuineness of Sisson's main series of documents." Indeed, the "ignorant layman" was so certain the documents were genuine that he arrogantly dismissed all critics of the verifying report either as dishonest and unscrupulous or as Bolshevik

79. See herein, pp. 67–68.
80. J. Franklin Jameson to Andrew C. McLaughlin, October 30, 1918, in Jameson Papers; Sisson (ed.), *The German-Bolshevik Conspiracy*, 29.

apologists.[81] Harper was right. It was by far a more terrible and significant casualty of patriotism and war for scholars really to have believed the unbelievable than for them simply to have acquiesced in the command of their government.

One final aspect of the scholars' cooperation with the CPI remains to be considered: their assistance in a project to implement the Espionage Act against the foreign language press of America. The project was initiated in May, 1917, before the passage of the Espionage Act but in anticipation of it. Ford stated that the project was being undertaken as part of the CPI survey of press opinion in the country, but also "with the possibility of having on hand definite information if later the advisability of a censorship law is taken up by Congress." More than fifty scholars throughout the country were assigned to read one or more local foreign language newspapers in their geographic area daily and to submit periodic reports concerning such questions as the papers' editorial policy, the nature and sources of their news from Europe and America, and their ownership, advertisements, and circulation. In September the focus was narrowed, and readers were instructed to concentrate mainly "on material which may fall under the Espionage Law." They were to send verbatim translations of any articles or editorials "which might be construed as advocating insubordination or opposition to the execution of the laws or regulations of the United States Government or halting the work of enlisting men in either the Army or the Navy."[82] Excerpts from the Espionage Act were provided as a guide in selecting articles for translation, and readers were told to report daily.

The readers included, among others, Herman V. Ames (Pennsylvania), Henry Bourne (Western Reserve), A. L. Kohlmeier (Indiana), Edward Krehbiel (Stanford), L. M. Larson (Illinois), William Lingelbach (Pennsylvania), George H. Sabine (Missouri), and Bernadotte Schmitt

81. J. Franklin Jameson to Samuel N. Harper, December 11, 1918, November 30, 1918, and Jameson to Richard W. Hale, November 25, 1918, December 3, 1918, all in Samuel N. Harper Papers, University of Chicago Archives; Jameson to Andrew C. McLaughlin, October 30, 1918, and Jameson to Claude H. Van Tyne, December 3, 1918, both in Jameson Papers.
82. Guy Stanton Ford to J. S. Bassett, May 17, 1917, Ford to A. L. Kohlmeier, August 8, 1917, Ford to G. H. Sabine, September 21, 1917, and Ford to Francis Allinson, September 13, 1917, all in CPI Papers.

(Western Reserve). The only objection to this enterprise came from the members of the history department of the University of Wisconsin. When Paxson was asked to appoint readers from his department, he answered that his colleagues believed that "it would perhaps be unwise for the Department as such to place itself in a position of naming individuals to watch over the actions of our German citizens, and that this nomination ought to be the work of agencies whose business it is to do this thing." Ford described this unwillingness to cooperate as the "only discordant note I have received in a correspondence with . . . academic men all over the country."[83]

The professors' reports appear to have carried weight in decisions about whether to enforce the Espionage Act against particular foreign language papers. In a letter of thanks for their "utmost assistance to the Government," the readers were informed that their reports were the "determining factor in the settlement of the treatment to be given to these papers" by the two executive departments concerned (Post Office and Justice).[84] The reports continued to be used even after the professors were released from the job, when the Trading-with-the-Enemy Act transferred responsibility for reading the papers to the postmaster general. In the case of their work on the foreign language press, the general willingness professors so frequently expressed to "do anything" to help the cause resulted in their helping the government in espionage hunting and in censorship. Perhaps it was not a very long road to have traveled, after all.

So long as American scholars thought that intellect derived its social legitimacy from demonstrably "useful service," they were able to contribute their professional talents to the NBHS and the CPI. They did not bother to explore the complexities surrounding the relationship of intellect to power. To some extent, the complexities were obscured during the First World War because the professors so fully concurred in the point of view they were promoting for the government. When they took the job of advertising the war as a struggle between autocracy and de-

83. Frederic L. Paxson to Guy Stanton Ford, May 24, 1917, and Ford to A. C. Krey, June 2, 1917, both *ibid.*
84. William Churchill, director of the CPI Division of Foreign Language Publications, to H. C. Brooks, November 13, 1917, *ibid.*

mocracy, upon whose outcome the survival of freedom depended, they advertised their own convictions as well as the government's official message. This was true, for example, even of Becker and Beard. They knew that the way the autocracy-democracy antithesis was being formulated was superficial and deceptive; nevertheless, Becker interpreted the war as essentially a fight to determine whether democratic and peaceful or autocratic and military ideals would shape the future of Europe and America, and Beard thought that Germany was a "merciless military despotism" that threatened the peace and freedom of all mankind.[85] By defining propaganda as lies, when they believed the official version of the war to be "true," professors satisfied themselves that their professional and promotional roles were not incompatible.

By contrast, some of the complexities of the relationship between intellect and power were exposed during the Second World War when a group of writers resigned from the Office of War Information (OWI) because they were *not* permitted to tell the truth about the war as they saw it. They were committed to portray the deeper issues of the struggle, but the administration had decided to avoid giving the war an ideological tinge. In this instance, what the government expected and demanded of the writers was inconsistent with their own views, and they had to quit the agency to maintain their integrity. Elmer Davis, head of the OWI, put his finger squarely on the problem when he wrote President Franklin D. Roosevelt: "Such a man [an intellectual] is very apt to insist that he must proclaim the truth as he sees it; if you tell him that so long as he works for the Government he must proclaim the truth as the President . . . [sees] it, he may feel that this is an intolerable limitation on his freedom of thought and speech. In that case, he must go. . . . In an organization that is going to get any work done you cannot do much with people who are convinced that they are the sole authorized custodians of Truth."[86]

85. Carl L. Becker, "The Monroe Doctrine and the War," *History Teachers Magazine*, IX (February, 1918), 87–90; Charles A. Beard, "A Call Upon Every Citizen," *Harper's*, CXXXVII (October, 1918), 654–56.
86. Sidney S. Weinberg, "What to Tell America: The Writer's Quarrel in the Office of War Information," *Journal of American History*, LV (June, 1968), 73–89.

If one assumes that absolute dedication to discover the truth and proclaim it as he sees it is a distinguishing characteristic of the scholar and that this habit of mind is inconsistent with being a servant of the state, then the logical conclusion would appear to be that a scholar should not offer his services to the government. But approaching the question from that perspective is inappropriate for the historian and quickly becomes a dead end. It is more profitable to begin by pointing out that a scholar who decides to become a servant of the state stands to lose his professional autonomy for the duration of his service and then to study the immediate and long-range consequences of such a decision. For the period of the First World War, the immediate consequences have been demonstrated above, conclusions about the long-range consequences are more elusive.

Studies of historians who promoted the war in America in 1917–1918, both as independent scholars and as servants of the state, have demonstrated that the historians' subsequent careers were unaffected by the experience. William Hutchinson maintains that with few exceptions the reputations of the men who "tried to use history for victory" were uninjured by their wartime roles. Indeed, he states that, "if their names are placed in one column and the names of their colleagues who remained aloof are placed in a parallel one, the first list will be the more impressive both on the score of its length and of its eminence, whether viewed from the standpoint of 1917 or 1942," when Hutchinson was writing. George Blakey traces the subsequent careers of the wartime historian-propagandists and demonstrates that their service left no appreciable mark—the lesser talents among them returned to their former positions, neither degraded nor enhanced by the experience; the greater talents went on to receive the highest rewards of the profession.[87]

These observations would seem to support the conclusion that the implications of the historians' wartime propaganda did not extend beyond the duration of their service, which then may be viewed as an "aberrant" response to the crisis of war. However, the opposite conclusion

---

87. Hutchinson, "The American Historian in Wartime," 182; Blakey, *Historians on the Homefront*, 140–48.

may be drawn from the fact that serving as government propagandists did not injure the reputations and careers of American scholars; the result testifies to the endurance among academic intellectuals of the view that it is professionally appropriate to make themselves available as servants of the government. The basic conviction upon which the professors' propaganda work rested—that their highest professional obligation was to provide useful service in the emergency—was not challenged after the war. Even those, like Becker and Beard, who came to regret their service did so primarily because they had changed their minds about the cause they had promoted, not because they had reevaluated the question of their social role itself.

There was no equivalent to the CPI in World War II. Ideological propaganda fell into disrepute after the Great Crusade and Franklin Roosevelt was determined to avoid having the propaganda stigma attached to his administration's prosecution of the war. He denied Creel a position in the OWI, in order to convince a wary press and Congress that his administration's publicity agency was not going to be another Creel Committee designed "to manufacture war propaganda."[88] Nevertheless, scholars flocked to government service once again, this time as experts rather than as ideologues and in much larger numbers than during the First World War; and once again government service undermined their professionalism. For example, social scientists who worked for the overseas branch of the OWI to provide a "scientific" foundation for its operations quickly discovered that they could not function as social scientists at all; those who decided to remain with the agency, nevertheless, "allowed most of their social science skills to hibernate, even as men and women in the armed forces were compelled frequently to forget their professions, trades or personal preferences."[89] The large number of historians who worked as professional experts in the more

88. Weinberg, "Wartime Propaganda," 228.
89. Leonard W. Doob, "The Utilization of Social Scientists in the Overseas Branch of the Office of War Information," in Lerner (ed.), *Propaganda in War and Crisis,* 302. For the contribution of social scientists in the Second World War, see also Loren Baritz, *The Servants of Power: A History of the Use of Social Science in American Industry* (Middletown, Conn., 1960), 143.

than forty governmental agencies that set up historical offices served a purely utilitarian function and practiced a severely restricted version of their craft.[90]

H. Stuart Hughes, reflecting on the experiences of American intellectuals in government service during the New Deal and the Second World War and on recent conditions as well, has concluded that the intellectual's "calling" is not compatible with government service. Speaking of the years 1933–1945, he points out that intellectuals in government service functioned as "mental technicians" and not as intellectuals. "They had assigned jobs to do," he says; "they were not free to speculate as their fancy directed. . . . By serving their country they lost some of their independence; as *intellectuals* their position was diminished rather than enhanced."[91] Hughes is not speaking in the name of the sacrosanctity of intellectuals, and he is not arguing that to preserve their "purity" intellectuals must remain aloof from the pressures of the real world. On the contrary, it is because he thinks that intellectuals have an essentially social function—to "corrupt" youth, and presumably the rest of us as well, through profound social criticism—that he insists on the necessity for them to remain free from obligations to "reasons of state."

In World War I American academic intellectuals committed themselves to serving the needs of the state. The role they played committed them to priorities that fettered their critical intelligence and warped their judgment; the work they produced in the service of the state seriously departed from responsible scholarship. The experience was not an ultimately insignificant interlude in their professional careers; their conduct in 1917–1918 is an important part of the history of a problem that remains very much alive today.

90. William C. Binkley, "Two World Wars and American Historical Scholarship," *Mississippi Valley Historical Review,* XXXIII (June, 1946), 3–26.

91. H. Stuart Hughes, "Is the Intellectual Obsolete?" *An Approach to Peace and Other Essays* (New York, 1962), 165. Hughes himself had served in the Office of Strategic Services during the Second World War; presumably he was writing partly out of his own experience.

V

Academic Freedom Under Fire

IF, AS WAS OBSERVED earlier, the war experience appeared to confer benefits in some areas of the professional life of American scholars, in one crucial area no such claim could be made. Academic freedom was a precarious ideal in the best of times; it was rendered more precarious still when the United States entered the war. The war, with its attendant excitation of public opinion, made professors even more vulnerable to assaults from the surrounding community and from the governing bodies of their own institutions than they were in normal times. The story of academic freedom during the war is part of the history of continuous assaults on professors by hostile outsiders.[1] But events during the war also demonstrate that the state of academic freedom depends largely on the professoriate itself, for they reveal the extent to which professors themselves were involved in wartime violations of academic freedom. The crisis of war exposed the repressive underside of majority sentiment on the campus; it exposed a lack of commitment to academic freedom within the profession at large and a willingness even of its chief defenders to bend the principle to the pressures of the

1. The standard source for the subject is Richard Hofstadter and Walter P. Metzer, *The Development of Academic Freedom in the United States* (New York, 1955).

163

moment; and it exposed an absence of collective consciousness and solidarity within the American academic profession.

It might have been expected that the AAUP would defend academic freedom during the war, for the protection of academic freedom was the *raison d'être* of the new organization. According to the historian of the AAUP, of all the problems confronting the academic profession in the early years of the twentieth century, the need for "self-defense" provided the organizing principle of the new association. Metzger writes that, despite opinion in favor of organizing the association around professional self-improvement or professional self-government, the AAUP "carved its niche in the academic world primarily as an agency of self protection" and dedicated itself chiefly to the tasks of "professional vigilance and redress." One of its earliest and most important pronouncements was a principled and procedural defense of academic freedom as the essential precondition of the academic profession; this pronouncement has remained the bedrock of the defense of academic freedom to our own time.[2]

The 1915 report of the AAUP Committee on Academic Freedom and Academic Tenure described the academic profession as holding a public trust that could be discharged only if the "absolute freedom of thought, of inquiry, of discussion and of teaching" of its members was guaranteed. The committee declared that an essential condition of this guarantee was that the "initial responsibility for the maintenance of its professional standards . . . [must be] in the hands of its own members," and the committee set forth four practical proposals by which this condition could be fulfilled. At the outset the report declared that its pronouncements governing freedom of teaching within the university were intended to apply to a professor's extramural activities as well, for, as the committee later elaborated, it was unthinkable that a professor should be deprived of the ordinary political rights of citizenship.[3] Al-

2. Metzger, "Expansion and Profession," 33–36, 48–50. See Walter P. Metzger, *et al., Dimensions of Academic Freedom* (Urbana, 1969), 1–33, for a cogent argument that it is time to revise the "classic" defense of academic freedom in accordance with modern conditions in the academic world.

3. "Report of the Committee on Academic Freedom and Academic Tenure," 39, 34, 20.

though the report is notable for its circumspection and moderation, particularly in its frequent reminders that freedom entails responsibility, it firmly insisted that without complete academic freedom no professor could fulfill the functions of his calling and that no institution depriving him of that freedom deserved to be called a college or university.

Several months after America intervened in the war, AAUP President Frank Thilly reported that the association began receiving notification of "action . . . taken against members of faculties on account of their public utterances with reference to the war" and requests for clarification of the "hopeless confusion of issues." Remarking that in advance of a formal declaration by the association he could express a personal opinion only, Thilly appealed for restraint of the passions and for fulfillment of the university's obligation to ensure "tolerance and fairness." The main burden of Thilly's recommendation was that the "professor accused of wrongdoing [must be granted] the right to a fair hearing and to a report of the facts coming from his colleagues." He insisted, in accordance with previous AAUP guidelines, that the faculty and not the administration must determine a professor's fitness for his job. But, although his call for a fair defense against specific charges accorded with the AAUP's procedural guidelines for the protection of academic freedom, in a subtle way his remarks reneged on the AAUP's insistence on the principle that a professor's position should not be jeopardized by his opinions on public issues. By calling for tolerance for those "scholars who are loyal at heart but whose opinions on secondary issues may not meet with our approval," Thilly implied that "loyalty" was a qualification for an academic position. The same disturbing implication was present in his insistence that the administration leave it to the faculty to draw the line "between the allowable and unallowable in speech and conduct" and in his objection to the "dismissal of professors unless there is a just ground for their dismissal and unless their guilt has been clearly established."[4]

The implicit in Thilly's remarks was made explicit a month later when the AAUP issued a formal report on academic freedom in wartime. The report opened with the observation that the state of war

4. "Report of the President," *ibid.*, III (November, 1917), 18, 19.

created "special obligations . . . for members of our profession"; it was an acknowledged retreat from the unconditional position of the 1915 academic freedom report. The heart of the document lies in the statement that the "committee believes that there are four grounds upon which the dismissal of a member of a faculty of a college or university by the academic authorities, because of his attitude or conduct in relation to the war, may be legitimate. Of these grounds, three presuppose no prior action on the part of any government official."[5] In other words, the committee had decided not only that a professor's attitudes and actions on a public issue could legitimately cost him his job, but that there were, legitimately, special restrictions on members of the academic profession as such, in addition to those imposed upon all citizens by the state. The report is sufficiently significant to warrant detailed discussion of both its substance and implications.

The first ground for dismissal concerned professors who fell afoul of the law. "Those who are convicted of disobedience to *any* statute or lawful executive order relating to the war may [with one qualification] . . . legitimately suffer deprivation of academic office," the committee declared. "Teachers under indictment for such offenses, but not yet convicted, may properly be suspended from their duties until their cause is legally determined." With the exception of the qualification (which will be discussed later) the committee did not elaborate on this issue, for it considered the reasons underlying the principle "to be too evident to require explanation." One may, however, question this justification for reticence, considering that the principle contradicted the most significant procedural proposal of the 1915 declaration, which had stated that "official action relating to reappointments and refusals of reappointment should be taken only with the advice and consent of some board or com-

5. "Report of Committee on Academic Freedom in Wartime," *ibid.*, IV (February–March, 1918), 29–47. The report was written on December 24, 1917, and approved by the association on December 29, 1917, at its annual meeting. The chairman of the three-member committee that issued the report, Arthur O. Lovejoy, was one of the two principal authors of the 1915 declaration. He was, as well, in the vanguard of those who fought to organize the AAUP around the issue of academic freedom. See Metzger, "Expansion and Profession," 34–36.

mittee representative of the faculty."[6] For the AAUP, which had previously insisted that professors themselves must determine their professional standards, it was a major capitulation for the association in effect to turn over the determination of a professor's fitness for his job to the public prosecutor and the lay jury.

The committee next declared that "members of college or university faculties should ... be required by their institutions to refrain from propaganda designed, or *unmistakably tending,* to cause others to resist or evade the compulsory service law or the regulations of the military authorities; and those who refuse to conform to this requirement may be, and should be, dismissed, even before any action has been taken against them by the law-officers of the state." Oliver Wendell Holmes's "clear and present danger" standard was not yet available as a guideline; even so, the AAUP departed very far from the spirit of the constitutional protection of free speech. The hardness of its line is illustrated in the elaboration of the main point:

> To prove an *intent* to encourage opposition to the enforcement of this measure it is not ... necessary that a speech or other public utterance should contain, in so many words, an exhortation to disobey the law. If, for instance, a speaker should declare that all participation in war is immoral, or should praise the example of the Russian troops who deserted their posts and betrayed their allies, or should assert that the payment of war taxes is contrary to sound ethical principles—such a speaker may be presumed to know that the *natural tendency* of his words is to stir up hostility to the law and to induce such of his hearers as are influenced by him to refuse to perform certain of the obligations of citizenship.

The committee went so far as to bring under its ban "those who seek to convert the people of the country to the *creed* of absolute nonresistance—to the *theory* that lending assistance to any war, in whatever cause, is unjustifiable." Dismissal of a professor on these grounds in advance of action by the state was justified with the argument that any institution retaining a professor whose "activities are clearly contrary to the law, and manifestly threatening to the public safety in a time of spe-

---

6. "Report of Committee on Academic Freedom in Wartime," 34–35, italics added; "Report of Committee on Academic Freedom and Academic Tenure," 40.

cial peril . . . would clearly involve itself to some extent in complicity in those activities." Here, the committee might have taken a leaf from Harvard President A. Lawrence Lowell's categorical insistence that the university, in time of war as well as peace, was in no way responsible for the extramural utterances of its faculty, which if they contravened the law, belonged like those of all citizens in the domain of the public authorities.[7]

In its third ground for dismissal, the committee extended the prohibition on free speech to "those who, because of opposition to the war, seek to dissuade others from rendering voluntary assistance to the efforts of the government." It explained that the "government would be wholly unable to carry on war unless individual citizens in large numbers voluntarily performed certain acts which are not required of them by law." Professors who engaged in propaganda to dissuade others from purchasing government bonds, for example, or supporting war charity organizations, or observing restrictions on the consumption of particular commodities, the committee declared, were performing an action that was "dangerous to the public security . . . [and] *irreconcilable with good citizenship*," and, even though that action was not forbidden by law, deserved to be removed from their posts, "provided that a deliberate purpose to impede the government's activities in the prosecution of the war is shown by conclusive evidence."[8]

Finally, the committee turned its attention to professors of German or Austro-Hungarian birth or parentage, some of whom still were citizens of the enemy nations and some of whom, "blinded to the moral aspects of the present conflict by their affection for the land of their origin . . . desire the victory, or at least the partial success, of the Central Empires, and by implication the defeat of the United States and its allies." The situation, the committee declared, required that these men "abstain from

7. "Report of Committee on Academic Freedom in Wartime," 37, 38, 39, italics added; A. Lawrence Lowell, "Academic Freedom," *At War with Academic Traditions in America* (Cambridge, Mass., 1934), 267–72. The AAUP printed Lowell's article in the same issue of the *Bulletin* as the "Report of Committee on Academic Freedom in Wartime" under the title "Recent Academic Freedom Discussion."

8. "Report of Committee on Academic Freedom in Wartime," 40. Italics added.

any act tending to promote the military advantage of the enemy or hamper the efforts of the United States."

> [They must] take care not to give, by their *utterances* or *associations,* reasonable ground for the belief that they *contemplate* such acts or are conspiring with other disloyal persons . . . refrain from public discussion of the war; and, in their *private intercourse* with neighbors, colleagues and students . . . avoid all hostile or offensive expressions concerning the United States or its government. Teachers of enemy alien nationality should be put upon their parole to observe these restrictions; and if they or others of pro-German sympathies fail to observe them, they should promptly be removed from their posts.[9]

The committee thought the likelihood of pro-German sympathies among professors who were first-generation American citizens, naturalized Americans, or aliens was sufficiently great and the actual threat to national security sufficiently probable to justify restricting not only their right to publicly discuss the war but also their right to express opinions about it in private conversation. Short of proscribing people's thoughts, it is hard to imagine any further possible violation of civil liberty.

It is only fair to point out that the committee warned, in the beginning of its report, against the danger of wartime passions imposing limitations on freedom of thought and discussion beyond those absolutely dictated by wartime necessity and tried to soften the specific limitations it recommended by stipulating conditions for their application. For example, the committee urged that conscientious objectors convicted of violating the Conscription Act (*i.e.,* those who did not have the religious qualification for C.O. status under the law) be exempted from the double penalty of losing their jobs. Although the committee regarded the attitude of these men as "ethically indefensible" and "gravely dangerous to the public safety," viewing them in a practical sense as "enemies of the state" in time of war, it acknowledged that such men frequently were "exceptionally public-spirited and useful citizens" in peacetime and urged the university to respect their claims of conscience.

9. *Ibid.,* 40–41. Italics added.

Further, the committee insisted on such procedural safeguards as prior description by the university of prohibited behavior and the establishment of judicial proceedings on specific charges for those accused of engaging in that behavior. Finally, concerning individuals of known or probable pro-German sympathy, the committee insisted that they be penalized only for engaging in the proscribed activities and not solely "because of subjective sentiments which it is not within their power to alter."[10]

However, what the committee failed to recognize is that the passions roused by the war, on and off the campus, would make the discriminating application of its principles, as well as the careful distinction between subjective states and objective dangers, very difficult. Herein lies the larger significance of the report. Given the likelihood that freedom of thought and expression would be jeopardized by an excited public and limited by the state—a likelihood that already had materialized by the time the report was written—an association that constituted the sole organizational defense of academic freedom might reasonably have been expected to believe that its function was to protect professors from anticipated assaults, and not to go even further than the state in limiting their freedom. In effect, the AAUP was opening the floodgate of repression, or at least was stepping aside, when it might have been expected to make every effort to hold back the waters.

When the *Nation* charged that the AAUP report "jeopards the very conception of a university," Lovejoy, as chairman of the drafting committee, replied that "such a war as this, in which the entire world is involved and the future character of human life and relations upon this planet is at issue, alters many things and suspends some of the rules of less critical and perilous times." Even more than the editorial attack, Lovejoy's defense laid bare the implications of the report: "The college cannot escape the hard necessities of the situation. It must either be . . . an accomplice in activities, which, if successful, would

10. *Ibid.*, 35–36, 42.

bring about the defeat and the dishonor of the republic and do immeasurable injury to the cause of freedom throughout the world; or else it must determine that it will not give countenance and aid to those who are clearly proved to be engaged in such activities—whether or not they have already come within the reach of the law."[11]

To be sure, in 1918 the AAUP had only a fraction of all the American professors on its membership list, could not be called representative of the academic profession, and was not its official spokesman. But it was the only professional agency in a position to provide a principled defense of academic freedom, in wartime as well as peacetime, and its failure to do so left a critical vacuum. If even the most committed supporters of academic freedom were ready to bow to the "extraordinary situation created by the war," then no effective source of protection against the extraordinary passions roused by the situation could be expected. The only clue to the AAUP's ready concessions to what were hard choices imposed by war seems to lie in the conviction that the "present war is far more than a clash of national interests," the very future of democracy appearing to be at stake in its outcome.

> When . . . a democracy finds itself forced into war in defense of its rights, of the integrity of the law of nations, and of the safety of democracy throughout the world, it will, if it has any practical wisdom, temporarily adapt its methods of political action and of governmental procedure to the necessities of the grave and perilous business immediately at hand. It can scarcely be deemed loyalty to democracy to place the future of democracy in jeopardy by an uncompromising adherence in time of crisis to the external forms of democratic government, which have their reason for being in their adaptation to wholly different conditions and wholly different ends.

Once the AAUP made plain its belief that, in this war, "to desire anything less than the realization of the essential objects which have been set forth by the President of the United States is to desire the

---

11. "The Professors in Battle Array," *Nation,* CVI (March 7, 1918), 255; Arthur O. Lovejoy, letter to the editor, *Nation,* CVI (April 4, 1918), 402.

triumph of moral evil in the world,"[12] then its decision that an unconditional dedication to academic freedom was among the luxuries of
peacetime is less surprising. What may be viewed as surprising, however, is that, in the face of all indications to the contrary, Lovejoy, as
spokesman for the report's drafting committee, raised the specter of the
presence in American universities of professors whose activities actually
might threaten to "bring about the defeat and the dishonor of the republic and do immeasurable injury to the cause of freedom throughout the
world."[13] That individuals who did not support the war (who were, in
any event, few among American professors) might conceivably pose
such a threat is a startling conception. More than commitment to the
principle of academic freedom was involved. The AAUP committee and
the membership that accepted its report revealed the same warped judgment and failure to consider coolly all the relevant facts, for which
Lovejoy himself had so sternly called the German professors to task.

There was widespread acceptance among American professors of the
Wilsonian view that a moral issue was at stake in the war, and there was
very little tolerance among them for colleagues who questioned the morality of the American cause or the necessity to unstintingly support every measure enacted to promote it. There are many indications that
professors who held dissenting views simply remained silent for the
war's duration.[14] In circumstances where doubt was considered evidence
not of possible error, let alone of legitimate difference of opinion, but of
questionable patriotism and even questionable morality, prudence
seemed to dictate silence on the part of doubters.

The situation of Edward Potts Cheyney is particularly revealing,
because of his prominence and the high esteem in which he was held by
his colleagues. He was professor of European history at the University

12. "Report of Committee on Academic Freedom in Wartime," 29, 41, 32.
13. Lovejoy, letter to the editor, *Nation*, CVI (April 4, 1918), 402.
14. See Edward Potts Cheyney, *History of the University of Pennsylvania,
1740–1940* (Philadelphia, 1940), 380–81; W. Freeman Galpin, *Syracuse University*
(Syracuse, 1960), II, 379; M. L. Larson to Guy Stanton Ford, April 20, 1918, in
CPI Papers.

of Pennsylvania, an influential member of the AAUP and the AHA, and an intimate of the leading historians of his time. His colleagues were totally out of sympathy with his pacifism. He wrote Jameson that his belief that "we ought not have entered the European war, that the compulsory military draft is a blot on our national escutcheon . . . and that the war between German autocracy and Allied democracy is largely a mythical conception" was considered by his fellow historians to be evidence of lack of patriotism. Cheyney protested strongly against this judgment. "I feel," he said, "that the most patriotic man is the one who clings most firmly to the *highest* ideals of his nation, not the one who 'goes along' most ardently when she is at war any more than when she is at peace." Because of his colleagues' opinion, he said, he was forced to conclude that "the less we see of one another—except for a few especially intimate friends—the better," and he regretfully decided not to attend the "historians' retreat" at Branford, Connecticut, in the fall of 1917. "I am sick and disheartened with it all . . . and yet I am not inclined to yield my judgment or go backward in the process of trying to think things out," Cheyney lamented. A comment by Turner suggests that Cheyney was not mistaken about his colleagues' views of his position on the war. Informed by Jameson that Cheyney's son had been committed to a federal penitentiary (apparently in connection with pacifist views or activities), Turner replied: "I am truly sorry for Cheyney, but I presume it is one of the crosses that he will have to bear as a part of his Quaker inheritance. I do not know his son . . . but I cannot help feel that Cheyney is partly responsible himself. The attitude which he took grieved me more than anything that has happened in the circle of my personal acquaintances in connection with the war. It is impossible for me to think myself into his state of mind."[15] If Cheyney's doubts about the war were so incomprehensible and unpalatable to his col-

15. Edward Potts Cheyney to J. Franklin Jameson, August 30, 1917, and Frederick Jackson Turner to Jameson, November 2, 1917, both in Jameson Papers.

leagues that he avoided discussion of the issues, certainly men who had similar doubts and were less secure than he in their academic positions could be expected to keep their views to themselves.

In the light of evidence suggesting that doubt about the war was effectively silenced by the pressure of opinion, it is unwarrantable to measure the state of academic freedom on American campuses during the war simply by known cases of individuals who were fired from their jobs. Surely, where opinion is being stifled, even by indirect means, academic freedom cannot be said to exist.[16] Even such tangible evidence as known firings can be misleading, for not taken into account are cases that did not enter the public record, either because they were isolated and obscure or because, instead of being fired outright, individuals simply did not have their contracts renewed. The historical record suggests that there were more cases of persons losing their jobs because of attitudes or activities relating to the war than previously have been accounted for.[17]

Among the known cases of professors who lost their jobs because of suspected or acknowledged lack of enthusiasm for the American cause were the following: Ernst Feise (Wisconsin); Allen Eaton (Oregon); Leon Whipple (Virginia); C. E. Eggert, W. W. Florer, E. A. Boucke, John Dieterle, W. W. Kusterman, Herman Wiegand, and Richard Ficken (Michigan); E. E. Hopt, C. E. Persinger, and G. W. A. Luckey (Nebraska); four faculty members at the University of Illinois; William A. Schaper (Minnesota); James McKeen Cattell and Henry Wadsworth Longfellow Dana (Columbia). There were three other significant ter-

16. Similarly, we would not think of drawing conclusions about the climate of opinion on American campuses in the 1950s solely on the basis of the number of professors who lost their jobs during the McCarthy era.

17. For example, the article "Report of Committee U on Patriotic Service," 32, states that a "considerable proportion of the institutions [polled] state that professors were discharged or that they resigned because of pro-German sympathy." And Grubbs's casual mention, in *The Struggle for Labor Loyalty,* 52, that Professor L. M. Keasbey of the University of Texas was fired because he worked for the People's Council for Peace and Democracy suggests that there may be more such instances.

minations of academic careers because of the war that were not ordinary dismissals. Scott Nearing, who had been fired from the University of Pennsylvania in 1915 because of his socialist beliefs, resigned from his position as professor of social science and dean of the College of Arts and Sciences at the University of Toledo in March, 1917, because he felt he could no longer function effectively in the overwrought interventionist environment of the university.[18] The active pacifist Emily Balch, a member of the Wellesley College faculty for twenty years and head of its Department of Economics and Sociology at the time of the war, took a leave of absence during the academic year 1917–1918 to spare the college the embarrassment she thought might be caused by her opposition to American intervention. When her appointment came up for renewal in the spring of 1918 the trustees postponed the question for one year, at the end of which they decided not to reappoint her.[19] The trustees of the University of Pennsylvania forced Simon N. Patten out of the Wharton School of Finance and Commerce ostensibly because he had reached the mandatory retirement age. In fact, they were "offended" by his "defense of German values" during the neutrality years (although he had been willing to accept American intervention in the war since 1916), as well as by his unorthodox economic and social views, and "capitalized" on his "tactical error" of introducing the pacifist David Starr Jordan at a public meeting on the eve of intervention.[20]

In some cases the faculty opposed the trustees' action and tried to protect its colleagues. For example, both the faculty and president of the University of Oregon repudiated the charges of disloyalty against Allen Eaton, who had attended a Chicago meeting of the People's Council for Peace and Democracy and had written a letter about it to an Oregon newspaper; they tried, without success, to prevent his dismissal. In other instances, the faculty itself insisted upon the dismissal. At the University

18. New York *Times,* March 10, 1917, p. 2.
19. See Mercedes M. Randall, *Improper Bostonian: Emily Greene Balch* (New York, 1964), Chap. 11.
20. Fox, *The Discovery of Abundance,* 124, 126–27.

of Virginia all the faculty members joined in a condemnation of Leon Whipple's pacifist sentiments, which he had expressed in an address to the Current Events Club at Sweet Briar College and summarized in a statement sent to several Virginia newspapers. They denounced him as a discredit to the university and a threat to its effort to instill the spirit of loyalty in the students and to present a united front to the enemy.[21] In the Schaper and Cattell cases, the action against professors accused of "disloyalty" was so peremptory and so severe and was accomplished with such blatant disregard of rights accrued from long years of distinguished service that the failure of the faculty in each case to join forces in defense of their ousted colleagues deserves close study. Both the Schaper and Cattell cases expose faculty willingness to sanction assaults on the rights of colleagues who were personally unpopular and had unpopular opinions about the war.

William A. Schaper was the American-born son of German parents who had emigrated to the United States during the revolution of 1848. After receiving a doctorate in political science from Columbia University, he joined the faculty of the University of Minnesota in 1901, was promoted to professor of political science in 1904, and subsequently became chairman of the department. Not a productive scholar, he was a recognized authority on state and municipal government and frequently was called as a consultant in Minnesota on such subjects as municipal charters and railroad and public utilities regulation. In that capacity and as an active member of the Nonpartisan League, he is reputed to have publicly crossed swords with Pierce Butler, who was then a St. Paul railroad attorney and member of the university board of regents, and generally to have provoked the ire of the Minnesota corporate interests. Schaper's colleagues appear to have regarded him as a conscientious and able teacher, but an undiplomatic and ungenerous man. Although a former student assistant maintains that those who were close to Schaper

21. Oswald Garrison Villard, letter to the editor, *Nation,* CV (November 15, 1917), 537–38; Philip Alexander Bruce, *History of the University of Virginia, 1819–1919* (New York, 1922), V, 365–67.

knew him as warm, sympathetic, modest, and reserved, he was apparently generally disliked and had no close friends on the faculty.[22]

By his own testimony, when the war broke out Schaper sympathized with the German cause, at least to the extent of repudiating the Allied version of the origins of the conflict, and on two occasions he publicly clashed with pro-Allied colleagues, among them a member of his own department. Although he was known to hold "pro-German" views, there never was any question of his having introduced them in his classes or of his attempting to indoctrinate his students in any way. He apparently participated in antiwar demonstrations and in March, 1917, he signed a petition urging Wilson not to take America to war. Upon intervention, he stopped his antiwar activities and accepted the necessity of supporting the government. He even recommended to several students that they join the armed forces. He later described his position by saying, "My convictions are not subject to repeal by act of Congress; but my duties most certainly were changed the moment war was declared."[23]

In the summer of 1917 an unidentified informant to the Minnesota Public Safety Commission denounced several members of the faculty, Schaper among them, for "infection" with the "germ" of disloyalty. A

22. Schaper's relations with his colleagues were described by Professor Emeritus William A. Anderson in an interview with the author, September 19, 1964. See also "The 'Schaper Case,' " recollections of William Anderson, April 11, 1958, in Schaper Case Papers, University of Minnesota Archives. The recollections of Schaper's student assistant are contained in Arnold J. Lien to Anderson, June 11, 1958, in Schaper Case Papers. Lien concedes that Schaper could be dogmatic and stubborn "in the face of highly irritating provocations." The existence of the Schaper Case Papers is the result of the efforts of Professor Anderson, who was a member of the political science department when Schaper was dismissed. Anderson collected the existing documents and solicited recollections from surviving principals for deposit in the University of Minnesota Archives in the 1950s.

23. William A. Schaper to Max Lowenthal, January 29, 1923, and Schaper to Arthur O. Lovejoy, December 11, 1917, both in William A. Schaper Collection, Western History Collections, University of Oklahoma Library. (The Schaper Collection was generously microfilmed and lent to me by the University of Oklahoma Library.) There are occasional references to Schaper as a "pacifist," particularly by Anderson, who goes so far as to conjecture that Schaper would have opposed war even with Britain, his *bête noire*. Anderson, interview with the author.

member of the commission brought this charge before the chairman of
the board of regents. It is important to note that the president of the
University of Minnesota, M. L. Burton, had just assumed office and by
all accounts was not well suited for the job. Not only was he rabid on
the subject of the war (he is reputed to have declared in public that in
the event of a German invasion he would shoot his family), but his correspondence reveals that he was under the thumb of the board of
regents, particularly its chairman, Fred B. Snyder, and Pierce Butler,
whom Burton consulted before making decisions.[24] At three o'clock in
the afternoon on September 13 President Burton told Schaper to appear
in fifteen minutes before the regents. According to Schaper, when he arrived the chairman told him that the board was trying to get rid of
disloyal men on the faculty, and when Schaper asked if there were any
charges against him, the chairman answered no.[25]

Schaper recounted that when he was asked by the regents to describe
his attitude toward the war he declared that, though he had opposed it
from the very beginning and certainly opposed American intervention,
after April 6 he had insisted that the law must be obeyed and the government in no way hindered in its war activities. He was informed that
this was not enough; what the regents wanted to know was how he personally felt about the war. To this he claims to have replied that, with
first cousins in the German army and several close friends in the American army, he was in "a delicate position" and consequently "could not
boost for the war." By that, he explained, he meant that he could not
"go out to harangue the street crowds, stirring up hate, and spreading
the Hun propaganda." This response apparently infuriated Butler, and
Schaper described the rest of the two-hour session as an angry inter-

24. John F. McGee to Fred B. Snyder, July 13, 1917, M. L. Burton to Snyder,
October 3, 1917, and November 15, 1917, Burton to Pierce Butler, December 6,
1917, and December 19, 1917, all in Presidents' Papers, University of Minnesota
Archives, hereinafter cited as Minnesota Presidents' Papers; Anderson, interview
with the author.
25. For what transpired we have only the testimony of Schaper since, as is
characteristic of star chamber proceedings, no transcript of the session was taken.
Aside from the accuracy of his quotations, considering the outcome we have no
reason to doubt the main outline of his story. My account is based on Schaper to
Judiciary Committee, United States Senate Subcommittee on Appointment of
Pierce Butler to the Supreme Court, December 7, 1922, in Schaper Collection.

change between them, during which Butler accused Schaper of being "the Kaiser's man" and of having "lived off the public money of this State" for the sixteen years of his tenure at the university. To this onslaught Schaper said he replied: "Regent Butler, you assume the role of prosecuting Attorney and assign to me the position of criminal at the bar. I desire to remind you that . . . I am the Professor of Political Science of this University, and you, sir, are a member of the Board of Regents."[26] Rumor colored the episode differently. Reports circulated the campus that Schaper had been deliberately provocative; for example, it was rumored that, when asked what he thought about the invasion of Belgium, he denounced the action of the Allies in Greece.[27] (Schaper's version is that, when asked about Belgium, he replied that she was not the only country being wronged.) Given Schaper's temperament and the vexatious manner of the board, and of Butler in particular, it is quite likely that the tone of his responses was not so lofty as his testimony suggests. Even if there were some substance to the rumors, however, they only help to recreate the atmosphere of the session, not alter the issue—that the board of regents thought that Schaper's personal opinion about Belgium, for example, was relevant to his tenure at the university.

Schaper was dismissed from the meeting; when he was called to reappear in an hour or two, he was read a short resolution expelling him from his job at the university for demonstrating to the board that "his attitude of mind . . . and his expressed unwillingness to aid the United States in the present war, render him unfit and unable rightly to discharge the duties of his position." The resolution explained that the "Board holds that the best interests of the University, the State, and the nation require unqualified loyalty on the part of all teachers in the University, coupled with willingness and ability, by precept and example to further the national purpose in the present crisis." Schaper requested that the charges be put in writing and that he be given an opportunity to reply to them. Not only was his request denied, but the resolution of ex-

26. *Ibid.*
27. Guy Stanton Ford to James W. Garner, September 28, 1917, in CPI Papers.

pulsion was immediately released to the press and broadcast throughout the country. On the following day, Butler printed a personal statement in a St. Paul newspaper describing the action as part of an effort to silence disloyalty and branding Schaper a "blatherskite."[28]

Both the principle on which the expulsion was based and the procedures by which it was accomplished had serious implications for academic freedom at the University of Minnesota. Schaper lost his job because he did not share the political views of the board of regents, not because he had done anything to disqualify him for the professorship of political science. He was dismissed summarily from the high office he had conscientiously filled for sixteen years with no advance notice, with no formal charges lodged against him, in closed session of which no record was taken, and without the opportunity to defend himself. He received one month's pay for the academic year and was automatically deprived of the pension that he would have been entitled to upon retirement. The consequences for Schaper were dreadfully severe even beyond these considerations. Having been declared publicly to be a disloyal American, his career was effectively wrecked, certainly at the very least for the duration of the war. Under the circumstances, the faculty might have been expected to make some joint effort to defend Schaper and secure redress for him.

Years later Ford recalled that two professors, one of them a member of Schaper's department, had tried to rouse the faculty to urge the administration to reconsider Schaper's expulsion. They were unable to do so, he said, because of "war hysteria" and Schaper's personal unpopularity with his colleagues. William A. Anderson explored faculty response in greater depth during a 1964 interview I had with him. With the faculty overwhelmingly in favor of the war as well as out of sympathy with Schaper on personal grounds, Schaper was left without support from his colleagues. Anderson conceded that the faculty had no influence over the board of regents, but he believed that the situation would have been different if Schaper had had backing from his colleagues. As it was, he recalled, faculty members shed no tears over Schaper. Anderson at-

28. Resolution of expulsion, September 13, 1917, and Schaper to Judiciary Committee, December 7, 1922, both in Schaper Collection.

tributed the faculty's failure to see the implications for themselves in Schaper's dismissal to more than personal dislike for a colleague. Recalling the state of academic freedom and of professional consciousness at the time, Anderson remarked that in 1917 professors were not vigilant in defense of academic freedom because it was not yet clearly defined and there were no guarantees of a professor's position. Furthermore, he said, the faculty was more interested in its own scholarship than in the profession as a whole and essentially accepted its employee status in the university hierarchy.[29]

The failure of the faculty to grasp the fundamental issue of the Schaper case—that the regents presumed the right to question a professor about his "patriotism" and to make his academic position dependent upon the acceptability of his response—is pointed up best by the reaction of Guy Stanton Ford, who was a senior faculty member and a dean at the University of Minnesota. When the Schaper case occurred Ford was in Washington with the CPI; he learned about the dismissal from the press and from reports from colleagues at the university. What is most striking about Ford's response is that, although he regretted the action of the regents, in his analysis of the case he put the onus on Schaper.

In correspondence with colleagues and with Schaper himself Ford dwelt exclusively on Schaper's poor handling of himself, his "prickly hairsplitting" (as he later described it), which prevented him from taking the opportunity to clear himself as the other "suspects" had done in five minutes and which, Ford said, brought about results no one on the board had anticipated or desired. This interpretation by implication supported the board's right to inquire into Schaper's beliefs, a conclusion that is suggested further by advice Ford offered to Schaper: "I am hoping that before this was is over you are going to do something, engage in some activity, that by its nature will bespeak your true and loyal sentiments and end all quibbling over things said. You must not care what it is so long as it is distinctly war service work."[30] Schaper, who

29. Guy Stanton Ford to Charles A. Beard, August 16, 1937, in Minnesota Presidents' Papers; Anderson, interview with the author, September 19, 1964.
30. Guy Stanton Ford to William A. Schaper, March 12, 1918, in CPI Papers.

claimed to have been willing to do war work, quite naturally was outraged at Ford's advice and replied, "I have a right to something worthy of me. I am not approaching you as the guilty one approaches the judge. You have no right to put me in the attitude of one that has to prove his innocense [sic]. . . . I offer [my services] . . . to be of use to my country, not to clear myself of any charge or any guilt."[31] At bottom, Ford sympathized with Schaper's predicament and very much regretted the serious consequences of the expulsion. The episode, he wrote a Minnesota colleague, would make a "complete shipwreck . . . of this man's whole career, for the future must be practically closed in any and every avenue in which he has hitherto worked after an American University has dismissed him for disloyalty."[32]

Ford's prediction was fulfilled. There was no possibility of Schaper being offered a position at any other university during the war, and his correspondence bears witness to the pathetic decline in his fortunes. At first he had hoped to use his unwelcome leisure to do writing he previously had no time for and had planned to use the libraries at the University of Wisconsin for research. When he was informed by friends on the faculty there that his appearance in Madison would provoke newspaper charges against the university, which already was under considerable fire, he decided not to place his undergraduate alma mater or his friends in jeopardy. He made several unsuccessful attempts to go into business and finally undertook the manufacture of a patent washboard; the business did badly because of wartime conditions. In the meantime, he discussed his case and his situation with friends and relatives all over the country. What he lamented most was the slur on his patriotism. "That my Americanism should ever be questioned," he wrote a friend, "is one of the griefs of my life. . . . I felt that I was heeding my country's call when I tried to prevent us from being dragged into the struggle." To another he wrote, in words reminiscent of Cheyney's:

31. William A. Schaper to Guy Stanton Ford, March 28, 1918, in Guy Stanton Ford Papers, University of Minnesota Archives. Ford replied, "My suggestion about active service was not in any way to indicate that you had to prove your innocence but rather that it was the most direct way of proving the Regents were entirely wrong."
32. Guy Stanton Ford to W. S. Davis, September 25, 1917, in CPI Papers.

"Who is the real patriot anyhow, the man who waves the flag and shouts on the side that will profit him the most or the man who risks the loss of old and dear friends, the ill-will of his superiors, the abuse of the press, and finally his only source of income to keep his country out of the most awful war in all history? No one who has ever known me will ever doubt my devotion to my country. It was because of my intense Americanism that I tried to keep my country out of the European war."[33]

Efforts by a federal labor commission, which was in Minneapolis on other business and one of whose members was a friend of Schaper's, to informally intercede in his behalf came to nothing. The AAUP took testimony on the case with the intention of discussing it in the report on academic freedom in wartime, but went no further than the initial investigation.[34] Schaper knew nothing would be done for him during the war,

33. William A. Schaper to Rinehart J. Swenson, October 10, 1917, Schaper to Charles A. Beard, October 11, 1917, Schaper to Rateaver, October 12, 1917, and Schaper to Maro, October 18, 1917, all in Schaper Collection.

34. William A. Schaper to Rinehert J. Swenson, December 19, 1917, Schaper to Judiciary Committee, December 7, 1922, Arthur A. Lovejoy to Schaper, December 4, 1917, all *ibid.*; Lovejoy to M. L. Burton, November 8, 1917, December 4, 1917, and December 18, 1917, all in Minnesota Presidents' Papers. Schaper's public statements dwelt entirely on the procedural aspects of the case. See his statement for the press, reprinted in *School and Society*, VI (July–December, 1917), 443–45. This really was the only issue, for Schaper's opinions should never have been subject to examination. In his correspondence with Lovejoy, however, who wanted to reconstruct precisely what had transpired, Schaper dwelt in detail on the substance of the charges against him. In reply to Lovejoy's question whether, in fact, he did desire the success of the German Empire, he wrote:

If by the success of the German Empire you mean a complete victory on the field of battle which would give her power to dominate the world or lay the foundation for such a consummation later, or a victory that would enable her to crush the political system of her enemies or even to seriously endanger such system or systems, or a victory that would enable her to compel all nations to continue their huge military establishments then I would answer unhesitatingly no. If by success of the German Empire you mean on the other hand the preservation of Germany from complete annihilation such as the extremists among her foes have often threatened her with, then I would be a common renegade to say I desired her defeat. I want my country to come out of this war crowned with the glory of a real victory and a real peace worthy of her great traditions.

Schaper to Lovejoy, December 11, 1917, in Schaper Collection. Whether this distinction made Lovejoy uncertain about Schaper's loyalty and unwilling to defend him is unclear; whatever Lovejoy's original intention, no mention of the

but hoped to bring legal suit against the regents after it was over. In the meantime the years passed. In 1923 he wrote James McKeen Cattell: "My equipment in Political Science, gained after so many years of toil lies there in the scrap heap. The doors of the University world seem to be locked and barred against me. My slender savings are melting away, as losses in a business enterprise that has not prospered or in meeting living expenses."[35] Two years later he was rescued from this condition when he received an appointment as professor of finance at the University of Oklahoma, which he filled, without incident, until his retirement in 1938.

At the University of Minnesota, threats to academic freedom did not end with the Schaper expulsion. Three months later an incident occurred concerning Wallace Notestein, whom Ford subsequently described as having been the "most outspoken Anglophile and pro-Ally on the Minnesota campus."[36] In December, 1917, Notestein delivered a paper before the AHA in Philadelphia in which he quoted from several Pan-German writers. A reporter in the audience undoubtedly did not listen carefully, for the following headlines appeared in the Philadelphia *Record* the next day: "Britain is branded as Instigator of War. Minnesota Educator accuses England of Forcing Great Conflict on World. Defends Pan-Germans. Scathing Arraignment of America's Ally shocks Conference of Savants." A "loyal Philadelphian" sent the article to the Minnesota regents, and at first President Burton was "rushed off his feet" (by Pierce Butler and an ally on the Public Safety Commission). It appeared as if the Schaper episode was about to be repeated. Only intervention by Notestein's colleagues, who succeeded in demonstrating the absurdity of the charges, ended the matter. It is notable how quickly and forthrightly his colleagues came to the defense of a man who per-

Schaper case was made in the "Report of Committee on Academic Freedom in Wartime."

35. William A. Schaper to James McKeen Cattell, April 6, 1923, Schaper Collection. This lament should not be taken as an indication that Schaper's spirit had been broken. Even when his health failed and his prospects looked hopeless, he did not sink into despair. His correspondence reveals plenty of the pugnacity that apparently had irritated his colleagues.

36. Guy Stanton Ford to William A. Anderson, May 5, 1958, in Schaper Case Papers.

sonally was popular and had popular views about the war. Several faculty members used the occasion to raise the broader issue of academic freedom with the president.[37] But the situation was so unimproved that in June, 1919, a committee of the faculty charged that threats to academic freedom had created for the university "a real and serious problem." A year later Notestein reported, "Things are going very badly here. The Regents are interfering and will soon spoil a pretty good University. Proud men are eager to leave."[38] Conditions did not change until the Farmer-Labor party assumed control of the state government and gained representation on the board of regents in the 1930s, when the final chapter was written in the Schaper case.

For years it had been rumored that Schaper's dismissal was motivated by larger political considerations than his views on the war alone. In 1937 the Farmer-Labor press in Minnesota brought to light old charges that reactionaries in the state had taken the opportunity presented by war hysteria "to rid the university of liberal professors," of whom Schaper distinctly was one. Professors Ford and Anderson point out that Schaper was considered a radical by the old-line Democrats and the Republicans who ruled the state and the university and that one of the functions of the Public Safety Commission, a member of which originally denounced Schaper, was to crush radicalism.[39] There can be no doubt that Schaper's politics increased his vulnerability in the same way as his personal unpopularity did. But his lack of commitment to the prevailing interpretation of the war was the offense that cost him his job. His political and personal unpopularity only weakened his position with the regents and the faculty, making it even more difficult to defend his rights before the charge of "disloyalty." Too, for many years, his politics

37. M. L. Burton to J. Franklin Jameson, January 19, 1918, in Jameson Papers; Cephas D. Allin to Guy Stanton Ford, February 4, 1918, January 23, 1918, both in CPI Papers.

38. James Gray, *The University of Minnesota* (Minneapolis, 1951), 257; Wallace Notestein to George B. Adams, May 5, 1920, in Adams Papers. Notestein left Minnesota at the end of the academic year and joined the history department at Cornell.

39. Clipping from the *Minnesota Leader,* December 25, 1937, in Comptroller Papers, University of Minnesota Archives; Anderson, interview with the author; Guy Stanton Ford to James L. Lee, November 5, 1957, in Schaper Case Papers.

prevented him from clearing his name of the charge. It is a matter of record that numerous attempts to secure redress for Schaper, particularly by the lawyer Max Lowenthal and Schaper's colleagues C. D. Allin and William Anderson, were unsuccessful until the conservative ruling parties, both Republican and Democrat, were unseated by the Farmer-Laborites. At that time the case was reopened and had a quick and happy denouement. With the cooperation of the governor of the state and after an opening salvo had been fired by Charles Beard in the *New Republic,* the board of regents rescinded the resolution of expulsion, reinstated Schaper as professor emeritus of political science, and awarded him $5,000 as reparation for his salary loss for the academic year 1917–1918. The board used the occasion to pass a broad resolution on academic freedom that protected a professor's freedom of teaching, research, and outside utterance and established procedures for faculty review and open hearings of any charges against one of its members.[40]

The luster of this sequel was tarnished slightly by Guy Stanton Ford, then acting president of the university, to whom Beard wrote for details when he was asked by friends of Schaper's to assist in reopening the case. In 1917 Ford had been on the payroll of the U.S. government and may have felt that he was not in a position to make a ringing defense of a professor's right to immunity from investigations into his loyalty. In 1937 he was not under such a constraint; yet, instead of welcoming the opportunity to publicly repudiate the presumption of the 1917 board, he expressed great reluctance to see the Schaper case reopened. His reply to Beard's request for information began with the observation that he very much doubted whether "real and discriminating" friends of Schaper wanted to reopen the case, for he supposed that Schaper "would be willing to let bygones be bygones." Ford then went on to say, in great detail, that Schaper's difficult personality largely was responsible for the expulsion. "If you knew Schaper," he wrote Beard, "you could easily understand how the whole German nation might become obsessed with

40. Guy Stanton Ford to Charles Beard, August 16, 1937, and Governor Elmer A. Benson to L. E. Lohmann, November 30, 1937, Minnesota Presidents' Papers; Charles A. Beard, "Mine Eyes May Behold," *New Republic,* LXXXIX (January 19, 1938), 306; and text of resolution passed by the Board of Regents of the University of Minnesota, January 28, 1938, Minnesota Presidents' Papers.

the encirclement idea."[41] The point here is not to make Ford appear to be a villain—in his own way he had tried to help Schaper through the years and had written him a strong recommendation for the Oklahoma position—but to demonstrate that the personality issue, which should never have been permitted to obscure the principles of the case, twenty years later still was uppermost in Ford's mind. Beard at first was given pause by Ford's reply, but he recognized that "we are all human and no case is 'perfect' " and went ahead with the job. In addition to the article in the *New Republic*, he wrote a strong editorial for the AAUP *Bulletin*, in which he hailed the reinstatement as more than righting an individual wrong, in itself "a magnificent gesture," but also as providing a set of resolutions on academic freedom, which should bind forever and serve as a "guide to other trustees in dark days when the angry passions of men rage again and the murky night of war closes in upon us."[42]

The case of James McKeen Cattell in many respects was different from Schaper's and certainly infinitely more complicated. It was preceded by a long history of difficulty between Cattell and the president and trustees of Columbia University and was intertwined with a struggle by the Columbia faculty, itself divided on tactical questions, to win some protection against assaults on academic freedom by the trustees. The Cattell case was part of an intricate and important chapter in the history of university politics at Columbia.[43] But, like the Schaper case, it also was an important part of the history of the academic com-

41. Guy Stanton Ford to Charles Beard, August 16, 1937, in Minnesota Presidents' Papers. However, when the reinstatement was made part of a principled defense of academic freedom and won widespread applause, Ford did not hesitate to bathe in its light. "Of course I was glad to see the Schaper case come up for its liquidation was long over due, both in justice to the man and for the honor of the University." Ford to A. J. Carlson, March 1, 1938, and Ford to Harold J. Laski, March 1, 1938, both in Minnesota Presidents' Papers.

42. Charles Beard to Guy Stanton Ford, September 6, 1937, in Minnesota Presidents' Papers; "A Ray of Light," *American Association of University Professors Bulletin*, XXIV (March, 1938), 294.

43. I have argued elsewhere that the Cattell case suggests the need for historians of academic freedom to pay more attention than they have in the past to intrafaculty politics. See my "Academic Freedom at Columbia University, 1917–1918: The Case of James McKeen Cattell," *American Association of University Professors Bulletin*, LVIII (September, 1972), 297–305.

munity during the war. Its development was part of a larger story, but its denouement must be seen against the background of the tensions, uncertainties, and prejudices spawned by the war.

James McKeen Cattell was one of the leading psychologists of his time. A pioneer in American experimental psychology and an early advocate of its practical application, he held the first professorship wholly in psychology to be established in the United States, at the University of Pennsylvania. Professor of psychology at Columbia University since 1891 and for a time chairman of the philosophy and psychology department, he established and directed a famous psychological laboratory at the university, in which he trained many of the next generation's outstanding psychologists. He edited two weekly and two monthly scientific and educational journals, among them the important publications *Science* and *Popular Science Monthly*, and was an active member of numerous professional organizations, including the American Psychological Association, of which he was a founder and past president, the American Association for the Advancement of Science, and the National Academy of Sciences. In addition, he was the acknowledged and tireless leader of the early twentieth-century movement for faculty control of the universities. Within psychology, Cattell was widely respected for the quality of his professional work and his intellectual fairness. At a time when many psychologists urged their own sectarian claims on all their colleagues, Cattell exercised his leadership in a statesmanlike fashion and helped to keep the profession open to many points of view.[44] On the issue of university administration and among his colleagues at Columbia, however, he was something of an *enfant terrible*, a gadfly who was uninhibited by the social amenities that ordinarily govern speech and behavior.[45] Long a trial both to his colleagues and the administration, in 1914 he was offered as "living proof" of the existence

44. Michael M. Sokal, "The Educational and Psychological Career of James McKeen Cattell, 1860–1904" (Ph.D. dissertation, Case Western Reserve University, 1972); Joncich, *The Sane Positivist,* 114–16, 220; Metzger, "Expansion and Profession," 21–22. I am indebted to Dorothy Ross, who has written an article on Cattell for the forthcoming supplement to the *Dictionary of American Biography,* for the evaluation of Cattell's role and reputation in the psychological profession.

45. Just as his nondoctrinaire position in his work in psychological organizations stemmed from his evaluation of the needs of the discipline of psychology, so

of academic freedom at Columbia. On October 1, 1917, the start of the new academic year, he was dismissed summarily by the trustees on the serious grounds of "sedition," "treason," and "opposition to the effective enforcement of the laws of the United States" and deprived of the pension to which twenty-six years' service to Columbia had entitled him. The issue of Cattell's patriotism was intertwined with the issue of his radical stance on university reform and with his role and conduct within the university; he himself described the reasons for his dismissal as "personal and complicated."[46]

The Cattell case occurred when there was conflict between the Columbia faculty and trustees over the issue of academic freedom and division among the faculty as to how the conflict should be resolved. For some time prior to the case, the trustees had been attempting to oversee instruction in the social sciences; in defense, the faculty had been trying to establish procedures to curb the trustees' arbitrary exercise of power.[47] In the spring of 1916 Charles Beard was summoned before a committee of the trustees on the charge of having defended a speaker who allegedly said "to hell with the flag" at a public meeting. After having successfully answered the charge, Beard was subjected to a half-hour inquisition into his beliefs and teaching. The meeting ended with Beard being admonished to warn all the members of the faculty of political science against teachings "likely to inculcate disrespect for American institutions." Shortly before this episode, two faculty members, Leon Fraser and Benjamin B. Kendrick, had been required to explain to the trustees remarks criticizing military training which they had made before a student meeting earlier in the year. When some of the younger faculty members wanted to make an open protest against the trustees' tactics, the leaders of the faculty of political science, E. R. A.

---

was his pugnacious behavior in his own university a product of his evaluation of the condition of American professors. This explanation of Cattell's behavior will be explored later in this chapter.

46. Frederick P. Keppel, *Columbia* (New York, 1914), 160; James McKeen Cattell to Allyn A. Young, November 11, 1917, in Hart Papers.

47. The outlook of the trustees was captured beautifully in a remark by trustee Francis S. Bangs to President Butler. "A little academic freedom in changing the Department of Economics and History for the good of the University would not be amiss," Bangs wrote. Francis S. Bangs to Nicholas Murray Butler, July 16, 1917, in Columbia University Archives.

Seligman chief among them, cautioned that such action would
jeopardize the progress being made toward academic freedom and
assured them that the trustees would cease their attacks on the faculty.[48]

Despite this assurance, in March, 1917, after considerable student and
faculty disapproval was voiced at the official rescinding of a speaking invitation to the pacifist Count Ilya Tolstoy, the trustees appointed a committee of their members to inquire whether doctrines subversive of the
Constitution and of the federal and New York state governments were
being taught at the university. The University Council, a quasi-faculty
body, then appointed the Committee of Nine (initially composed of four
deans and five professors), with Seligman as chairman and including
Professor John Dewey, to "cooperate" with the trustee committee and to
prevent it from taking any arbitrary action against the faculty. After the
faculty of political science passed a unanimous resolution condemning
the threat of a "general doctrinal inquisition," the trustees, temporarily
chastened, abandoned their plan.[49]

Cattell's position on the faculty had been precarious for at least seven
years before his dismissal; since 1910 the trustees had considered retiring Cattell from the university on three occasions. The issue was first
raised by President Nicholas Murray Butler, who was reacting against
Cattell's vociferous differences with administration policy and
procedures. Although a trustee committee considered at length the possibility of retiring Cattell, the matter was held in abeyance. The issue
was raised again in 1913, after Cattell's publication of a radical critique
of the structure and nature of American institutions of higher learning.
In *University Control* Cattell advocated a total restructuring of American higher education. Under the present system of administration, he

48. "A Statement by Charles A. Beard," *New Republic*, XIII (December 29,
1917), 249–51; Thomas Reed Powell to E.R.A. Seligman, November 13, 1917, in
James McKeen Cattell Collection, Special Collections, Columbia University
Library.
49. For the appointment of the Committee of Nine, see "A Statement by
Charles A Beard," 250; New York *Times*, March 24, 1917, p. 10; petition to the
trustees, undated, in Seligman Collection. The University Council comprised the
heads of the various academic divisions and a number of elected faculty members.
The trustee Special Committee to Inquire into the State of Teaching in the University remained in operation and played a role in the Cattell case.

wrote, the universities fail to guarantee the independence, security, and self-respect of the professoriate, to attract men of character with first-rate minds to the faculty, and to realize their full social value. "The university," he said, "should be a democracy of scholars serving the larger democracy of which it is part." One of his proposals toward this end was the strict curtailment of the power and perquisites of university presidents and trustees.[50] On this occasion, the trustees attempted to force Cattell's retirement but were prevented from doing so by the protest of several faculty members. The trustees tried to retire Cattell once more in March, 1917, after the first stages of an episode that may have been, as Cattell himself described it, "absurdly trivial" and "a childish matter," but which came close to exhausting the patience of his colleagues.[51]

In January, 1917, in response to an announcement by Butler that the Faculty Club was to be taken away from its members, who were thereafter to be relegated to a corner of the Commons, Cattell sent a confidential memorandum to the club members, in which, among other things, he ironically suggested that they confiscate the president's house for their own use. Only the utterly humorless could have taken this modest proposal seriously, and the faculty, accustomed to Cattell's publicizing techniques, chose to ignore the memorandum. However, almost two months later, one spiteful member released the offending document to the press, and, since it contained a characterization of Butler as "our many-talented and much-climbing president," it seemed to call for an answer. Twenty-eight members of the Faculty Club, including such

50. Extracts from minutes of the Committee on Education, February 3, April 26, November 30, December 22, 1910, and January 14, 1911, in Cattell Collection; James McKeen Cattell, *University Control* (New York, 1913), 62. The latter has yet to receive the attention it deserves. It is a seminal critique of institutions of higher learning and is relevant today. In Cattell's eyes its appearance provided the impetus for the 1913 expulsion attempt.

51. Extracts from minutes of the Committee on Education, May 1 and 3, 1913, Nicholas Murray Butler to George L. Rives, May 6, 1913, Butler to James McKeen Cattell, May 9, 1913, E. L. Thorndike to Butler, May 12, 1913, F. J. E. Woodbridge to Butler, May 13, 1913, M. I. Pupin to Butler, May 19, 1913, Edmund B. Wilson to Butler, May 20, 1913, extracts from minutes of the Special Committee to Inquire into the State of Teaching in the University, March 5, 1917, and Cattell to Young, November 11, 1917, all in Cattell Collection.

luminaries as Shotwell, Dewey, Seligman, Michael Pupin, William A. Dunning, and Giddings, wrote Cattell dissociating themselves from the sentiments of the memorandum and disapproving of its language and gave a copy of their rebuke to the press.[52]

The news that the trustees again were trying to oust Cattell convinced the Committee of Nine of the importance of defending him as part of its campaign to secure faculty control over appointments and dismissals. The faculty had mixed feelings about Cattell's tenure, but the sentiment was universal that any action against him should be taken only on the initiative of its own representatives. The Committee of Nine itself was divided at first about its recommendation. Dunning proposed that Cattell be retired for having ignored the "most elementary proprieties of decent society" and for having "rendered personal relations with most other Professors difficult and with the President inconceivable." But Dewey strongly objected to retiring a scholar for his eccentricities, and Seligman questioned the wisdom of retiring a man because he had become an unwelcome presence to the president and trustees. After persuading Cattell to sign an apology written by Seligman, the committee recommended that the trustees take no further action.[53] The trustees decided to hold the matter for further consideration. The issue between Cattell and his colleagues, however, erupted again over a difference about what constituted proper conduct. Cattell had been persuaded to sign the apology only by the argument that his successful defense, which the apology would make possible, would be an important victory for academic freedom. He had understood that the apology was to be shown only to the trustees. But the document was sent, on Committee of Nine recommendation, to the more than four hundred members of the Faculty Club and subsequently was published in the press. Its wide cir-

52. Confidential memorandum to resident members of the Faculty Club, January 10, 1917, James T. Shotwell *et al.* to James McKeen Cattell, March 3, 1917, both *ibid*. Cattell was referring to Butler's political ambitions. The full charge was: "If our many-talented and much-climbing president should be swept into the national vice-presidency by a reactionary wave, it is not likely that his successor will care to live in such a mausoleum."

53. F. J. E. Woodbridge to E. R. A. Seligman, March 28, 1917, *ibid*.; Minutes of the meeting of the Committee of Nine of the University Council to cooperate with the committee of the trustees, May 8, 1917, Report of the Committee of Nine on Professor Cattell, May 18, 1917, both in Seligman Collection.

culation without explanation made it appear to be an abject confession of bad judgment, and this Cattell would not tolerate. He accused Seligman of violating his agreement to show the apology only to the trustees and sent the accusation, supported by copies of his correspondence with Seligman, to the Faculty Club members.[54]

The distribution of Cattell's apology was viewed as perfectly legitimate because there was such widespread distaste for Cattell's tactics and his now-public confidential memorandum. Cattell's response was taken as further evidence of his unfitness for membership in the university community. To publicly accuse the powerful and highly respected Seligman of breaking his word and to circulate Seligman's correspondence were viewed as intolerable personal assaults, and Seligman was sent numerous letters of commiseration denouncing Cattell as an ass, an egotist, an ingrate, a scoundrel, a man with a "queer" mind, and even as insane.[55]

There can be no disputing that Cattell was a difficult man to get along with. He was combative, blunt, and altogether lacking in tact, and his colleagues had been disturbed by his incessant agitation for several years. But they missed the point when they dismissed him as having an "ungenerous and irrational mind," as being "ungentlemanly," "irretrievably nasty," and "lacking in decency."[56] When Cattell broke the rules of polite conduct he did so not because he had a personality defect but because his diagnosis of the ills of American higher education and his prescription for their cure made it obligatory for him to do so. Cattell described himself as being on the "extreme left wing" of the spectrum of academic politics. He advocated the complete dismantling of presidential and trustee control of the universities, which he characterized as

54. James McKeen Cattell to E. R. A. Seligman, June 16 and June 23, with enclosures, both in Cattell Collection. The report of the Committee of Nine on Professor Cattell [draft], undated [ca. May 11, 1917], and Seligman to Cattell, May 14 and June 14, 1917, all in Seligman Collection, make plain that Seligman dealt with Cattell duplicitously, but without actually lying to him.

55. See, for example, Richard Gottheil to E. R. A. Seligman, June 19, 1917, Howard Lee McBain to Seligman, June 24, 1917, and Thomas Reed Powell to Seligman, June 29, 1917, all in Seligman Collection.

56. F. J. E. Woodbridge to E. R. A. Seligman, March 28, 1917, S. W. Lambert to Seligman, May 17, 1917, George P. Krapp to Seligman, June 22, 1917, and H. E. Hawkes to Seligman, June 20, 1917, all *ibid.*

"autocratic." Its product, he said, was a state of humiliating dependency and subserviency among the faculty. To Cattell, the code of "gentlemanly conduct," with which faculties regulated their profession, further undermined their character and independence. He advocated the tactical use of ridicule and irony to break down this stultifying "gentlemanliness." He insisted upon the necessity for complete truth, openness, and publicity about the internal affairs of the university. "It is better to wash your dirty linen in public," he wrote, "than to continue to wear it."[57]

These convictions led Cattell to play the role of a relentless critic and propagandist. He repeatedly gave widespread publicity to every issue that seemed to suggest the need for university reform. As the editor of numerous periodicals and president of a printing company, he did not lack outlets for publication. Further, he refused to be satisfied with appearances and insisted on seeking out and calling attention to the implications of things. For example, when the Committee of Nine circulated his apology among the Faculty Club members, Cattell reflected on the inappropriateness of regarding the committee as a faculty watchdog when the majority of its members were "deans who are nominated by the president and, according to the statutes, must 'act in subordination to the president.' "[58] When this observation was interpreted (with magisterial indignation) as a personal assault on the integrity of five deans, Cattell dryly observed, "A committee of this character cannot represent the teachers of the university unless it is chosen by them."[59]

That Cattell's agitation so infuriated his colleagues suggests that, consciously or unconsciously, they were reacting to his principles as well as to his tactics. Otherwise, it is difficult to explain the depth of their feel-

57. James McKeen Cattell to John Dewey, May 14, 1913, Confidential memorandum, May 26, 1916, and Cattell to E. R. A. Seligman, March 8, 1917, all in Cattell Collection; Cattell, "Academic Slavery," *School and Society*, VI (October 13, 1917), 421–26; Cattell, *University Control*, 59.

58. James McKeen Cattell to E. R. A. Seligman, June 13, 1917, in Cattell Collection. By this time the composition of the committee had changed, so that deans and acting deans (of whom Seligman was one) made up the majority.

59. E. R. A. Seligman to James McKeen Cattell, June 14, 1917, and Cattell to Seligman, June 23, 1917, both in Seligman Collection. The Committee of Nine was not an elected body; it was appointed by the University Council from its own members.

ing as reflected in their almost indecent characterizations of him and their suggestions that he was insane. Cattell's colleagues appear to have responded to his statements as implicit accusations of cowardice. His repeated characterization of professors as "clerks" of the administration implied that if they *really* were "gentlemen"—*i.e.*, principled men— they would rise and demand their rightful place in university government. Cattell's personality is not irrelevant to his conduct. He had the kind of temperament that enabled, even impelled, him to speak his mind regardless of the impression made on others. Whether this reflected courage or insensitivity is a matter of opinion. But he is an example of a perfect marriage of temperament and point of view. Only a very few of his colleagues could appreciate that his behavior was inseparable from his principles.

After his exposure of Seligman, two men, both of whom disapproved of his manner and manners and admired Seligman, came to Cattell's defense. W. P. Trent, professor of literature, expressed complete agreement with Cattell's assessment of the "subserviency and the sycophancy of academic life," and Franz Boas wrote that on account of Cattell's "unusual courage and singleness of purpose . . . we should not only be willing to bear with his personal peculiarities . . . but be glad to have him and be grateful for what he gives to us."[60] These were voices in the wilderness.

On June 18, seven members of the Committee of Nine (the other two were unavailable) notified the trustees that they were "convinced that it is impossible for Professor Cattell to respect the ordinary decencies of

60. W. P. Trent to E. R. A. Seligman, June 20, 1917, and Franz Boas to Seligman, June 23, 1917, both *ibid.* Trent's observation deserves to be quoted at length: "It ought not to be possible for a man of my training and temperament to feel that at bottom despite all his defects and missteps, my sympathies are steadily with Cattell rather than with the ostensible attitude of a majority of my colleagues and with the officers of administration. I like peace and order and in many ways am conservative, I have filled, in a small way, administrative positions myself, I practically do not know what friction with my colleagues and the administration means, yet in my fifty-fifth year I find myself continually impressed by the subserviency and the sycophancy observable in academic life, by the parasite nature of the typical professor, by the growth of a spirit of censoriousness and revolt in myself. This is not as it should be, but self-examination does not leave me convinced that the fault lies entirely with me."

intercourse among gentlemen" and had concluded that "his usefulness in the University is ended." The committee members promised to make a formal report recommending Cattell's retirement at the beginning of the new academic year.[61] It is clear that the trustees were determined to get rid of Cattell and would seize any opportunity to do so and that the willingness of Cattell's colleagues to defend him had been stretched to the limit. The committee established to protect the academic freedom of the faculty concluded, in spite of Cattell's professional qualifications, that his personal peculiarities rendered him unfit for continued membership in the Columbia community. At this point Cattell took a step that introduced the issue of "loyalty" into his case, which then became more complicated as it was subject to the pressures of external opinion and the passions of wartime.

In August Cattell sent a letter to a number of congressmen urging them to "support a measure against sending conscripts to fight in Europe against their will." Cattell had been a long-standing critic of German militarism. With an unfailing instinct for the ironic, he pointed out: "I opposed the German Kaiser and his military bureaucracy when Theodore Roosevelt was dining with him, the trustees of Columbia University were naming a chair in his honor, and Dr. Nicholas Murray Butler was saying that 'he would have been chosen monarch—or chief executive—by popular vote of any modern people among whom his lot might have been cast.' " Cattell also was a critic of the war, and during the years of American neutrality he had urged an end to hostilities and a negotiated peace. Although he claimed to be still opposed to the war when the United States intervened, he became an active member of the National Research Council psychology committee, which organized and supervised psychological research and service for the emergency. Cattell clearly did not share the prevalent view that the war was a fight for civilization and morality, but his reservations about it did not extend so far as to preclude his performing professional service "to promote national efficiency."[62] Cattell's letter to the congressmen is a good exam-

61. E. R. A. Seligman *et al* to the subcommittee of the trustees, June 18, 1917, in Cattell Collection.
62. James McKeen Cattell to Julius Kahn, August 23, 1917, Cattell to Young, November 11, 1917, both *ibid.*; Yerkes, "Psychology and National Service."

ple of his independent posture on the war. Notwithstanding charges that it was intended to cripple the war effort, the letter asked neither for repeal of the Conscription Act nor for legislation against sending armies abroad. But its petition for a bill to relieve draftees from fighting abroad against their will clearly expressed support for conscientious objectors and thus was likely to be suspect in the eyes of those who saw the war as a great crusade to which it was impossible in conscience to object.

Cattell exercised his constitutional right of petition on stationery that identified him with Columbia. The record bears out his claim that he did not use official university letterhead, but rather personal stationery on which he had printed his "New York City address" (Columbia University, Division of Philosophy, Psychology and Anthropology) in small letters in the corner.[63] Nevertheless, Cattell previously had stated that a professor should try not to involve his institution in his political statements and had said that he therefore sent his own communications on public issues from his home address in Garrison, N.Y.[64] The point here is not to argue that the use of stationery identifying himself with Columbia was a serious offense on Cattell's part, but that he was not unaware of the difficulties it would create. The question then is why he acted in a way that he might have suspected at the very least would not help his already precarious position at Columbia. Perhaps he was not overly concerned about his tenure. When it was threatened in 1913 he wrote Dewey: "I have not been comfortable in the university in recent years, and if . . . [the trustees] do see fit to retire me on a pension . . . I shall not suffer seriously." He further asserted, "I do not want to be retained by Butler as he might a cook who promised not to get drunk again."[65] Cattell had twenty-eight years of university teaching behind him, an active professional life outside the university, and an adequate private in-

63. See his discussion of this issue, which he calls "trivial," in Cattell to Young, November 11, 1917, in Cattell Collection, and a copy of his letter to the congressmen in its original form, Cattell to Willard Saulsbury, August 23, 1917, in Columbia University Archives.

64. See copy of a letter to Seligman, early in 1917, in J[ames] McK[een] C[attell], *Memories of My Last Days at Columbia: Confidential Statement for Members of the Faculty Club* (Garrison-on-Hudson, N.Y., 1918), 8, in Cattell Collection.

65. Cattell to Dewey, May 14 and May 15, 1913, *ibid.*

come. Under these circumstances, circumspection in judgment and action, always uncongenial to his temperament, on this occasion may have seemed not worth the effort.

Cattell's affiliation with Columbia, in any event, already was known publicly. It had been displayed prominently in the press on June 1, the day after his son Owen, together with two other Columbia students, was arrested and indicted under the Conspiracy Act for authoring a pamphlet supporting draft resistance.[66] The pamphlet had been prepared following a meeting of the New York branch of the Collegiate Anti-Militarism League, held ten days before the Conscription Act was passed, at which two Columbia faculty members, Henry R. Mussey and Henry Wadsworth Longfellow Dana, had spoken. Mussey's role was minimal; he had no connection with the Anti-Militarism League and had appeared at the meeting to advise those present not to disobey the Conscription Act in the event of its passage. Dana's position was different. He had been associated with the league for several months and openly opposed conscription, although he did not counsel the students to resist the draft after it became law. He subsequently became affiliated with the radical-pacifist People's Council for Peace and Democracy, and during the summer of 1917 he attended its meetings in various parts of the country.[67]

Cattell's petition to Congress and Dana's affiliation with a pacifist organization brought the two professors under the ban of a wartime moratorium on academic freedom that had been announced by Butler on June 6 in a commencement day address to the alumni. Comparing the status of free assembly, speech, and publication before and after inter-

66. See, the banner headlines and detailed story in the New York *Herald*, June 1, 1917, p. 11. See also New York *Times*, June 1, 1917, p. 1, June 2, 1917, p. 2, June 3, 1917, p. 1, June 19, 1917, p. 2, June 20, 1917, p. 5, June 21, 1917, p. 9, June 22, 1917, p. 1, and June 23, 1917, p. 8. Cattell's eldest son McKeen interrupted his studies in physiology at Harvard to enlist in the army and served in France. But it was the activities of Owen, an officer of the Collegiate Anti-Militarism League, that received attention. Seligman declared that Owen's support of draft resistance threatened "social anarchy" and was "little short of treason." E. R. A. Seligman to James McKeen Cattell, June 11, 1917, in Cattell Collection.

67. For the program of the People's Council see Chatfield, *For Peace and Justice*, 27–28, 59. Chatfield demonstrates that although the People's Council was "billed as radical and subversive by fervent patriots and conservative labor leaders" this reputation was exaggerated.

vention, he had said: "What had been tolerated before becomes intolerable now. What had been wrongheadedness was now sedition. What had been folly was now treason. . . . There is and will be no place in Columbia University . . . for any person who opposes or counsels opposition to the effective enforcement of the laws of the United States, or who acts, speaks or writes treason. The separation of any such person from Columbia University will be as speedy as the discovery of his offense." Butler's conception of intolerable behavior, sedition, and treason was suggested by his conclusion: "This is the University's last and only warning to any among us . . . who are not with whole heart and mind and strength committed to fight with us to make the world safe for democracy."[68]

Although scholars have treated this pronouncement with the disapproval it deserves,[69] they have not noted that the initiative for it came in part from faculty members. Butler's pronouncement was made on the unanimous recommendation of the Special Committee to Inquire into the State of Teaching in the University (trustees) and the Special Committee of the University Council (Committee of Nine), which met jointly after the three students were indicted for preparing the draft resistance pamphlet. Furthermore, at a later date, the Committee of Nine not only met to investigate Dana's role at the Collegiate Anti-Militarism League meeting, but also issued the following warning: "If, in the future . . . [Dana] or any other colleague of ours acts in any way contrary to the letter or the spirit of the President's [commencement day] declaration, we shall be prepared to bring him before the authorities of the university for necessary discipline."[70]

68. Extracts from a speech at the alumni luncheon, Columbia University, June 6, 1917, in Cattell Collection.

69. Walter P. Metzger, *Academic Freedom in the Age of the University* (New York, 1955), 255; Richard Hofstadter and Wilson Smith (eds.), *American Higher Education: A Documentary History* (Chicago, 1961), II, 843–44; and William Summerscales, *Affirmation and Dissent: Columbia's Response to the Crisis of World War I* (New York, 1970) 88.

70. For a description of the joint meeting see E. R. A. Seligman to James McKeen Cattell, June 11, 1917, in Seligman Collection, and Nicholas Murray Butler to John G. Milburn, October 21, 1919, in Columbia University Archives; E. R. A. Seligman, "Report of the Committee of Nine in re participation of Columbia professors at the Meeting of the Anti-Militaristic League on May 8th, 1917," in Seligman Collection.

Concern about Columbia's reputation for patriotism was clearly beginning to be felt in several quarters at the university. After consulting with some of his fellow trustees, George L. Ingraham urged Butler to call Professors Mussey and Dana before the trustees and notify them that "either they must disassociate themselves from all these associations which are opposed to the war or opposed to conscription or opposed to a full and explicit obedience to the laws of the United States and the State of New York and the constituted authorities in relation to the war, or they must separate themselves from Columbia. Any association that opposes conscription or opposes the prosecution of the war by the President and other federal authorities, is really committing a crime, and I do not think that we should allow any professor, or anybody else connected with the University, to be connected with such an association." Ingraham's concern about Columbia's reputation led him to exercise absolutely improper influence on a judicial proceeding. He told Butler that he had had a long talk with the judge who was to preside at the trial of the three young people who "are spoken of all over as 'students of Columbia,'" and that "some time during the trial . . . [the judge] is going to make some sort of a statement about the defendants' connection with the University and to call attention to what the University had done in aid of the Government." He continued, "I thought it would be a good thing to get him to make such a statement in the course of the trial, as that would emphasize the fact that these few individuals do not at all represent the feeling in the University itself."[71]

President Butler clearly was becoming increasingly agitated by the public attention that Dana and Cattell drew to Columbia. He received communications from several congressional recipients of Cattell's petition, implicating the university in the professor's action. One congressman characterized the sentiments of the petition as seditious and treasonous. A newspaper clipping about Minnesota's expulsion of Schaper was sent to Columbia by a member of the New York Chamber of Commerce, with the message: "This is what you should do with *Cat-*

---

71. George L. Ingraham to Nicholas Murray Butler, June 11, 1917, in Columbia University Archives. The judge's role in this affair will be passed over in silence.

tell et al." Butler expressed extreme chagrin that Dana was "reported day by day in the public press as engaged in activities which throw doubt upon his sanity and which tend to bring the University into contempt" and declared, "Prompt action is imperatively demanded in the cases of Cattell and Dana." Butler's increasing anger was reflected in an outburst to Francis S. Bangs:

> Words without deeds are futile. My statement at the Alumni Luncheon on June 6th was perfectly definite and final. I then stated that it was the last and only warning that would be given. Since that time my warning has been openly flouted by Professor Cattell in letters addressed to various members of Congress, and by Professor Dana in a number of public acts. I must insist that both men be dismissed peremptorily at the first meeting of the Trustees. If this is not done, the whole world will laugh and laugh loudly at our pretense of patriotism. My patience is exhausted.

Butler made it known that at the next meeting of the trustees, on October 1, he would call for the immediate dismissal of Dana and Cattell.[72] That the two men were going to be fired was common knowledge across the campus throughout September.[73]

Trustee John Pine's exultation, "We have got the rascal this time," would leave no doubt, if further proof were needed, that the trustees were determined to get rid of Cattell on any ground. But to say, as Cattell did, that they "hid behind the flag to assassinate" and used "the prejudice, the passion and the blind patriotism of war" to conceal their objective[74] is misleading, because the statements are only partly true. Butler and the trustees clearly believed that Cattell's activities were damaging Columbia's reputation for patriotism, and they felt called upon

72. Julius Kahn to Nicholas Murray Butler, August 27, 1917, clipping, on Chamber of Commerce letterhead, undated [ca. September 15, 1917], Butler to Francis S. Bangs, September 3 and 19, 1917, and Butler to A. L. Walker, September 24, 1917, all *ibid.* The last letter was a response to a petition to the president from eight members of the Committee on Instruction for the mines, engineering, and chemistry schools, which claimed to speak for the faculty of these schools, asking for the expulsion of Dana and Cattell under the provisions of the commencement day address. See Walker *et al.* to Butler, September 19, 1917, in Columbia University Archives.

73. Levering Tyson to John G. Saxe, November 29, 1919, in Cattell Collection.

74. John Pine to Nicholas Murray Butler, September 21, 1917, in Columbia University Archives; Cattell to Young, November 11, 1917, in Cattell Collection.

to dismiss him to protect the university. Even if they had other reasons for firing Cattell, it is significant that they were able to rely on patriotism to accomplish their objective. Patriotism was available as a weapon because the Columbia faculty, with few exceptions, agreed that Cattell, and Dana as well, deserved to be fired because his activities were injurious to the university.

The conduct of the Committee of Nine makes it clear that the expulsion of Dana and Cattell cannot be separated from the patriotism issue. On the initiative of one of its members, the committee met to consider asking the trustees to dismiss Dana and Cattell for bringing the university into disrepute by their apparently "treasonable conduct." Dewey was becoming increasingly concerned about the committee's activities, in which until now he had concurred. He objected to the meeting, declaring that he had never supposed that the object of the committee "was to do espionage work" and that "a meeting for such a purpose is wholly *ultra vires*."[75] None of Dewey's fellow committee members objected to the proposed meeting. One of them commented that "enough rope has been paid out to Cattell & Dana and some one should put his foot on the slack." Although the committee did not mention the issue of patriotism in its reports, it nevertheless moved to recommend the dismissal of both men—of Cattell on the grounds of personal unfitness, as revealed in his imbroglio with Seligman, and of Dana, who the committee thought had behaved "irresponsibly," because his "usefulness" to the university was at an end.[76]

Despite the attempt to take a high ground, the committee's posture clearly was disingenuous. In July, before Cattell wrote his controversial letter to the congressmen, Seligman had expressed second thoughts about the committee's earlier decision to request Cattell's dismissal because of Seligman's own personal quarrel with him and had just about

75. For the proposal to call the meeting see James C. Egbert to E. R. A. Seligman, September 4 and 15, 1917, both in Seligman Collection; John Dewey to Egbert, September 15, 1917, and Dewey to Seligman, September 16, 1917, both in Cattell Collection.

76. S. W. Lambert to E. R. A. Seligman, September 9, 1917, minutes of the meeting of the Committee of Nine appointed to cooperate with a special committee of the trustees, September 24, 1917, and Seligman to George L. Ingraham, September 28, 1917, all in Seligman Collection.

decided to ask the committee to "stick to [its] original report" urging the trustees not to fire Cattell.[77] Considering Seligman's personal influence on the committee, both as chairman and as a powerful and highly respected figure in the faculty, it is more likely than not that his wish would have prevailed. However, Cattell's petition obviously changed the situation. Seligman's correspondence with Frederick Woodbridge about the projected meeting indicates that they expected the committee to take "decisive action" concerning both Dana and Cattell. Seligman, knowing of Dewey's objections to the committee meeting, urged Woodbridge to try to bring Dewey "around to your point of view." Seligman himself tried to mollify Dewey about the proposed meeting with the following observation: "The situation is, in my opinion a very complicated one and it needs a great deal of wisdom. We have lost our heads in this war and it is going to be a very difficult thing to keep our balance."[78]

To take the committee's recommendations for dismissal of Dana and Cattell at face value is difficult, since the meeting from which they issued was convened precisely to consider the "unpatriotic" activities of the two men. Furthermore, if the committee had been genuinely uninfluenced by the treason charge, its members surely knew that, under the circumstances of widespread disapproval of the actions of Dana and Cattell and of widespread knowledge that the Columbia president and trustees were about to fire them for treason, their recommendation for dismissal couldn't possibly be dissociated from the patriotism issue. When Cattell was about to be spuriously branded a traitor, it was inappropriate, to say the least, for the committee to recommend his dismissal for personal unfitness. As for Dana, it is unclear in what way his behavior was "irresponsible" unless, in the eyes of the committee, association with a politically unpopular organization constituted irresponsibility.

77. E. R. A. Seligman to F. J. E. Woodbridge, July 24, 1917, in Cattell Collection.
78. E. R. A. Seligman to F. J. E Woodbridge, September 6, 1917, Woodbridge to Seligman, September 7, 1917, Seligman to Woodbridge, September 11, 1917, Woodbridge to Seligman, September 12, 1917, Seligman to Woodbridge, September 15, 1917, Seligman to John Dewey, September 18, 1917, all in Seligman Collection.

The conclusion is inescapable that the Committee of Nine believed that Cattell's petition and Dana's political affiliation were improper and injurious to Columbia; their language disguised their reasoning.[79]

On October 1 the trustees dismissed Dana and Cattell for activities tending to promote disloyalty in defiance of Butler's commencement day address. Given the language of the address, the terms of the dismissal amounted to a charge of sedition, treason, and opposition to the enforcement of the laws of the United States. Although they had acted entirely on their own, the trustees issued a statement to the press that mendaciously implied that they had acted on the recommendation of the Committee of Nine. That the trustees had not consulted the committee and had then misrepresented its formal position to give legitimacy to their action were resented deeply by the faculty. The trustees' conduct created considerable discontent on the campus, giving rise to new efforts to secure machinery to defend faculty rights.[80] The most dramatic consequence of the trustees' conduct was the resignation from the faculty, on October 8, of Charles Beard. Beard resigned not in support of Dana and Cattell personally, but because the expulsions were the last straws in a series of episodes that had proven to him that the university was "really under the control of a small and active group of trustees who have no standing in the world of education, who are reactionary and visionless in politics, narrow and medieval in religion."[81] However, in spite of the widespread resentment among the faculty over the manner in which the expulsion of Dana and Cattell had been accomplished, there was very little feeling that the expulsions themselves were unjustified. There is every indication of considerable faculty agreement that the opinions and activities of the two men were improper and injurious to Columbia University and to the nation.

79. Dewey refused to support the deception. He resigned from the committee and unsuccessfully urged Seligman to join him. See John Dewey to E. R. A. Seligman, September 25 and October 3, 1917, both in Cattell Collection.

80. See heading Committee of Reference in catalog to Columbia University Archives.

81. Charles Beard to Nicholas Murray Butler, October 8, 1917, in *Minutes of the Trustees of Columbia University*, XXXVIII (1917–18), 89. For the details of the Beard resignation and the differing interpretations among the faculty of the circumstances surrounding the Dana-Cattell-Beard episode see Gruber, ' Academic Freedom at Columbia," 303–304.

There were individuals who objected to the firing of Dana and Cattell. On the eve of the expulsions Franz Boas appealed to Butler in Cattell's behalf. After the two professors had been fired, the press carried statements critical of the action by Beard, Dewey, James Harvey Robinson, and Professor of Philosophy W. P. Montague.[82] Dewey, Robinson, and Thomas Reed Powell requested the AAUP to investigate the two cases.[83] But these were isolated, individual, and ineffective protests. There was no collective faculty effort to defend Dana's right to belong to a legal political organization. It remained for Randolph Bourne to make a principled statement in Dana's behalf. "Professor Dana's only offense," he wrote, "was that he retained his pacific and internationalist philosophy in wartime and associated with other radicals who had retained theirs. . . . He was charged with no specific offense against his country. The only charge is nonconformity." There was no collective faculty effort to defend Cattell's right to petition Congress on a matter of public concern. Indeed, the faculty had never objected to the outrageous commencement day address, under the terms of which Dana and Cattell were fired. Woodbridge described the opinion in the university about the firings as follows: "All those who had full and personal knowledge of the facts concluded that the usefulness of Professors Cattell and Dana in the University had ceased. . . . Apparently the greater part of the University concurs in it. The claim that . . . an injustice has been done these men has too little support to warrant serious attention."[84] Giddings was more explicit when he wrote that Dana and Cattell had overstepped the limit of legitimate free speech and that "their dismissal from the Univer-

82. Franz Boas to Nicholas Murray Butler, September 29, 1917, in Columbia University Archives; New York *Evening Post,* October 4, 1917, p. 5; New York *Tribune,* October 4, 1917, p. 2; and New York *Times,* October 9, 1917, p. 1.

83. John Dewey, James Harvey Robinson, and Thomas Reed Powell to A. A. Young, undated [October, 1917], in Cattell Collection. The AAUP acted on the request, but considered the case of Cattell alone and reported it without mentioning the name of either the university or the professor involved. In its "Report of Committee on Academic Freedom in Wartime," 45–46, the AAUP briefly condemned the action of an "important university" in firing " a distinguished man of science," on the charge of sedition and treason when all he had done was exercise his constitutional rights of citizenship.

84. Randolph Bourne, "Those Columbia Trustees," *New Republic,* XII (October 20, 1917), 329; F. J. E. Woodbridge, report, October 16, 1917, in Columbia University Archives.

sity was the plain duty of the trustees . . . every loyal alumnus of the university and every loyal student, whatever position he may take upon the question of academic freedom, should make perfectly clear to the public that he does not stand by men who disobey law and obstruct government."[85]

To say that patriotism was simply a cloak behind which the Columbia trustees hid their "real" motives is insufficient. They used the patriotism issue because they thought it was legitimate, and they were able to do so because of the climate of opinion about the war in the community and on the campus. Seligman was right when he said, "We have all lost our heads in this war"; the equanimity with which the faculty accepted Butler's statement (which had itself been recommended by some faculty members) that dismissal from Columbia awaited any professor who was not "with whole heart and mind and strength committed to fight with us to make the world safe for democracy" is proof enough of the accuracy of Seligman's observation. That the university's affairs were aired daily in the New York City press increased the difficulty of maintaining a sense of balance and proportion on the campus during the tense period of the war. The public was made privy to Columbia's domestic quarrels, often in a way that could only increase their intensity. Butler recounted that in the days following the October 1 meeting of the trustees "the University was literally infested with armies of reporters" and said he had reason to believe that the Committee of Nine report on Dana and Cattell had been leaked to the press even before it was presented to the council.[86] In a glare of publicity, on the basis of the most serious charges that can be leveled against a citizen in wartime, Dana and Cattell were discharged from Columbia, with the acquiescence of most of their colleagues, who seem to have believed that the fate was merited.

85. "The Public, the University, and the Professor," *Independent*, XCII (October 20, 1917), 118. Giddings' authorship of this editorial is revealed in Giddings to Butler, October 18, 1917, in Columbia University Archives. Giddings wrote Butler to dissociate himself from the last lines of the editorial, which praised the "courage and self-sacrifice" of Beard's resignation; these, he says, "were added in the office without my knowledge."

86. Nicholas Murray Butler to John Pine, October 23, 1917, in Columbia University Archives.

The wartime history of academic freedom is not complete without an account of the campaign against Senator Robert M. La Follette by members of the faculty of the University of Wisconsin. Although not an instance of the abridgment of academic freedom, the incident is relevant to the issue as a striking example of the lengths to which wartime intolerance could carry American professors. Accounts of the wartime relations between the university and the senior senator from Wisconsin are usually confined to a discussion of the famous faculty round robin of January, 1918.[87] In response to widely publicized charges throughout the state and elsewhere in the country that the faculty's failure to repudiate La Follette's opposition to the war was proof that the university supported La Follette's stand, a subcommittee of the university War Committee drew up and circulated a petition that read: "We, the undersigned resident members of the faculty of the University of Wisconsin ... protest against those utterances and actions of Senator Robert M. La Follette which have given aid and comfort to Germany and her allies in the present war; we deplore his failure loyally to support the government in the prosecution of the war. In these respects he has misrepresented us, his constituents."[88] The petition, which conspicuously echoed the Constitution's definition of treason, was signed by over 90 percent of the faculty, including the president of the university and the deans. The petition alone is a serious indictment of the faculty, for it demonstrates that in order to protect their own reputations for patriotism the professors were willing to besmirch the patriotism of another, who was one of Wisconsin's outstanding public servants and a long-time friend and protector of the university. In addition to the attack on La Follette in the round robin, however, faculty members were engaged in an aggressive campaign to destroy him and his supporters politically, a campaign that included a sub-rosa investigation of the senator to which the NBHS lent its support.

87. See especially Curti and Carstensen, *The University of Wisconsin*, II, 115, 201; Charles G. Sellery, *Some Ferments at Wisconsin, 1901–1947* (Madison, 1960), 7–8; and Richard T. Ely, *Ground Under Our Feet* (New York, 1938), 217–18.

88. Petition in Wisconsin Presidents' Papers.

The campaign was initiated in the fall of 1917 by Ely, Commons, and Fish.[89] Its purpose, as expressed by Ely, was "to purge the state politically . . . [to] put La Follette and all his supporters out of business." To this end, in January, 1918, the Madison chapter of the Wisconsin Loyalty Legion was established with Ely as president. It pledged "to work against La Follettism in all its anti-war forms, realizing that any encouragement to the supporters of La Follette is in fact support of La Follette himself." The professors conducting the campaign hoped to attract followers by substantiating their charge that La Follette "has been of more help to the Kaiser than a quarter of a million troops." Ely asked Dana C. Munro, of the NBHS Committee on Research, for assistance in gathering facts to show that La Follette's "influence has been pernicious, and that he has been encouraging our foes and discouraging the government in its war activities. . . . We want a record of his speeches and efforts, and we want to know what has been printed in German newspaper[s], indicating the encouragement he has given Germany. Especially do we want to know the kind of influence which he has exerted against our country in Russia." Munro turned the appeal over to the CPI, and Ford put Ely in touch with Victor Clark, who was gathering a file of German and Austrian newspapers and periodicals for the NBHS. This fact-finding campaign, which Ely admonished Ford to keep secret, also enlisted the aid of E. M. Coulter of Marietta College in Ohio and James G. Randall of Roanoke College in Virginia; but all the effort failed to uncover evidence to support the indecent charge against La Follette of giving aid and comfort to the German (and Russian) enemy.[90]

89. Carl Russell Fish to Mr. Bloodgood, October 4, 1917, in Fish Papers.

90. Richard T. Ely to Albert Shaw, January 21, 1918, Madison Chapter of the Wisconsin Loyalty Legion, Ely to Shaw, January 29, 1918, Ely to Dana C. Munro, January 20, 1918, Munro to Ely, January 23, 1918, Guy Stanton Ford to Ely, January 30, 1918, Ely to Ford, February 6, 1918, Victor S. Clark to John S. P. Tatlock, February 12, 1918, Clark to Tatlock, February 14, 1918, James G. Randall to Tatlock, February 16, 1918, all in Ely Papers; Carl Russell Fish to E. M. Coulter, February 20, 1918, and Coulter to Fish, February 27, 1918, both in Fish Papers. Coulter illuminated the spirit that animated the investigation. "Of course," he wrote Fish, "I understand it is to be an unbiased and candid account of the Senator's course and its effect—but we all know it can lead but to one conclusion—something little short of treason."

Meanwhile, the leaders of the Madison chapter of the Loyalty Legion organized to enlist support within the university. The campus was "farmed out," building by building, to faculty members—often the same ones who had solicited signatures for the round robin—who tried to sign up whole departments for membership.[91] However, the avowedly political purpose of the Madison chapter (as opposed to the purely patriotic purpose of the parent body, the Wisconsin Loyalty Legion) raised suspicion in some faculty members that the war was being used as a cover by the Wisconsin stalwarts to destroy Progressivism.[92] Those who had witnessed years of virulent attacks on La Follette Progressivism understandably were wary of a movement whose announced purpose was to crush La Follette and all his followers, even if it was led by such notable Progressives as Ely and Commons. Several Wisconsin men refused to join the Madison branch for this reason.[93] The plan to discredit La Follette failed, and after the war he was reelected by a resounding majority.

The round robin is a serious reflection of the wartime state of mind of the Wisconsin faculty. It is another indication of the sensitivity of members of the university community to the pressure of outside opinion. The grossness of the petition's suggestion that La Follette's position on the war constituted treason also is worthy of note, for it indicates an intolerance of political differences that borders on the pathological. The interest of the professorial attempt to destroy La Follette politically lies elsewhere. The campaign to gather facts—exact dates, exact quotations, exact references—from La Follette's speeches and from German and Russian newspaper sources is a remarkable example of the uses of scholarship for espionage. It was a far cry from the disinterested pursuit of truth for a group of professors to mobilize a secret research campaign

91. See Madison Chapter of the Wisconsin Loyalty Legion, reports for February 7 and 23, 1918, in Ely Papers.

92. This suspicion was given detailed exposition in Horace M. Kallen, "Politics, Profits, and Patriotism in Wisconsin," *Nation*, CVI (March 7, 1918), 257–59.

93. Edward A. Birge to G. M. Hyde, February 1, 1918, in Wisconsin Presidents' Papers; Charles Van Hise to Richard T. Ely, February 1, 1918, A. R. Hohlfeld to Ely, February 8, 1918, and J. S. Evans to Ely, January 31, 1918, all in Ely Papers.

to find ammunition to destroy the political career of a United States senator who did not share their view of the war.

In later years, Ely, the chief instigator of the campaign against La Follette, attempted to justify his role in the most dubious fashion. Writing about the episode in his autobiography, he mentioned only having signed the round robin, which he explained as follows: "My son John experienced some of the heaviest fighting of the war, and naturally I joined the ninety-two percent of the faculty which signed a protest to the United States Senate. . . . I was not one of the ring-leaders, as La Follette thought, in circulating this petition among the faculty, but I certainly was in sympathy with them." At the time he was writing, postwar revisionism was the popular cause, and Ely managed again to come out on the winning side. He acknowledged the failure of the American attempt to make the world safe for democracy and announced, "I am ready to throw a wreath on [La Follette's] grave."[94]

The Great Crusade was so popular on the American campus that those professors who did not share the prevailing enthusiasm were suspected of being mentally or morally deficient, or even dangerous. The climate of opinion on the American campus was so conformist that neither tolerance nor respect was allowed for differences of opinion about the war. And, in cases when a person's job was at stake, there was clearly such insufficient dedication to the principle of academic freedom that a professor couldn't count on his colleagues to insist that his job must be immune from political considerations. Even the traditional spokesmen for academic freedom took an ambiguous position because they thought that the war had created new priorities. It stands to reason that academic freedom is threatened most in times of social crisis, when threats to the community's life and values weaken the resistance of the university and its faculty to outside suspicion and hostility and expose internal rifts in the profession itself. The response to the war on the

94. Ely, *Ground Under Our Feet*, 217, 218. For an account that accepts this explanation, see Benjamin B. Rader, *The Academic Mind and Reform: The Influence of Richard T. Ely in American Life* (Lexington, Ky., 1966), 183. See also the account by Sellery, one of the authors of the round robin, in *Some Ferments in Wisconsin*, 7–8.

American campus exposed an absence of professional cohesiveness among professors that has implications extending beyond the history of academic freedom during the war.

Early in the century Dewey wrote an article on academic freedom that perceptively made the point that genuine academic freedom was threatened less by assaults from without than by conditions within the profession—specifically, institutional loyalty, disciplinary specialization, and administrative centralization—which weakened the independence, initiative, and responsibility of the faculty. The corrective he urged was a recognition by professors that they belonged to a suprainstitutional community of scholarship. "The consciousness of being a member of an organized society of truth-seekers," he wrote, "will solidify and re-enforce otherwise scattered and casual efforts."[95] In an argument with implications remarkably similar to Dewey's, Cattell insisted that professors had less to fear from sporadic dismissals for unpopular points of view than from a process of subtle enslavement by the conventions of the university. "It is not academic freedom in the classical sense which is seriously in question, but the limitations in speech and conduct which university routine imposes," he said. "It is not dismissal which is the difficulty, but the dependence on favor for advancement in position and in salary and for the little offices and honors about the institution which serve in lieu of salary. . . . It seems at times as though the whole organization of the university is better suited to the courtier, the adventurer or the mediocrity than to the man of genius or of fine temperament."[96] Each in his own way, Dewey and Cattell were both saying that academic freedom would be only an ideal until professors themselves, united in a collective consciousness and élan, resisted the intimidating influences that undermined their own independence and freedom of thought and conduct. The history of academic freedom during the war demonstrates that there was a political collective consciousness among American professors; indeed, that was part of the problem. But this his-

95. John Dewey, "Academic Freedom," *Educational Review,* XXIII (January, 1902), 14.
96. Cattell, "Academic Slavery," 426.

tory also demonstrates that a professional collective consciousness, which might have enabled professors to defend the rights of the politically and personally unpopular colleagues in their midst, was lacking.

VI

Colleges and
Commandants

IN THE FALL of 1918 the nation's institutions of higher learning performed the ultimate act of service to the cause: They turned their intellectual and physical resources over to the War Department and became centers for military training. On October 1, at simultaneous assemblies at 516 colleges and universities throughout the country, 140,000 male students were inducted into the U.S. Army and assumed the novel status of student-soldiers, in a program known as the Students' Army Training Corps (SATC). There was no mistaking the significance of the event. For the students, as President Wilson's message said, the step signified that they had "ceased to be merely individuals . . . [and had joined] with the entire manhood of the country" as participants in the Great Crusade. For the colleges and universities, which would be devoted primarily to training the student-soldiers under the War Department's direction, the step meant becoming "like the railroads, essentially government institutions."[1] If the face of higher education had been altered previously by cooperation with the cause, it now was transformed

1. U. S. War Department, Committee on Education and Special Training, *A Review of Its Work During 1918 by the Advisory Board* (Washington, D.C., 1919), 135, cited hereinafter as Committee, *A Review*; Thwing, *The American Colleges and Universities in the War*, 57.

totally, as the colleges and universities relinquished their function as centers for the higher learning and dedicated themselves to serving the needs of the War Department. That the SATC was in operation a bare three months before its liquidation at the end of the war should not minimize the significance of the program. It was the fulfillment of the higher education's service ideal. By the fall of 1918 the colleges and universities were hostage to the commitment they had already made to the cause and the cooperation they had already given to the government; they had no principled position from which to resist the last assault on their autonomy. Nicholas Murray Butler's offer of his "army of students and teachers" for any act or service the government might require[2] turned out to be prophetic.

The SATC originated in the National Army Training Detachments, which were established in April, 1918, by the War Department Committee on Education and Special Training. The committee had contracted with 157 colleges, universities, and technical and trade schools to provide training to drafted men in such subjects as radiotelegraphy, carpentry, automobile repair, and sheet-metal work. The men received seven hours a day of vocational training; in addition, three hours of military drill were provided by army officers detached to the schools. The schools were paid a fixed price per man per day for housing and subsistence of the student-soldiers. After two months of training the men were distributed to the various branches of the service. Shortly after the program was inaugurated Professor Frank Aydelotte of the Massachusetts Institute of Technology was requested by the committee to organize a brief course on the historical background of the war and the social philosophies of the belligerent nations. The War Aims Course, as it was called, was tried in May at a technical institute in Boston and was so successful in enhancing morale that it was extended to all the detachments, becoming mandatory for at least one hour a week. In developing this course as well as every other phase of the program, the committee, which comprised three army officers, was aided by a seven-man civilian

2. See p. 100 herein.

advisory board, on which James R. Angell, dean of faculties at the University of Chicago, represented the universities and colleges.[3]

As early as March when the National Army Training Detachments were still in the planning stage, the committee, realizing that the army also faced a shortage in the higher technical professions and in candidates for officers' training camps, decided to extend its program. On May 8 the secretary of war announced that a "comprehensive plan . . . to provide military instruction for the college students of the country" would be implemented at the beginning of the fall semester. The new plan had the twofold objective of developing "as a great military asset the large body of young men in the colleges and . . . [of preventing] unnecessary and wasteful depletion of the colleges through indiscriminate volunteering, by offering to the students a definite and immediate military status." The final details, embodied in an announcement from the adjutant general of the army to the presidents of American colleges on June 29, provided that a Students' Army Training Corps unit be established at all colleges of arts and sciences and at technical and professional schools enrolling one hundred or more able-bodied male students over the age of eighteen. These men were to enlist in the United States Army and were to be placed on furlough status without pay, not to be called into service until after they had received their diplomas or reached the draft age of twenty-one, whichever occurred first. In addition to their regular studies, the students were to receive ten hours a week of military training—six of practical work and four of academic studies of military value—to be supplemented by six weeks of intensive training in a summer camp.[4] President Richard C. Maclaurin of MIT, who was chosen educational director of the collegiate section of the SATC, appointed twelve district directors, one from each of the geographical districts into which the nation's higher educational system had been divided, to help administer the new corps.

3. The National Army Training Detachments are described in C. R. Dooley, *Final Report of the National Army Training Detachments, Later Known as Vocational Section S.A.T.C.* (Washington, D.C., 1919), and Ralph Barton Perry, "Students' Army Training Corps," *National Service, with the International Military Digest*, VI (August, 1919), 77–85.
4. Committee, *A Review*, 57, 60–64.

As initially conceived, the plan would have called for a certain amount of adjustment in the colleges but would not have interrupted academic work significantly or involved major changes in educational policy. President Van Hise, for instance, observed that the government was simply adopting the policy, which had been pursued by the University of Wisconsin since America had entered the war, "of holding the young men . . . [in college] until they are ready to take the training for officers or to enter special service."[5] In the beginning of August, however, after 250 institutions had already received authorization for an SATC unit, a sudden change in manpower policy necessitated completely revamping the program. The War Department asked Congress to lower the draft age to eighteen and announced that the men within the enlarged draft range would all be called into service within a year. This step threatened the existence of the very institutions that were being counted on to provide the immediate and intensive training for the large number of officers and specialists who would be needed. Under the new manpower bill the colleges would be emptied of their able-bodied male students over the age of eighteen, and new students would be discouraged from enrolling because of the certainty of being drafted within the year. At three great regional meetings at the end of August, representatives of the army presented the presidents of the nation's educational institutions with a hurriedly devised plan that stressed mutual interest and need.

The aim of the new Students' Army Training Corps was to utilize effectively the plant, equipment and organization of the colleges for selecting and training officer-candidates and technical experts for service in the existing emergency. Two types of divisions were established: Sections A (collegiate) and B (vocational). Section B, comprising the old National Army Training Detachments and designed to provide vocational training to grammar school graduates, is not of interest for this study.[6] It is Section A that represented a radical departure for the nation's higher educational institutions. As under the earlier plan, units of

5. Charles Van Hise to the members of the instructional staff, May 28, 1918, in Wisconsin Presidents' Papers.
6. Committee, *A Review*, 65. For a history of SATC Section B, see Dooley, *Final Report of the National Army Training Detachments*.

Section A were to be established at colleges and universities, normal schools, and graduate and professional schools requiring for admission graduation from a standard four-year secondary school or its equivalent and enrolling at least one hundred able-bodied male students over the age of eighteen. All men students who entered qualifying institutions in the fall of 1918 as freshmen, upperclassmen, or graduate or professional students, who were physically fit and eighteen or over, would become privates on active duty in the United States Army. As such, they would wear uniforms, live in barracks (which were to be improvised by the colleges), eat at a common mess, receive a monthly allowance of thirty dollars, and be subject at all times to military regulations and discipline.[7] Each institution was to be assigned a commanding officer and as many junior officers as were necessary and available to take charge of the military aspects of the program. The rest of the program was to be under the direction of the regular academic faculty.

Normal academic organization, including the four-year course of study and the classification of students by academic maturity as freshmen, sophomores, juniors, and seniors, was to be abandoned. The academic year was to be divided into four quarters, and the schedule was arranged so that students would be ready for a regular military assignment at the same time when all other men of their age were called. It was planned that students who were twenty and older on September 18 would remain in school for one quarter (October–December), those of nineteen for two quarters (October–March), and those of eighteen for the maximum period of three quarters (October–June). They were to follow a course of study strictly prescribed according to their ages and to the program in which they were enrolled. This could be one of five officers' preparatory courses or a professional and technical course.

The schedule was to consist of eleven hours of military drill a week and forty-two hours of "essential" and "allied" subjects, which varied according to the program the student entered. The "essential" or primar-

7. A special congressional fund was established, from which tuition, room, and board were to be paid to the colleges and uniforms, army equipment, and wages were to be provided. The cost per student was estimated at $900 a year. See Thwing, *The American Colleges and Universities in the War*, 60.

ily military subjects, which included military law and practice, hygiene and sanitation, surveying and map making, and modern ordnance, had to be taken in the first quarter by the twenty-year-old students; the nineteen- and eighteen-year-olds could distribute the subjects over two and three quarters respectively. Although each program had a different curriculum, every student was required to take the War Issues Course, an adaptation and extension of the War Aims Course that had originated in the National Army Training Detachments. The schedule of fifty-three hours a week included two hours a night of "supervised study," when the men were to be assembled in large halls by the commanding officer and guided, if necessary, by faculty members in individual study. At the end of his school term the student-soldier, on the basis of his performance as judged by the commanding officer, would be assigned to an officers' training camp, a noncommissioned officers' training school, or a depot brigade or would be permitted to continue such special studies as engineering, medicine, and law.

President Maclaurin remained educational director of the collegiate section and retained the twelve district directors he had chosen for the original program.[8] An attempt was to be made to provide the usual educational activities for civilian students (women, physically disqualified men, and men under eighteen), but the needs of the SATC were to be given priority.

Although the "allied" subjects in each program included such academic courses as modern languages, mathematics, physical and natural sciences, economics, history, and government, they all were to be adapted to the military programs. As a result, the colleges and universities would lose their academic character and become military training institutes, under the direction of the War Department, and the official bulletins describing the SATC made this quite clear. A memorandum from the chairman of the Committee on Education and Special Training to college presidents and commanding officers, dated September 28,

8. For example, Dean Charles H. Haskins of Harvard was director of District 1 (New England States), President Edward K. Graham of the University of North Carolina directed District 4 (Virginia, North Carolina, South Carolina, Georgia, and Florida), and President Ray Lyman Wilbur of Stanford directed District 11 (California, Nevada, and Utah).

1918, unequivocally stated that since the SATC was established to "hasten the mobilization and training of our armies . . . its value cannot be appraised by ordinary academic standards of college admission or the requirements for academic degrees. . . . The courses must not be considered, or their results measured, from the ordinary standpoint of college standards and customs."[9] The general plan of operation declared: "Fundamental changes must be made in college and school practices in order to adapt them to effective service in this emergency. . . . Academic instruction must necessarily be modified along lines of direct military value. The War Department will prescribe or suggest such modifications. . . . The colleges are asked to devote the whole energy and educational power of the institution to the phases and lines of training desired by the Government."[10]

Under the pressure of the abnormal conditions of wartime, it was probably too much to expect the institutions of higher learning to resist the implementation of the SATC. The direct pressure of the manpower needs of the government, combined with the indirect influence of prospective benefits that the SATC seemed to offer, smoothed the way for acceptance of a program that made the institutions of higher learning an arm of the military establishment. In one important respect the way already had been prepared by college and university presidents themselves, who for several years had been advocating military training in the institutions of higher learning. Their lack of resistance to the SATC was related in part to this previous hospitality to the military on the campus.

Under the terms of the Morrill Act of 1862, military training had been a required subject at land-grant institutions since they had begun to be established in the latter part of the nineteenth century.[11] Early in

9. Memorandum from Committee on Education and Special Training to college presidents and commanding officers, September 28, 1918, in Wisconsin Presidents' Papers.

10. Committee, *A Review*, 75, 77.

11. Although the War Department insisted that the Morrill Act made military training compulsory and the state legislatures supported this interpretation, some state university presidents believed that it was a misreading of the provisions of the act. The dispute will be discussed later in the chapter. There are indications

the twentieth century, as part of the campaign for military preparedness, efforts were made to extend the training to students at all institutions of higher education. In 1912, General Leonard Wood devised a plan to build a national military reserve among college students. Beginning in 1913, five-week summer camps were established for college and university students (and high school graduates over the age of eighteen), where, according to the War Department, in addition to providing military drill army officers were teaching the students "the true military history of the country, not the illusive school-book version of our few victories, but the real accounts . . . of our many defeats . . . military policy past and present, [and the] necessity of some sound, definite military policy." The Plattsburg System, whose essential purpose for the War Department was to promote preparedness, gained the support of leading college and university presidents.[12] The seven-man Advisory Committee of University Presidents, including John G. Hibben (Princeton), A. Lawrence Lowell (Harvard), Arthur T. Hadley (Yale), George H. Denny (Alabama), Harry B. Hutchins (Michigan), Henry S. Drinker (Lehigh), and Edward W. Nichols (Virginia Military Institute), popularized the program among students and fellow administrators.[13]

After the outbreak of the war, as agitation for preparedness increased, so too did discussion of universal military training. The attitude of the military authorities was conveyed by General Wood, who told delegates of the National Education Association that universal military training was essential because war, though unpleasant, was a reality, because we had to "nationalize" our "individualistic" people, because we had to be qualified to win against a first-rate power, which we had never done (although, he reproved his audience of educators, our history books failed

---

that military training was not taken very seriously at the land-grant institutions, particularly by the academic faculty. Wyatt Rushton, "Training College Students," *American Review of Reviews*, LIII (February, 1916), 202.

12. Arthur Wallace Dunn, "Military Camps for College Students," *American Review of Reviews*, XLIX (March, 1914), 322. Although the enterprise originally was called Army Camps for College Students, it became known popularly as the Plattsburg System after the eastern regional camp in Plattsburg, N.Y.

13. For example, in 1915 the committee sent a letter to univeristy and college presidents all over the country urging them to encourage their students to attend the summer training camps. See New York *Times*, November 18, 1915, p. 3.

to point out this fact), because of the obligation of citizenship, and because of the need to defend our overseas possessions.[14]

Civilian advocates of military training, including publicists, college presidents, and professors, tended to stress its nonmilitary benefits. Although they mentioned such military considerations as the inadequacy of the volunteer system and the necessity for a peaceful country to be prepared to defend itself against aggression, by and large they portrayed military training as being of great educational value, as conferring physical and moral well-being, and as promoting order, punctuality, and cooperation.[15] A favorite argument of university proponents of military training was that it would provide college students with sorely needed discipline. As President Benjamin Ide Wheeler of the University of California expressed it, "the atmosphere of the drill ground is a fine corrective upon the usual laissez-faire of the college yard."[16] Their most imposing argument was that universal military service, including training, would promote democracy, for it would create a citizens' rather than a professional (class) army, where the rich man's son and the poor man's son, standing shoulder to shoulder in khaki, would be indistinguishable.[17]

In the beginning of 1915, prompted by President Hibben's public ad-

14. Leonard Wood, "Universal Military Training," *National Education Association Addresses and Proceedings*, LIV (1916), 159–65.

15. See George Creel, "Military Training for Our Youth," *Century*, XCII (May, 1916), 20–26; Jacob Gould Schurman, "Every College Should Introduce Military Training," *Everybody's Magazine*, XXXII (February, 1915), 179–83; and Albert Bushnell Hart, "Please, Mr. President," New York *Times*, February 11, 1917, Sec. 5, p. 2.

16. New York *Times*, January 31, 1915, Sec. 4, p. 5. The same point was made more picturesquely in a popular anecdote, which described the Harvard and West Point football teams facing each other at the start of a game. " 'Are you ready, West Point?' called the referee. 'Yes, sir,' came the answer. 'Are you ready, Harvard?' And the Harvard captain answered, 'Yep.' " "Harvard and Preparedness," *Outlook*, CXII (January 12, 1916), 66–67.

17. Franklin H. Giddings, "The Democracy of Universal Military Service," *Annals of the American Academy of Political and Social Science*, LXVI (July, 1916), 73–80, and Munroe Smith, "Universal Military Service and Democracy," New York *Times*, July 23, 1916, Sec. 5, p. 16. This argument was not advanced by the spokesmen for the sons of the poor—labor leaders, socialists, social workers—who, in fact, opposed universal military training and service largely on the grounds that increased numbers of trained men would provide a weapon *against* democratic aspirations; they could be used to quell labor disorders and in other ways to keep the people in line.

vocacy of military training at the colleges, the New York *Times* polled
the heads of what it considered to be the most important educational institutions in the country and concluded that two-thirds of them were in
favor of universities providing military training. Included, among others,
were the presidents of Chicago, Cornell, Johns Hopkins, MIT, Notre
Dame, Purdue, and the leading state universities. Among them was
President Edmund James of the University of Illinois, who felt so
strongly on the subject that he appeared before the House Committee on
Military Affairs with a proposal for increasing the usefulness of the
land-grant institutions in providing trained military personnel.[18]

Considering the sentiment among college and university presidents in
favor of military training in the schools, it is not surprising that beginning in 1915 the heads of several institutions worked closely with
General Wood to establish extracurricular student military units and
introduce accredited military courses into the curriculum. During the
academic year 1915–1916 Princeton offered a course in military history
and policy, which included rifle practice and tactical excursions into the
surrounding countryside; Harvard offered a military science course and
established a regiment for the preparation of students as reserve officers,
which by the spring of 1916 numbered close to one thousand men; and
Yale formed four student artillery batteries; which were mustered into
the Connecticut 10th Field Artillery of the National Guard.[19]

The situation at Yale reveals the lengths to which a determined president would go, in the face of reluctance and even opposition within his
university, to secure military training for the students and to introduce
military subjects into the curriculum. At the Plattsburg Camp in the
summer of 1915 President Hadley of Yale, entirely on his own responsibility, began what George W. Pierson describes as "quiet negotiations"
with General Wood for the establishment of an artillery battalion. It was

18. New York *Times,* January 24, 1915, Sec. 4, p. 5, January 31, 1915, Sec. 4,
p. 5; "President James and the Land Grant College," *Outlook,* CXII (March 8,
1916), 536–39.
19. "The Colleges and the War," *Outlook,* CXX (September 11, 1918), 48–50;
John G. Hibben, "The Colleges and National Defense," *Independent,* LXXXII
(June 28, 1915), 532–33; "Harvard and Preparedness," 66–67; and George W.
Pierson, *Yale College: An Educational History* (New Haven, 1952), I, Chap. 23.

organized on a voluntary, extracurricular basis during the following academic year. In the fall of 1915 Hadley tried, with the support of powerful alumni, to persuade the Academic Board to approve the introduction of military subjects into the curriculum, but the most he could secure was approval for a single course in American military history or policy, to be taught by the army officer training Yale's artillery battalion.[20]

In June, 1916, prompted partly by the Mexican crisis, Congress authorized establishment of the Reserve Officers' Training Corps (ROTC) at educational institutions to provide a reservoir of officers. The plan was to provide accredited military training for undergraduates, who would continue their regular studies in a prescribed four-year course under the direction of an army officer who would be appointed professor of military science and tactics. Hadley was most eager for Yale to have a regular ROTC unit, which would replace the extracurricular militia batteries, and in his correspondence frequently stated that he wanted Yale to take the lead among universities in cooperating with the War Department in its officer-training program. The problem, as he bluntly put it, was that, although at state universities the "contributions from the public treasury . . . are so large that the Government can exercise direct control over the course of study and requirements for a degree," at Yale curricular changes had to be approved by the faculty. This did not prove to be an easy matter. According to Hadley, the Yale faculty and corporation were divided on the subject of accredited military instruction, with about 40 percent in each body supporting it, 20 to 25 percent strongly opposed on "pacifist" grounds, and the remainder somewhat uncertain.[21] The matter was referred by the corporation to the Faculty

20. Pierson, *Yale College,* I, Chap. 23. Hadley had been encouraging Wood's efforts to introduce credit courses on military science into college curricula since January, 1915, and even advised the general how to fit such work into the intricacies of the elective system. See Arthur T. Hadley to Leonard Wood, January 11, 1915, in Yale Presidents' Papers.

21. Arthur T. Hadley to Brigadier General Albert L. Mills, September 5, 1916, and Hadley to Leonard Wood, August 31, 1916, both in Yale Presidents' Papers. Hadley thought that he had a good chance of securing a majority in favor of the ROTC. However, when the War Department postponed the mustering out of the Yale Battalion, which had spent the summer at a training camp in Pennsylvania, he feared the whole maneuver would fall through. He wrote urgent ap-

Committee on the Course of Study, which acquiesced reluctantly. After long deliberation, it issued a unanimous report approving the granting of seven hours' credit toward the bachelor's degree for military study but providing all sorts of conditions to guarantee the seriousness of the work.[22]

Pierson recounts that the vote on the committee's report in the general faculty meeting was thirty-eight to zero, with twenty-four present and not voting, and that the faculty made a statement that it was only implementing a policy recommended by others. Indications are that faculty opposition was more serious than Pierson's account suggests. William E. Dodd wrote Oswald Garrison Villard that a Yale professor told him in confidence that a majority of the faculty was opposed to granting the credit and capitulated only after Hadley threatened to resign if the measure weren't approved. Villard tried to verify the story when he was in New Haven but reported that the "professors are under seal of secrecy and cannot talk." He was, however, able to get an "intimation" from some of them that Dodd's story was accurate and that the "initiative was taken not by the faculty but by the president and presidential committee of the corporation."[23] At the beginning of the second

peals to Generals Wood and Mills, explaining that the postponement would antagonize the faculty and corporation. The battalion was mustered out in September, and the issue of the ROTC came before the corporation in the same month and before the faculty in December.

22. Unanimous report of the Committee on the Course of Study to the general faculty on the subject of academic credit for the proposed course in military science, December 14, 1916, in Faculty Records, Reports, Historical Manuscripts Collection, Yale University Library. One of the conditions was that credit be given only for work that required a "genuine intellectual effort and may conceivably result in what is not improperly called learning." It did not seem to the committee that equitation, pistol practice, and other such practical work was of this character.

23. William E. Dodd to Oswald Garrison Villard, January 25, 1917, and Villard to Dodd, February 1, 1917, both in Oswald Garrison Villard Papers, Houghton Library, Harvard University. Dodd was especially sensitive to the issue of military training in the colleges. In addition to publicly protesting against the nationwide preparedness campaign, he actively but unsuccessfully, opposed Wood's and President Judson's attempts to introduce military training into the Chicago curriculum. See William E. Dodd, "The United States of Tomorrow," *Nation*, CIV (January 18, 1917), 74–75, entries for October 10, 1916, and January 7, 1917, in Mabry (ed.), "Professor William E. Dodd's Diary," and Dodd to Claude Kitchin, June 2, 1916, in Dodd Papers. Dodd frequently expressed the

semester, in February, 1917, the Yale chapter of the ROTC got under way. Yale was one of 115 institutions of higher learning participating in the War Department's officer-training program.

It is not surprising that the SATC, which superseded the ROTC, received support from presidents of ROTC institutions, as well as from many other presidents who for years had favored military training at colleges and universities. The importance of a long-standing presidential commitment to campus military training in facilitating acceptance of the SATC must not be underestimated. Yet, additional considerations inclined college and university presidents to accept the plan, which seemed to offer solutions to problems on the campus that appeared to have reached crisis proportions. A year and a half of wartime conditions had taken a terrible toll on the institutions of higher learning. They were experiencing a heavy loss of students, faculty, and administrative personnel; consequently their functions were seriously impaired, academic standards everywhere were declining, and an apparently insurmountable financial crisis threatened. In each of these areas the SATC promised relief.

Shortly after American intervention, Herman Ames predicted: "The progress of the war is likely to affect seriously the attendance and work in all our colleges and universities." At his own institution, he said, intervention was followed by a reduction of the student body, and the students who remained "might as well have gone, as the current excitement prevents their giving any very serious attention to their work." Comments from faculty in institutions all over the country substantiate Ames's prediction about students. As the war progressed, increasing numbers of faculty members left for war service, and an added burden

---

opinions that university presidents (together with bankers and businessmen) were advocates of preparedness because they were among those reactionaries who feared democracy and that the preparedness campaign was being waged not for defense, but against "too much liberty at home" and "for offense in the world of commerce." See Dodd, "The United States of Tomorrow," 74–75. Although such a charge is impossible to document, it was the president of Dodd's own university who suggestively wrote, in support of universal military training: "The countless implications resulting from such organizations in time of peace as well as in time of war need no comment, as they must be obvious to all." Harry Pratt Judson to Albert Bushnell Hart, December 30, 1916, in Chicago Presidents' Papers.

was placed on the already strained institutions. For example, Ferguson wrote that at Harvard the "war has played havoc with . . . [the History] Department," the field of modern European history alone having lost five men to war work. The faculty depletions had created such a "serious hole" in course offerings, Ferguson reported, that he would have to "borrow somebody to give at least a course or two on Modern European History."[24] In some places whole departments ceased to function because of student and faculty depletions.[25]

President Butler's description of the war's impact on Columbia during the academic year 1917–1918 can serve as a summary for conditions throughout the country. The effects of the war had been so great, he reported, "that the normal development of the University's life and work has been to all intents and purposes suspended. . . . Students by the hundred and prospective students by the thousand entered the military, naval, or civil service of the United States; teachers and administrative officers to the number of nearly four hundred sought and obtained leaves of absence or resigned their posts in order to enter the service of the Government; courses of instruction were modified or abandoned; habitual modes of procedure were altered; the whole University went upon a war footing." Butler was careful to point out that this description was not intended as a complaint. "We would not have had it otherwise," he said. "Columbia University . . . could have no end or purpose of its own to serve that would for a moment compare with its duty to assist the Government in the prosecution of the war to a victorious conclusion." However, his private evaluation of the situation was less cheerful. Early

24. Herman V. Ames to Augustus H. Shearer, May 4, 1917, Ames to D. C. Munro, May 14, 1917, both in Ames Papers; C. D. Allin (Minnesota) to G. N. Jones, April 27, 1917, in Minnesota Department of Political Science Correspondence; Thomas W. Page (Virginia) to Waldo G. Leland, May 15, 1917, Jonas Viles (Missouri) to Frederick Jackson Turner, June 2, 1917, and Raymond Cahall (Kenyon) to James T. Shotwell, August 25, 1917, all in NBHS Papers; W. S. Ferguson to W. C. Abbott, June 5, 1918, in Harvard History Department Correspondence; and Ferguson to Walter Lippmann, May 24, 1918, in Inquiry Archives.
25. For example, the Princeton School of Electrical Engineering had no students, and the University of Illinois School of Railway Engineering and Administration suspended operations because most of its faculty was away in war service. See "Notes," *Science*, n.s., XLVII (October 26, 1917), 498, and *University of Illinois Annual Register, 1917–1918*, 50.

in June he wrote John Erskine, "Columbia has been shot all to pieces by the withdrawal of so many men . . . from its teaching and administrative staff. . . . If we do not keep intact the University's organization, we shall lose our power to serve the nation. . . . Our finances are hopelessly disorganized by the war and the deficiency in the cost of operation for the year ending June 30 will be no less than $250,000."[26]

A serious side effect of the reduction in student ranks was the financial toll from the loss of tuition. At Yale, for example, where 40 percent of the students were away at war, the loss of tuition fees and dormitory rents for the academic year 1917–1918 was expected to be close to $300,000, and at Columbia the income from students' fees was almost $200,000 less than the preceding year. In addition, the universities were affected severely by wartime inflation. With the rise in cost of supplies and labor it was impossible to recoup tuition losses by economies elsewhere in the budget. Women's schools did not suffer from the depletion of their student bodies to the extent that those with male students did, and state universities did not get their operating funds from tuition fees, but both these kinds of institutions shared in feeling the effects of the general financial uncertainty and of rising costs.[27] To exacerbate the situation, wartime taxation took a heavy toll on receipts from gifts. University men throughout the country were so alarmed that they attempted to exert pressure on Congress to amend the tax laws, permitting the deduction of educational and charitable donations from taxable income and exempting such donations from the inheritance tax. Hadley admonished Senator George P. McLean to remind his colleagues that "the power to tax is the power to destroy." The ad hoc Committee on War Charity and Social Work, whose chairman was Samuel McCune Lindsay of Columbia and whose members included Johns Hopkins President Frank J. Goodnow and Harvard's President Lowell, urged university presidents to organize the support of prominent alumni for amendments to

26. "Annual Report of the President," *Columbia University Annual Reports, 1918*, 1–2, and Nicholas Murray Butler to John Erskine, June 7, 1918, in John Erskine Papers, Special Collections, Columbia University Library.

27. Arthur T. Hadley to the commissioner of education, March 14, 1918, in Yale Presidents' Papers; "Annual Report of the President [of Columbia]," 2–3; "Report of the [Barnard College] Dean for the Academic Year Ending June 30, 1918," *Columbia University Annual Reports, 1918,* 150.

the wartime tax measures.[28] The combined effect of these financial problems was serious. One college president, writing shortly after the war
ended, recalled that in the summer of 1918 higher educational institutions were in such a critical financial state that a "discontinuance of
activities seemed to many to be not far remote."[29]

The SATC promised relief from this critical situation. Most important, it offered a solution to the problem of student losses. That the new
manpower bill would administer the coup de grâce to already struggling
institutions was no secret, and Chicago's James Angell expressed the
sentiment of many university men when he said of the SATC: "The
only alternative to this general solution . . . [would be] to shut up the
colleges as far as concerns physically fit men subject to the draft."[30] Under the program not only would regularly enrolled students remain in
school, but those who never would have gone to college would be encouraged to participate. The American Council on Education undertook
a campaign to promote the SATC in the late summer of 1918; its slogan
was "It's Patriotic to Go to College." The campaign, conducted by college presidents and prominent educators in each state, popularized the
SATC on a local level through high schools, churches, and newspapers.
Even the most selective institutions made room for special SATC students. Lowell announced: "At the opening of the term on September
23, [Harvard University] will receive not only the regular candidates
for a degree who have passed the entrance examinations for the college,
but also as student members of the SATC applicants over eighteen years
of age who have graduated from any good high school or had an education equivalent thereto."[31]

The promotion campaign succeeded, and the SATC more than ful-

28. Arthur T. Hadley to George P. McLean, May 25, 1918, in Yale Presidents' Papers; Samuel McCune Lindsay to the president, June 29, 1917, in Chicago Presidents' Papers; Lindsay to the president, July 19, 1917, in Wisconsin
Presidents' Papers.
29. Kolbe, *Colleges in War Time,* 177.
30. James Angell to J. W. Linn, August 12, 1918, in Chicago Presidents' Papers.
31. See documents from the American Council on Education, Commission on
Students' War Service, in Minnesota Presidents' Papers; "Harvard University Students' Army Training Corps," September 9, 1918, in Lowell Papers.

filled expectations in keeping college doors open. At the larger institutions Section A units numbered in the thousands. At Minnesota there were 3,120 student-soldiers registered; at Wisconsin, 2,250; and, at Columbia, considerably more than 2,000.[32] At small and obscure colleges the program brought new life. For example, it was reported that, as a result of the establishment of an SATC unit, Transylvania College in Lexington, Kentucky, began the academic year with the "largest attendance in its history." Conversely, little colleges that did not qualify for a unit found themselves losing students to those that did. The president of the University of Omaha complained to the SATC director of District 12 that because students at other institutions in the vicinity "have the advantage over our students of receiving their tuition and thirty dollars a month . . . a considerable number of our students have asked for their credits" to transfer elsewhere.[33]

The SATC also promised to cut down faculty depletions. The government provided that faculty members of draft age who were needed for the program were to be given deferred classification. Those who might have volunteered for nonmilitary war work would be induced to stay, because university teaching itself had become a form of war service. At the University of Wisconsin the choice was not left to the faculty, which was notified that "every member must regard himself as in war service and assigned to duty here. No one can expect to be released by the university for service elsewhere unless he can show that he is not needed here."[34]

Finally, the SATC offered immediate financial relief for every institution that established a unit. The schools were guaranteed tuition, room,

32. Memorandum for report on Students' Army Training Corps, Collegiate Section, in Minnesota Presidents' Papers; Report on the Collegiate Section of the SATC at the University of Wisconsin, submitted by S. H. Goodnight, educational director of Section A, in Wisconsin Presidents' Papers; "Report of the Registrar for the Academic Year Ending June 30, 1919," *Columbia University Annual Reports, 1919* (New York, 1919), 308.

33. Joseph Myers to Guy Stanton Ford, September 25, 1918, in CPI Papers; D. E. Jenkins to E. E. Nicholson, September 14, 1918, in Dean of Students Papers, University of Minnesota Archives, hereinafter cited as Minnesota Dean of Students Papers.

34. Edward A. Birge to members of the faculty, September 3, 1918, in Wisconsin Presidents' Papers.

and board for every student-soldier enrolled in the program and reimbursement for administrative expenses and the use of university buildings and equipment.[35] Any additional expenses incurred, such as for
construction of special facilities, were to be paid for by the government.[36]

In addition to holding forth the promise of rescuing the schools from
their wartime difficulties, the SATC had a positive appeal. It offered an
unmatched opportunity for the institutions of higher learning to demonstrate their usefulness and, by implication, to lay the ghost of ivory-tow-
erism that haunted them. In general, the war experience was believed to
be narrowing the gap between the colleges and the public; in the opinion of one popular journal the war was "raising the window-shades that
hide the world from the class-room" and forcing the colleges to deal
with the problems and issues of "real life."[37] But the SATC in particular
could do more, since the program was an official acknowledgment by
the government that the nation's colleges and universities were vital to
the war effort. After its inauguration, university men and the popular
press commonly referred with pride to the institutions of higher learning
as "essential industries" of wartime. Princeton's President Hibben wrote
that at his university it was considered a "rare privilege" to be able to
place all the institution's resources and equipment at the disposal of the
War Department. "It has always been the tradition of Princeton that it
is our highest privilege to train men for the service of the state, for the
promotion of civilization in times of peace and for the preservation and
protection of our nation in times of war," he explained. In Hibben's

35. Substantial sums of money could be involved. The settlement made with
Wisconsin, for example, amounted to close to $500,000 for Sections A and B for
three months. H. J. Thorkelson, SATC settlement, June 20, 1919, in Wisconsin
Presidents' Papers.

36. This provision could be taken advantage of. The SATC inspector for District 8 reported that when he arrived at Morningside College in Sioux City, Iowa,
he found that "one *elegant* 150-men barracks building had already been completed without authority from the goverment and of a quality which indicates that
at least one-third of the money put into it was unnecessary." SATC district inspector, District 8, to Committee on Education and Special Training, September
25, 1918, in Minnesota Dean of Students Papers.

37. "A Legacy of the War to Our Colleges," *Outlook*, CXX (September 11,
1918), 46.

eyes, when the students took the oath of allegiance to the SATC, "the ceremony became sacramental."[38]

Appreciation for government recognition of the colleges' usefulness to the nation led educators to hail the SATC for the benefits it would confer on the institutions of higher learning—a complete misrepresentation of the program's purpose. "Now is the great day for American education!" trumpeted the director of the American Council on Education Students' War Service Campaign, and Charles F. Thwing characterized the program as the "richest gift which the Government had ever made to the higher education." Students made the same mistake. The student newspaper at Wisconsin, for example, proclaimed the SATC the "greatest opportunity ever offered to young men in the world's history.... For once in the history of our country ... a young man does not have to depend upon fortunate circumstances and environment to give him a higher education."[39] Although this misplaced emphasis regarding the purpose of the SATC ultimately led to disappointment and resentment, it made the program very attractive at the start and undoubtedly was a factor in its widespread acceptance. By the time the 1918 fall semester began, SATC contracts had been signed by administrators of 516 higher educational institutions, from the most prominent to the most obscure, all over the country.[40]

Although faculty members were understood to be less enthusiastic about the SATC than administrators,[41] professors did not protest the program; they were willing to cooperate and to give it a fair trial. That the SATC could rescue the colleges and universities from an exigent sit-

38. John G. Hibben and Jacob G. Schurman, "The University Cantonment, Princeton and Cornell," *Bookman*, XLVIII (November, 1918), 288–89.

39. Robert L. Kelly to the state directors and college presidents, August 29, 1918, in Philander P. Claxton Papers, National Archives; Charles F. Thwing, "The Colleges as War Camps," *Independent*, XCVI (October 5, 1918), 12; *Cardinal*, October 1, 1918.

40. It seems that only one institution, the Quaker Haverford College, was moved for reasons of principle to refuse to participate in the educational-military experiment. See "The Revolution in the Colleges," *Nation*, CVII (September 28, 1918), 338, and Rufus M. Jones, *Haverford College: A History and an Interpretation* (New York, 1933), 180.

41. See, for example, Thwing, "The Colleges as War Camps," and John Lee, "Drafted Universities," *Nation*, CVII (December 7, 1918), 695–97.

uation was certainly of direct and immediate concern to professors. Furthermore, for those who had found no opportunity for war service, the SATC promised to satisfy deeply felt needs to contribute to the national cause. Edward S. Corwin of Princeton wrote, "We are all now practically under the orders of the War Dep't., & have had to install an entirely new curriculum for the SATC. . . . Altogether Princeton is to be a very military place this winter. . . . But I'm mighty glad of it. The War Dept's need has saved our bacon as an institution, and for us individually our self-respect, by giving us some useful work to do while drawing our salaries." Cephas Allin of Minnesota expressed similar sentiments: "The truth is that we will be a military institution this coming year. . . . There is some small satisfaction, however, in feeling that possibly we may be doing a little something to assist in prosecuting the war. I have certainly felt restless through the last year over being a useless university man. The man in the trenches, the miner and the farmer seem to be so much more valuable members of society than we could possibly be."[42] The University of Wisconsin faculty discovered in the prospective militarization of their institution an opportunity to reap educational advantages. Acknowledging that the SATC would mean a complete reorganization of teaching methods exclusively for military ends, they declared that the experience would be an "admirable preparation" for the "task of readjustment" to the inevitably changed conditions of the postwar world. The experience would give them, they said, "new and broader views of our work and its possibilities" and would teach them something of "new methods and ideals, both in their strength and their limitation."[43]

The SATC changed the character of the institutions of higher learning and dramatically changed the function and responsibilities of the faculty. The sheer physical burden of initiating and implementing such a vast program in so short a time was enormous. Acting President Edward

42. Edward S. Corwin to Albert Beveridge, September, 22, 1918, in Beveridge Papers, and Cephas D. Allin to R. M. Alden, September 13, 1918, in Minnesota Department of Political Science Correspondence.
43. Minutes of the regular university faculty meeting, October 7, 1918, in Wisconsin Faculty Documents.

A. Birge's remark to the Wisconsin faculty that "no member . . . need fear that he will not be kept busy next year" was a gross understatement. At Wisconsin "all customary schedules of vacations, hours of teaching per week, subjects taught, etc." were abandoned as soon as plans for the SATC were announced. Faculty members were asked to indicate at least three subjects outside of their own fields in which they could give elementary instruction.[44] The number of courses offered was reduced, and the teaching hours were increased by at least one-third. At Minnesota, every social scientist in the vicinity of the campus in the late summer found his vacation ended; at Chicago, the faculty was reported to be heavily burdened by the tasks of organizing and implementing the new war courses; Clark was described as being in a state of "great confusion" because of the new courses, particularly the one on the issues of the war.[45] Throughout the country, faculty members had to revamp courses overnight, to hastily prepare themselves to teach unfamiliar subjects, and to arrange to provide special educational materials for what in some institutions amounted to thousands of students.[46] To add to the general chaos and confusion, when the semester began the influenza epidemic was at its height, delaying the opening of some schools for a week or more, putting others under quarantine, and daily depleting the student ranks at still others.

The faculties recognized that overwork and confusion were inevitable consequences of the emergency and generally accepted them with cheerful goodwill. But they found it difficult to adjust to the transformation of the universities into military camps. There is testimony from many institutions that they were being utilized almost entirely for the military

44. Edward A. Birge to members of the faculty, September 3, 1918, and war teaching registration, both in Wisconsin Presidents' Papers. It is not clear how many of these subjects professors then were assigned to teach.

45. Edward A. Birge to M. L. Burton, September 11, 1918, in Minnesota Presidents' Papers; W. S. Davis to Guy Stanton Ford, August 24, 1918, in CPI Papers; A. C. McLaughlin to G. B. Adams, October 3, 1918, in Adams Papers; and G. W. Blakeslee to A. A. Young, September 17, 1918, in Inquiry Archives.

46. Naturally, college administrators were at least as burdened as their faculties by the demands of the new program. For example, President James (Illinois) wrote, "I have been driven to the limits of my strength lately by the organization of our SATC." Edmund James to Sidney Mezes, October 2, 1918, in Inquiry Archives.

program. At Harvard, where Lowell originally had promised that for
civilian students the "educational offering will be substantially unim-
paired," there was hardly a department that did not adapt its curriculum
to the SATC. English courses were devoted to the writing of military reports, fine arts to military sketching, and modern languages to military
terminology. The significance of whatever regular courses remained can
be imagined from Ferguson's contemptuous dismissal of them as being
taken "mainly by undersized Jews and cripples." At Minnesota the registration for regular courses consisted almost entirely of young women,
but even they were remarkably few, it was explained, because "many
parents are afraid to send their daughters to the University at present
and . . . many young women have gone into some form of public service."[47]

The faculties soon began to chafe under inconveniences caused by apparently absurd military routine. Specifically, they became increasingly
impatient with the requirements that SATC students be marched to and
from class under military surveillance and stand at attention in class
when reciting and that the faculty, as civilians, had to show passes to
gain entrance to university buildings, which were under military guard.
Those among them who lived on the campus had difficulty returning to
their homes if they went out at night, because curfews were imposed.
One can imagine the reaction of the Yale faculty when informed by
Hadley that "a student in uniform carrying out the orders of his commanding officer has the right to expect the same prompt obedience from
members of the Faculty which he would exact from civilians not connected with the University."[48]

A more fundamental incompatibility between the SATC and academic life affected college presidents as well as faculties. SATC regulations
gave the military autonomy in its sphere, and the divided authority between academic and military men led to constant conflicts between

47. W. S. Ferguson to R. A. Newhall, September 28, 1915, in Harvard History
Department Correspondence; Cephas D. Allin to G. N. Jones, October 23, 1918,
in Minnesota Department of Political Science Correspondence.
48. See the sarcastic letter by "a mere professor" in the New York *Evening
Post,* October 23, 1918, p. 8; Arthur T. Hadley to the members of the Yale faculties, October 15, 1918, in Yale Presidents' Papers.

them. From the start, at one SATC institution after another, there were repeated complaints about serious military interference with academic work. The complaints essentially were twofold: that military duties (such as kitchen police, sentry duty, special drill, etc.) were assigned during class hours, with the result that students either were late or absent from regularly scheduled classes; and that military personnel were undermining the importance of academic work among the student-soldiers, with the result that academic performance was abysmally below normal standards.

The experience at Minnesota, which is amply recorded, clearly illustrates the academic-military conflict. During the very first week of the quarter President Burton wrote a lengthy memorandum to the commanding officer, Major R. R. Adams, outlining complaints from every department of the university about military interference with academic work. These included: getting students to class half an hour or more late; assigning students to military duty during class hours and telling them this was perfectly all right because they were at a military school; trying to persuade professional students to transfer to one of the war courses; and permitting roughhouse behavior during supervised study periods. Burton urged Adams to bring immediately to the attention of his officers the "absolute necessity of having the men delivered on time at their various classes, and also to request them to understand beyond all shadow of doubt that purely academic matters belong to the educational authorities and not to them, and that it is not part of their function or duty to advise students in regard to their academic work." But the complaints continued, and by the beginning of November the situation had so deteriorated that the faculty of the schools of science, literature, and the arts asked the dean for permission to make a formal complaint about the unsatisfactory work of the SATC students. The faculty insisted that the attitude of the officers was responsible for the poor performance of the students and that the "whole influence of the SATC has been to break down standards of work, and to destroy whatever seriousness of purpose the students have in coming to college."[49]

49. M. L. Burton to R. R. Adams, October 15, 1918, and Dean J. B. Johnston to Burton, November 7, 1918, both in Minnesota Presidents' Papers.

The "intense wave of indignation and dissatisfaction" described at Minnesota was apparently characteristic of faculty sentiment throughout the country, for on November 5 Brigadier General Robert I. Rees, chairman of the Committee on Education and Special Training, issued a memorandum directing commanding officers at all SATC institutions to immediately take steps to improve the academic work of the student-soldiers. Specifically, the officers were to reduce to the barest minimum any military duties that interfered with academic work and to cultivate a respect for academic studies among the men. Officers were ordered to "avoid remarks tending to create in their men the impression that academic work is comparatively unimportant, and [to avoid] all conduct conspicuously at variance with the established usages of the academic community." Rees announced a rating system for the selection of men for officers' training camps in which academic performance was rated highest among several criteria on a scale of one hundred. Military ability, for instance, was to receive twenty points as compared with thirty-five for academic record.[50]

When the memorandum was issued, President Burton was convinced that it would make possible the introduction of "immediate and radical changes . . . reducing the amount of interference with scholastic work." But Major Adams' response to being sent a list of conditions to be corrected demonstrated that the academic and military authorities continued to have conflicting conceptions of the program and that it would be impossible to resolve the conflict under the existing system of divided authority. The reason the deans and the faculty were so critical, Adams insisted, was that they were "chiefly interested in the advance to be made in their studies by their students. Further than that . . . they are not particularly concerned." Adams reminded Burton that for himself, "as commanding officer, there is one duty that supersedes all others, namely the health and welfare of my men." Then he speculated on the possible consequences of eliminating one form of interference with academic work, the posting of student guards at university buildings. "If

50. M. L. Burton to R. R. Adams, November 8, 1918, and Robert I. Rees to commanding officers, district inspecting officers, district educational directors, and heads of SATC institutions, November 5, 1918, both *ibid.*

the buildings are left unguarded . . . [and are] bombed with a resultant loss of life, I would unquestionably be brought before a Court Martial and my crime would be nothing less than murder." To make sure that his point would not be missed he added the observation: "Were men in my command here to lose their lives through gross negligence on my part and it came out in the examination that I was urged to such gross negligence by the deans and faculty of this University it would be a serious blot upon the fair record of the institution which you honor."[51] The problem remained unsolved, and the academic-military conflict at Minnesota and elsewhere continued until the SATC came to an end.

Faculty men everywhere were dissatisfied with the SATC because of the preeminence given to the military aspects of the program. The War Department had made it clear from the start that its objectives were exclusively military and that the institutions of higher learning were being asked to devote their "whole energy and educational . . . power to the phases and lines of training desired by the Government."[52] But academic men never faced the full implication of the kind of service they were asked to perform; instead, they idealized the program and looked for compensatory benefits from it. When these failed to materialize, even those who had initially welcomed the SATC as an opportunity to serve the cause finally were disenchanted with it. Corwin complained to Albert Beveridge: "Princeton . . . is not Princeton just now—only a cog of the military machine, & we professors are cogs within cogs. Of course, it's nice to feel useful—but I'll be glad when the Kaiser is definitely canned, just the same." After the program came to an end Allin declared, "The SATC was an educational affliction."[53]

The War Issues Course was the one redeeming feature of the SATC in the eyes of the faculty; it both gave professors an outlet for their pa-

51. See "Bulletin to the Deans," November 8, 1918, and R. R. Adams to M. L. Burton, November 11, 1918, both *ibid.* The absurdity of anticipating invasion on the eleventh of November aside, Adams failed to indicate just how, in the event of aerial bombardment, the posting of student guards would prevent loss of life.

52. Committee, *A Review,* 77.

53. Edward S. Corwin to Albert Beveridge, October 22, 1918, in Beveridge Papers; C. D. Allin to R. M. Alden, June 26, 1919, in Minnesota Department of Political Science Correspondence.

triotic enthusiasm and proved to have long-range educational implications. By suggesting the reform of the curriculum toward prescribed subjects and areas of study that would reflect the problems of the contemporary world, the course contributed to reassessments of the college curriculum in the postwar decade. In its immediate implications the course placed educators in the position of war propagandists, suggesting some of the same questions raised by scholars' activities for the National Board for Historical Service and the Ford Division of the Committee on Public Information.

When the plans for the SATC were first made public the Committee on Education and Special Training announced that an "integral part" of the program would be a course in the underlying and immediate causes of the war and in the conflicting points of view of the belligerent nations as expressed in their forms of government, their philosophies, and their literature. No syllabus was to be issued; each institution was to plan its own course and choose its own text. The committee wanted the course to reflect the complexity of the war's issues and recommended, therefore, that it be developed jointly by members of the departments of history, government, economics, philosophy, and literature (plus any others that the individual institution might think appropriate).[54] For guidance to the instructors the committee circulated a pamphlet composed by Wallace Notestein and NBHS representatives consisting of more than a hundred representative questions about the war and an annotated bibliography of sources where answers to the questions could be found.[55]

From the start, the Committee on Education and Special Training announced that its policy was to have the course "present facts rather than propaganda," and it advised instructors to use the method "of the teacher rather than of the orator." At the same time, the propagandistic purpose of the course was made clear in the committee's statement that the objective of the War Issues Course was "to enhance the morale of

54. Frank Aydelotte, *Final Report of the War Issues Course of the Students' Army Training Corps* (Washington, D.C., 1919), 42–44. Aydelotte was the national director of the War Issues Course; twelve district directors supervised the course in the educational districts into which the country had been divided.
55. U.S. War Department, Committee on Education and Special Training, *Questions on the Issues of the War* (Washington, D.C., [1918]).

the members of the corps by giving them an understanding of what the war is about and of the supreme importance to civilization of the cause for which we are fighting."[56] The thin line that separated factual means from propagandistic ends was suggested by an instructor who wrote:

> We were advised not to make the course one of propaganda, and yet it could not escape being propaganda. . . . When the war broke out, we [history teachers] were willing as neutral bystanders to present historical facts with great dispassionateness. But German atrocities were facts, and they were facts which opened our eyes as moral beings to the inhuman qualities of German militarism, and to the ideals of the State which bred militarism. We felt more and more willing to tell the ugly truth about Germany, and to put the Germans in the witness-box against themselves. Never before, have we felt more definitely that there are moral forces at work in history making. As a result, it may be that the teacher of history will, for at least a time, be also something of an advocate.[57]

Since the War Issues Course had a broad purpose and no uniform syllabus, it varied considerably from one institution to another. In dealing with the underlying issues of the war, for example, the course at different places began at different points in time. The Minnesota course began in 1870, with the creation of the German Empire (for which it was necessary to touch briefly on events in 1848) and the Franco-Prussian War; at Harvard, it was considered necessary to go back to the Old Regime and the French Revolution; at Columbia, the chronological section of the course focused on developments since 1815.[58] The level at which the course was given also varied considerably at different institutions. At Chicago, McLaughlin, who was in charge of the course, advised the instructors to keep the work below the ordinary college level. When he assigned Samuel Harper the lectures on the history of Russia

56. Aydelotte, *Final Report,* 46.

57. Albert Kerr Heckel, "The War Aims Course in the Colleges," *Historical Outlook*, X (January, 1919), 21–22. Heckel, who was a dean at Lafayette College, repeated the familiar admonition that the "historian cannot sacrifice truth—even to patriotism" and insisted that the course "has substituted a reasonable patriotism for chauvinism."

58. A. B. White to the teaching staff of the War Aims Course, undated, in Minnesota Presidents' Papers; problems and issues of the war, provisional program, October 4, 1918, in Hart Papers; Columbia University, *Outline of the Course on Issues of the War for the Students' Army Training Corps* (New York, 1918).

he reminded him that they "must be very simple, given very slowly, and thoroughly outlined ... [because] a lot of these fellows do not know Peter the Great from Temerlane [*sic*] the Great, or Odessa from Petrograd."[59] The published outline of the course at Columbia suggests that at that institution an attempt was made at a high-level presentation of nineteenth-century and early twentieth-century historical, political, and economic developments in Europe. But these local differences do not conceal the fundamental purpose of the course to present the war as a life-and-death struggle between democracy and autocracy, upon whose outcome the future of civilization depended. This purpose was logical for a course designed to enhance the morale of students being trained for combat.

Fortunately, full summaries of lectures in the University of Michigan War Issues Course have been preserved, making it possible to obtain an accurate picture of the nature of the course at one major institution. The Michigan course consisted of 21 lectures delivered to 2,200 Section A students by Professors Claude H. Van Tyne, Edward R. Turner, and William A. Frayer. Although the course included some fairly straight narrative lectures on such subjects as the formation of the alliance system, the resources of the belligerents, and the military history of the war, the interpretive framework into which the lectures were placed left no doubt that the war was a conflict between the forces of light and the forces of darkness.

The material in the first lecture, in which Van Tyne contrasted autocracy with democracy, included the topics, "How Autocracy Drills Its Subjects," "Dreams of World Power," "Superman," and "A State Without Moral Obligations." In contrast to the allegedly brutal and loathsome German regime, the Allies were portrayed as champions of humanity and of democratic self-government. Turner's lecture on England included the observation that "the English, more than any other people in the world, except the French and ourselves ... have the humani-

59. Andrew C. McLaughlin to Samuel Harper, November 5, 1918, in Department of History Papers, Intrafaculty Correspondence, 1910–1924, University of Chicago Archives.

tarian spirit, a desire for fair play and to do what is right, to help people who are weaker than themselves, not to take advantage of weaker people, in other words to do to others as they would be done by. I think you would find that the Germans carry on war as they have in France and Belgium because the German people do not have the humanitarian spirit of fair play, which the English, American and French do have." The troubles in Ireland, which might have cast some doubt on Turner's interpretation, were not simply ignored, but were attributed to the Irish who were declared not to have "a single grievance today that . . . [they] are not to blame for themselves." French history was given a novel twist when Frayer explained that the Revolution "went wild . . . because that same military autocracy, Prussia, which in 1914 had got its tentacles on a large part of central Europe, goaded the French people into fury by senseless interference." Turning his attention to more contemporary affairs he pointed out that the "subject people of France love their masters" and offered as proof the observation that the "people of Madagascar, Tunis, and Algiers sent their troops voluntarily and these troops fought gladly beside the French."[60]

After the war was over, the theme of absolute good versus absolute evil was retained by simply putting the Bolshevik in place of the Hun as the menace to democracy everywhere. Turner notified the students that the struggle against Bolshevism was more important even than the military struggle that had just been won and urged them to throw their influence "on the side which is most likely to maintain . . . [the better] forces, so that chaos, which has already ruined Russia, may not come to us." Frayer advised them to study "the wild excesses of the revolutionists," remarking that "a surprising number" of them were Jews. The Russian Jew was particularly dangerous, he said, because centuries of suffering at the hands of the government had made him a bitter man. The students were warned that Bolshevik friends and sympathizers "are everywhere—in Germany, in France . . . in Italy, in Holland, in England, in the United States—they are on the campus of the University of Mich-

60. Claude H. Van Tyne, "Causes and Issues of the War," Lecture 1, October 5, 1918, E. R. Turner, "England," Lecture 2, October 15, 1918, and William A. Frayer, "France," Lecture 3, October 17, 1918, all in War Aims Lectures, Michigan Historical Collections, Bentley Historical Library, University of Michigan.

igan." The great task of social reformation facing the world, they were told, must not be given to "men whose sense of honor, right and justice is utterly perverted."[61] The moralistic crudities of the War Issues Course at Michigan may not have been typical of the way in which the issues of the war were presented on every American campus, but the morale-building purpose of the course clearly lent itself to, and even suggested, an approach to historical and other subject matter that would not be likely to find a place in the curriculum in normal times.

Apparently it was precisely this purpose that partly accounts for the widespread popularity of the course among professors who taught it. When the armistice brought the SATC to an unexpectedly early end, only one part of the War Issues Course, the historical and economic causes of the war, had been given. Even after a partial trial only, the consensus among professors was that the course had been enormously successful. The final reports of the twelve district directors to the national director Frank Aydelotte indicate that a large part of the course's appeal was the opportunity offered to the instructors to imbue potential fighting men with their own passion about the war. Frank Bogardus, for example, reported that his objective as district director had been "to have the work done in such fashion that every student would become possessed of an overmastering desire to take some action, to do something for righteousness' sake. . . . The fact that they were about to become identified with a great world movement, one that involved the welfare of the whole human race was kept before the young men and it had an immense compelling power." Bogardus reported that the instructors in his district universally "felt that they were serving the great cause of establishing human liberty."[62] The image of tens of thousands of college students, wearing the uniform of the United States Army and under its discipline, being prepared for combat by professors whose purpose was to ennoble the cause, captures the contradictions on the American campus in the First World War. It perfectly illustrates the manner in which

61. E. R. Turner, "The First Year of the War, Part II," Lecture 14, November 26, 1918, and William A. Frayer, "Russia," Lecture 19, December 19, 1918, both *ibid.*
62. Aydelotte, *Final Report*, 99.

American professors compromised their professional function when they dedicated themselves to serving the state.

Beyond its appeal to professors as an outlet for their patriotism, the War Issues Course was praised for having demonstrated the desirability and feasibility of educational reform to breach the walls separating the disciplines, to introduce some order in the chaos of the elective system, and to make room in the curriculum for the problems of the contemporary world. Every district director's final report contained favorable comments about interdepartmental cooperation fostered by the course, which typically recruited faculty from several departments and disciplines. The course was said to have broken down departmental isolation, ended departmental jealousies and bickerings, and promoted harmony and cooperation that would benefit the departments, the institutions, and the students for years to come. The War Issues Course lent weight to arguments in favor of reintroducing prescribed courses in the undergraduate curriculum. It was praised for being a healthy departure from the elective system, because it promoted the idea that a certain amount of basic education should be required for every student. The course called attention, District Director William E. Hocking wrote, "to the fact that there are, after all is said, some essentials of a college course, some matters which colleges owe training in, as a duty, to those whom they under-take to fit for citizenship. It ought to burn up much of the rubbish of elective courses, and thus at the same time relieve the awful burden of imitation and pretense that weighs upon the smaller institutions."[63] Finally, the course was praised for demonstrating the need for making the undergraduate curriculum more relevant to problems of the contemporary world.

The introduction of the required course in contemporary civilization at Columbia illustrates clearly the relationship between the War Issues Course and curricular reform. While the course was in progress, Dean Woodbridge, who was its director and had been chiefly responsible for

63. *Ibid.*, 89–90. See also the observations about interdisciplinary cooperation by E. B. Greene, who directed the War Issues Course at the University of Illinois, in "Co-operation Between Colleges and Secondary Schools in Promoting Education for Citizenship," *Association of American Colleges Bulletin,* V (April, 1919), 104, 107.

preparing its syllabus, indicated that the course was beginning to be
viewed as a prospective basis for "a liberal education for the youth of
today." In the face of the confusion of ideas and standards left by the
demise of classical education, he said, the War Issues Course seemed to
afford the "opportunity to introduce into our education a liberalizing
force which will give to the generations to come a common background
of ideas and commonly understood standards of judgment." Woodbridge
met with other members of the staff and planned a course in peace issues that was designed, like its parent, to cut across departmental lines
and to introduce the student to the complex social problems of his
times.[64] A required course in contemporary civilization, offered by members of the departments of history, economics, government, and philosophy, was introduced at Columbia in the fall of 1919. Its purpose was to
survey the historical background of Western civilization and to acquaint
the student with current world problems. Its promotion as a bulwark
against radicalism betrayed its origins in the patriotic War Issues
Course. Dean Herbert E. Hawkes, one of the founders of the contemporary civilization course, described it as being intended to silence the
"destructive element in our society" by preparing students to "meet the
arguments of the opponents of decency and sound government" and
thus to make the college student a "citizen who shall be safe for democracy."[65]

The final reports of the district directors demonstrate that the War Issues Course, with all its problems, was generally regarded as the most
successful part of the academic side of the SATC program. An index to
the widespread approval of the course is provided by the comments in
every director's report that many institutions in their districts were continuing the course (studying the peace conference, problems of recon-

64. F. J. E. Woodbridge, "The 'Issues of the War' Course in the S.A.T.C.
Schedule," *Columbia Alumni News,* X (November 15, 1918), 217; Justus Buchler, "Reconstruction in the Liberal Arts," in Dwight C. Miner (ed.), *A History of
Columbia College on Morningside* (New York, 1954), 48–135.
65. Harry J. Carman, "The Columbia Course in Contemporary Civilization"
(Paper delivered before the Association of History Teachers of the Middle States
and Maryland, Bryn Mawr, May 2, 1925); Herbert E. Hawkes, "A College
Course on Peace Issues," *Educational Review,* LVIII (September, 1919), 144,
150.

struction, etc.) at least for the remainder of the year and, in several cases, were making a similar course on contemporary problems a permanent part of the curriculum. Aydelotte's summary of the reports included the announcement that between two hundred and three hundred institutions had decided to continue the course at least until the end of the academic year.[66]

When the armistice raised the question of the future of the SATC, however, the decision proved to be complicated, involving more than personal estimates of the program by the faculty and administrators of the various institutions. Because of its widespread unpopularity, the SATC's early demise should have been generally welcomed, but the prospect raised problems that demanded consideration. The government had contracted with the institutions for the SATC to run until June 30, 1919, and on the strength of these contracts millions of dollars had been borrowed for the construction of new facilities, the remodeling of existing ones, and the purchase of equipment. Special faculty had been hired for the year, and student-soldiers had joined the program expecting that their education would be supported by the government for anywhere from three to nine months. A man identified only as the "president of one of the oldest and largest of the universities" was quoted by the Committee on Education and Special Training as saying of the proposed abrupt termination of the SATC: "The institutions of higher learning throughout the United States are literally threatened with bankruptcy and receiverships."[67] The presidents of those colleges with great endowments and wealthy alumni thought that financial considerations should not be uppermost. Hadley wrote Lowell, for instance, that the primary consideration should be that the system was defective, and "the fact that many of our colleges will suffer financially by a premature termination of the contract ought not to weigh too heavily in our minds."

66. Aydelotte, *Final Report,* 18. J. H. Tufts was the only District Director to subject the idea of "success" to analysis. He pointed out that calculations of success should distinguish between patriotic and academic standards, for, while the course unmistakably was successful in enhancing morale, the same could not be said for the "ordinary academic standard of actual mastery of facts and theory." Aydelotte, *Final Report,* 101.
67. Committee, *A Review,* 47.

For the presidents of less affluent institutions, however, the choice was not so obvious. The president of Grinnell College was very much concerned with "what assistance the government will give the colleges that are certainly to lose heavily as a result of the experiment," and the president of Jamestown College (North Dakota) pointed out that, on the basis of the contract with the government, "our program has been adopted; new teachers have been employed; budgets have been made." He expressed concern about the fate of these arrangments and of the students, "who have now no other way of meeting their educational expenses."[68]

The committee was aware of some of these problems and sent a questionnaire to the heads of all SATC institutions asking them whether they wanted the program, with some modifications, to run until the expiration of the contract period. For some, the decision seems to have been easy to make. Continuation was opposed for such reasons as the unworkability of divided academic-military authority, the low quality of academic work, the demoralizing effect of retaining large numbers of unqualified students, and the deterioration of places of learning into "mere officer nurseries for a great army." Continuation was supported on the grounds that the SATC was a great educational publicity campaign, was an eloquent tribute from men to affairs to the necessity of college training, and instilled discipline and respect for law and authority in the students.[69] For many presidents the decision was difficult, complicated less by the financial issue than by the future role of military training in the colleges and the War Department's feelings about the subject.

Indications are that, because of the War Department's wish to perpetuate military training in the colleges, university presidents did not feel

68. Arthur T. Hadley to A. Lawrence Lowell, November 14, 1918, in Yale Presidents' Papers; J. H. T. Main to E. E. Nicholson, November 30, 1918, and B. H. Kroeze to Nicholson, November 27, 1918, in Minnesota Dean of Students Papers.

69. For an excellent sample of opinions favoring and opposing continuation of the SATC, see the letters from presidents of colleges in Minnesota Dean of Students Papers. The most novel opinion was offered by the president of Simpson College in Indianola, Iowa, who wrote: "Probably nothing else has happened to so thoroughly convince people of the unwisdom of Government ownership of our public utilities. If this should be the case probably the SATC has been worth all it cost." James W. Campbell to E. E. Nicholson, December 12, 1918.

free to express their views on discontinuation of the SATC. Although Hadley stated that his "definite conviction" was in favor of terminating the contracts, he wrote Lowell, "Of course we do what the War Department orders up to the first of July next, and I should naturally not like to have the contents of this letter made public." Similarly, Burton privately expressed the hope, even before the war had ended, that the War Department would demobilize the SATC as soon as peace came. Nevertheless, when Burton was rebuked by a district inspector for allegedly telling the Minnesota board of regents that he opposed peacetime continuation of the SATC, he denied the charge.[70] In his denial, Burton pointed to a report, which he had written for a committee of the National Association of State Universities, that supported continuing the SATC until the end of the contract period. However, this report urged such sweeping revisions of the SATC in all its aspects—recruitment and retention of students, curriculum, relation of military to academic work—that it appears to be less an approval of continuation than an attempt by the state universities to make palatable a program they thought they were expected to participate in. This impression is reinforced by an observation of Wisconsin's Acting President Birge, that to make the situation even tolerable, so the universities would continue to "endure" the SATC, the War Department would have to go much further in subordinating the military part of the program to the academic than even the committee had demanded in its resolutions.[71]

The matter of continuation was decided by the House Appropriations Committee, which ruled that since the SATC funds had been marked to train men for military service in France their use for any other purpose would be irregular. Accordingly, on November 26 the War Department issued an order to demobilize the SATC. Demobilization was begun on December 2 and was completed by December 26. The matter of military training in the colleges did not rest there. As soon as the demobili-

70. Arthur T. Hadley to A. Lawrence Lowell, November 14, 1918, in Yale Presidents' Papers; M. L. Burton to E. E. Nicholson, November 8, 1918, and Burton to J. W. McNeil, November 18, 1918, both in Minnesota Presidents' Papers.

71. See the report of a committee adopted by the National Association of State Universities at their annual meeting on November 11, 12, 1918, and Edward A. Birge to M. L. Burton, November 15, 1918, both in Minnesota Presidents' Papers.

zation order was issued, the Committee on Education and Special Training applied for and was granted authorization to reestablish the ROTC
and began to negotiate with the colleges. Before the war, ROTC units
had been organized on 115 campuses; immediately after demobilization
of the SATC was announced, 100 of these institutions applied for the
reestablishment of the units, and 200 more indicated their intention to
join the program.[72]

Partly, this willingness to participate represented the persistence of
the belief in universal military training among large numbers of college
presidents.[73] It also was the product of an active campaign by the War
Department to reestablish the ROTC, especially in the state universities.
This campaign was not without its critics. Originally there had been dissatisfaction, even among the supporters of universal military training,
with the War Department's conception and management of the ROTC,
and this dissatisfaction was heightened by experiences with the military
authorities under the SATC. President Lowell, certainly no opponent of
military training for college students, asserted, "The difficulty both with
the ROTC and the SATC was that they were dictated by the War Department without consultation with the colleges to be affected thereby."
He pleaded that the War Department "take into counsel those among
the educators of the country who are deeply interested in the improvement of military training . . . who believe that the colleges can take part
in the military training of the youth of the land as they do in its training
in every other direction."[74]

Criticism from the presidents of state universities was more significant, for in those institutions compulsion was involved. There seems to
have been a lack of agreement among state university presidents as to

72. Committee, *A Review*, 33; "Reserve Officers' Training Corps in the Colleges," *School and Society*, VIII (December 18, 1918), 765–66.
73. Such stalwarts as Schurman and Hadley were even more committed to universal military training than they had been before the war. See, for example,
Jacob Gould Schurman, "The Effect of the War on Education," *Association of
American Universities Journal of Proceedings*, XX–XXIII (1918–21), 60–64, and
Arthur T. Hadley to Colonel McCormick, November 25, 1918, in Yale Presidents' Papers.
74. A. Lawrence Lowell, "Discussion of Problems Presented by the Students'
Army Training Corps, and the Future Military Training of Students," *Association
of American Universities Journal of Proceedings*, XX–XXIII (1918–21), 122, 124.

the precise meaning of the terms of the Morrill Act. Burton, for example, was not sure whether the act made military training compulsory; Edmund James understood that it did; whereas Birge categorically stated that the War Department interpretation of the act as making military training compulsory was "entirely incorrect." Birge recalled that one of the things he had disliked most about the ROTC was "what seemed . . . to be an attempt to place the universities quite definitely under the control of the Secretary of War." Consequently, in dealing with the new ROTC, he made every effort to keep the hands of the university as free as possible. In his letter of application for the reestablishment of the program he stated that whereas "the University is quite ready to require a reasonable amount of drill from its students . . . it is not ready to admit that the law of 1862 requires this to be done as a legal obligation." He wrote Burton that, since "the War Department is anxious to . . . make the land grant colleges into military or semi-military institutions," it would be wise to "hold back and confine our military instruction to the minimum possible . . . [in order] to have a chance to see the development of the system elsewhere before we commit ourselves beyond recovery."[75]

The War Department did everything it could to encourage reinstatement of the ROTC. At the 1919 annual meeting of the Association of American Colleges, Colonel F. J. Morrow of the Committee on Education and Special Training assured the assembled presidents that the SATC experience would not be repeated and that the officers, as part of the regular faculty, would be under the jurisdiction of the university administration, which would have power in their selection and removal.[76] The War Department tried to quiet criticism of the SATC on the grounds that negative comments would interfere with plans to reinstate the ROTC. When Ralph Barton Perry requested permission of the War Plans Division to publish an article on the SATC, which included a

75. M. L. Burton to Edward A. Birge, December 14, 1918, Edmund James to Birge, December 16, 1918, Birge to Burton, December 17, 1918, Birge to F. J. Morrow, January 20, 1919, Birge to Burton, February 19, 1918, all in Wisconsin Presidents' Papers.
76. F. J. Morrow, "Military Training in the Colleges," *Association of American Colleges Bulletin*, V (April, 1919), 158–69.

brief reference to faculty dissatisfaction with the program, he was told that his article would serve no purpose but "non-preparedness propaganda" and would only regenerate the "hostile and resentful attitude toward the SATC" among the students and rekindle a "fresh acrimonious discussion" which would "no doubt very unfavorably influence the student class against the ROTC."[77] Army representatives were quite bitter about academic criticism of the SATC, which they said stemmed from a misconception of the program's purposes. Academic critics, one army man complained, "failed to recognize that the SATC was not an organization primarily to keep the colleges going, but it was . . . one of the agencies created by the General Staff to hasten the end of the war. It was in no sense an experiment in education to determine whether military and collegiate training could be combined."[78] Whether to keep in the good graces of the colleges to assure cooperation with the ROTC or for less self-interested reasons, the War Department helped the universities out of their financial distress by settling all contracts within the record time of six months of the SATC's disbandment. The business director of the Committee on Education and Special Training proudly announced, "The SATC contract is the first Government contract to be entirely cleaned up and settled."[79]

Twenty-three years after the war to end war came to a close the United States found itself once more mobilizing for battle. Once more the lack of a coordinated plan to both satisfy the government's immediate needs for trained manpower and preserve the integrity of the institutions of higher learning created a crisis on the American campus. If anything had been learned from the World War I experience, we are

77. E. S. Hartshorn, memorandum for the executive assistant to the chief of staff, May 19, 1919, and W. F. Clark, memorandum for the chairman, Committee on Education and Special Training, May 10, 1919, both in Ralph Barton Perry Papers, Harvard University Archives. Perry did publish the article, but he deleted all reference to academic criticism of the SATC, leaving a favorable narrative account of the experiment. Cf. Ralph Barton Perry, "The Students' Army Training Corps" (MS in Perry Papers), and Perry, "Students' Army Training Corps," *National Service, with the International Military Digest*, VI (August, 1919), 77–85.

78. Edward C. Smith, "The S.A.T.C. from the Military Viewpoint," *Educational Review*, LIX (May, 1920), 402.

79. E. K. Hall to presidents of SATC institutions, June 18, 1919, in Minnesota Presidents' Papers.

told, it either had been forgotten or discarded as inadequate. Concerning the problem of students and the draft, however, "one point was clear— that the experiment of World War I with the Student Army Training Corps . . . did not justify a repetition." Various expediencies were adopted—including the provision for certain student deferments, the inauguration of accelerated programs leading to early graduation, and the establishment of specialized training programs within the colleges and universities—that made unnecessary a repetition of the World War I solution of turning the institutions of higher learning into military training camps. Even with these expediencies, it appears that if the war had lasted beyond 1945 the continued existence of many of the nation's colleges and universities would have been in doubt.[80]

The real conflict between immediate military demands and long-range educational goals in time of war should make us wary of supposing that the SATC might simply have been rejected in the critical year 1918. Given the absence of a plan to reconcile immediate military and long-range educational needs and the crippling effect of wartime conditions on the American campus, to expect that representatives of higher education could resist the implementation of the SATC is probably unrealistic. Even so, the absence of a *principled* objection to the militarization of the campus, particularly by professors, is startling. One looks in vain for agonized appraisals by American professors of the results of turning colleges and universities into military training camps; one is struck instead by the alacrity with which the term "essential industry" was embraced to describe the university's role in wartime and by the implications of the belief that being a scholar in time of war was "useless" and unworthy of self-respect. It is true that professors became disenchanted with the SATC and denounced it as a failure; but one should note that they complained about the malfunctioning of the program, not about its purpose. Criticisms of the SATC were of a practical nature. Using them as criteria it is possible to imagine a "successful" SATC in which problems concerning standards, schedules, personnel, and equipment would have been eliminated and in which the military man and the academic

80. Isaac L. Kandel, *The Impact of The War Upon American Education* (Chapel Hill, 1948), 3–4, 128, 145–56, 159.

man would have worked for a common end, each in his own sphere of authority. Such an SATC, with the military officers training the bodies of the student-soldiers and the professors training their minds and infusing them with a passion for the American cause, could have satisfied the objections professors had to the program; such an SATC would also have been a symbolic summary of the American professors' wartime role—a perfect, harmonious union of Mars and Minerva.

Conclusion

IN THE SAME YEAR that Angoff and Grattan delivered their acerbic assault on American professors, the French philosopher Julien Benda charged the intellectuals of his generation with betraying their calling, and his term *trahison des clercs* has come to stand as an indictment against intellectuals who eschew the search for truth in favor of the service of power. A concluding assessment of the response of American academic intellectuals to their country's participation in the First World War must come to terms with the issue of "betrayal," for it is suggested by much of the material in this book. The concept of betrayal derives from the notion that the defining characteristic of intellect is its disinterested pursuit of truth. To me, disinterestedness has never meant a freedom from values, an ideological neutrality, or an apolitical approach to the world's issues and problems; it has meant, instead, independence from the sources of economic and political power, whose objectives are remote from, if not inimical to, the search for truth.

From this perspective, betrayal is not involved in American professors' partiality to the Allies and support of United States intervention in the war, which were matters of political opinion. To be sure, with some exceptions, American professors demonstrated surprising naïveté about

historical, political, and diplomatic issues, especially when they sub-
scribed to a simplistic and moralistic interpretation of the war's origin
and meaning as a conflict between democracy and autocracy and, consequently, between good and evil. It was reasonable to have hoped, even
if not to have expected, that of all individuals they would have been
able to best see events in all the complexity of historical perspective and
thus would have been skeptical of simplistic and moralistic interpretations of complicated issues. For this reason, one may easily share the
disappointment behind Randolph Bourne's observation that it was remarkable how little resistance American intellectuals offered to the institution of war and may sympathize with his bitterness at the willingness
of American intellectuals "to open the sluices and flood us with the sew-
age of the war spirit."[1] By the same token, it is surprising how readily
American professors evaded the issue of the real savagery and horror of
the First World War—the still-stunning casualties of the stalemated,
technological conflict—and succumbed to the easy path of outrage and
indignation against Germany for incidental *Schrecklichkeit*. American
professors lacked the skepticism that might have enabled them to recognize that the novelty of the First World War lay in the use by "civilized"
nations of tactics against each other that they all, particularly the English and even the dreadfully wronged Belgians, had been using against
"backward" peoples for decades. Because academic men saw the Germans as uniquely atrocious and menacing to "civilization," they were
able to reach the startling conclusion that to stop the slaughter and seek
a negotiated peace would be immoral.

It was suggested earlier that for professors to really have believed the
unbelievable indicated a subtle and profound corruption of their mental
processes. Even so, I believe that, if we are to level the charge of betrayal against them, it must be less for their response to the war and its
issues, which was ultimately a matter of political judgment, than for
their conception of the demands the war made on them as men of
knowledge. Even war supporters could conceivably have decided on the
incumbency of maintaining a posture of critical independence from official policies and positions; this stance could have given their support of

1. Bourne, "The War and the Intellectuals," 134.

the war the unique social value of providing a sorely lacking principled defense of the very ideals and freedoms in whose name the war was being fought. Instead, they concluded without hesitation that their social function should be to offer themselves without reservation to the state's pursuit of military victory. When they assumed this role as servants of the cause, they were bound to compromise their critical judgment and accommodate increasingly to the "reality" to which they had made themselves hostage. Nothing better illustrates the extent that academic intellectuals became apologists for things as they were than Dewey's treatment of the subject of rising popular hysteria in the United States. Instead of taking a principled position against intolerance and repression, which might have been expected from a man of his views, Dewey took it upon himself to explain that the overwrought state of public opinion was largely a product of American inexperience with war, justifying the spectacle as "not altogether unlovely." He commented, "The amusement aroused by the display is tinctured with affection as for all the riotous gambolings of youth."[2]

Once American professors decided upon the role of uncritical commitment to the cause and pledged themselves to do anything necessary to secure its success, they inevitably became implicated in a host of concessions and compromises of their professional commitments. It certainly is intriguing to speculate about why and how exemplary scholars like Turner, Beard, Ford, Jameson, McLaughlin, and Greene, to name but a few, could participate in the NBHS and the CPI and, at the same time, make protestations of scholarly objectivity about what they were doing. Were they hypocrites and opportunists or naïve, self-deluded, and credulous visionaries? The question, however, is almost incidental, for once they had committed themselves totally to the agencies' objectives it followed as a matter of course that they would be working for the pursuit of victory, which had little to do with the pursuit of truth. The crucial question concerns their decision in the first place to offer themselves carte blanche to the service of the cause.

The circumstances surrounding the fate of academic freedom during

2. John Dewey, "In Explanation of Our Lapse," *New Republic*, XIII (November 3, 1917), 18.

the war are more complicated, because professors did not have the same degree of control in this area as they had over the integrity of their own labors. A professor could, after all, have quit the service of the CPI if he felt his professional ethics were being violated; it is less reasonable to expect him to have resigned from a university that was jeopardizing academic freedom—a luxury of principle that can seldom be afforded. We have seen, however, that professors themselves had considerable complicity in the abridgment of academic freedom during the war, partly because they thought it incumbent on university men to give un-equivocal support to the cause. "We cannot take the same position in time of war as we take in time of peace," Richard Ely wrote. "We are fighting for civilization . . . and the struggle is a life and death one. A man who gives utterance to opinions which hinder us in this awful struggle deserves to be fired."[3] The AAUP reneged on a principled commitment to unconditional academic freedom, in part because the or-ganization identified itself totally with the government's purposes in the war and felt obliged to forestall even the most contingent threats to those purposes. The ultimate concession made by American professors to the cause was to acquiesce in turning colleges and universities over to the War Department. The SATC was both the logical conclusion to and the fitting symbol of the commitment of the talents and resources of American institutions of higher learning to winning the war. By the summer of 1918 university men had gone so far in that commitment that they had no principled position from which to resist their total sub-mergence in the war effort.

To describe the process by which American professors compromised the ideal of their calling is easier than to provide precise explanations for it. Clearly, however, the war came upon an academic community ill prepared to meet the challenge. The recency of the revolution in higher learning and its failure to establish clear and commonly accepted goals left the nation's colleges and universities without a secure sense of value and purpose and particularly susceptible to pressures from the world outside their walls. The response to the war of the institutions of higher learning suggests a quest for legitimacy; they appear to have seized the

3. Richard Ely to A. A. Young, November 1, 1917, in Ely Papers.

opportunity to demonstrate their worth to themselves and to the public upon which they depended for support.

The same lack of definition that characterized the institutions of higher learning characterized the academic disciplines, which also had only recently assumed their modern form. The ease with which professors adopted moralistic interpretations of the war suggests that their disciplines had not yet been clearly established on a scientific basis. Like the universities, professors appear to have been seeking legitimacy by demonstrating the "usefulness" of their disciplines to the cause. So, too, did professors seek through participation in the war effort to work out problems within the disciplines themselves: in psychology, to win recognition for new and unproved methods of testing; in languages, to push the claims of spoken, as well as written, work in instruction; in the social sciences, to focus attention in a way to make the subjects relevant to the problems of the contemporary world. Historians particularly were unsure of the value accorded to their discipline, especially during the war, because history was devoted to an exploration of the past. The war presented an occasion both for softening the tensions within the discipline, because orthodox and new historians alike thought they had a public educative role to perform, and for sharpening the tensions, because new historians seized the chance to press the claims of present-mindedness and relevance. In the several disciplines the response of professors to the war's challenge suggests a quest for an end to uncertainty about the nature and function of knowledge—the relation between facts and values and their articulation with and significance for the realm of social action. The quest was expressed explicitly by McLaughlin, when he called on historians to use their knowledge to provide "prophecy" and "actual guidance" for the future, and by Turner, when he urged historians to acquaint Americans with those "hopes and ideals and characteristics which have meant to us a nation worth fighting for."

Finally, when the academic community was faced with the fact of war, academic professionalism was in a rudimentary state, and professors lacked a sense of solidarity and group morale that might have given them the security and self-confidence to resist threatening outside pressures. Allin's despair at being a "useless university man" and his welcome of the SATC to provide him with a sense of purpose and Corwin's appreciation of the SATC for saving the professors' self-respect by giving them "some useful work to do" indicate an absence of professional élan. Lacking a conviction of the value of his work, the professor sought to establish his own value by participating in the world of affairs. Lacking a sense of community among his peers, he sought it in war service. The "demobilized professor's" lament at the disruption by the war's end of the "new comradeship" he had found in war service suggests that such comradeship, which he described as "springing from coordinated and enthusiastic effort," was not to be found on the campus.

The tensions inherent in the dual status of American university scholars as employees and as professionals contributed to their lack of professional élan. The AAUP, which set itself the task of mitigating those tensions, was in its infancy when America was at war and thus lacked authority among both professors and university administrators. The AAUP was certain that academic freedom was the essential precondition for the practice of the academic profession, but the professoriate appears to have had a limited understanding of the implications of academic freedom and certainly did not subscribe unanimously or wholeheartedly to its precepts. The tenuous comprehension of and commitment to academic freedom among American professors reflected and contributed to their lack of professional identity and security. Although the AAUP's 1915 declaration on academic freedom was a strong statement of principles, the rights and status of American professors were protected by neither custom nor law. Professors were at the mercy of the standards, even the whims, of administrators, trustees, and public officials. Within the universities, faculties were not accorded a meaningful decision-making role and had not come to regard themselves as a body of peers from whom power and protection flowed and upon whom they should rely as a court of appeal. Lacking a clear sense of professional identity, security, or solidarity, the professors, among them the leadership and membership of the AAUP, failed to defend academic freedom when it fell victim to the wartime national consensus.

The response of American professors to the challenge of the First World War reflected conditions in the academic world at the time. A mere glance around us at present, however, is sufficient to suggest that not all those conditions have been outgrown, even though the institutions of higher learning, the scholarly disciplines, and the academic profession have long since passed the age of immaturity. In the issue of continuing devotion of the talents and resources of the higher learning to the service of power lies the larger significance of this study. For, even though America's participation in the First World War was of relatively short duration, the articulation of interest between the higher learning and the world of power that took place during the war's span was not an ephemeral experience; established and exposed then were assumptions, attitudes, and expectations that would flower in the decades to come.

Behind this commitment of talents and resources to the uses of the state during the war—with all that that commitment implied for the ideal of disinterested criticism and the unfettered pursuit of knowledge and truth—lay the ideal of service. The service ideal might have led in a different direction had a distinction been made between service to society and service to the state and had scholars recognized that they could serve society best as free and independent thinkers, who contributed to the expansion of human knowledge and, from a broad spectrum of values and ideological perspectives, exercised the function of social analysis and criticism. Instead, professors assumed that knowledge is effective chiefly in association with power, and they ultimately came to serve the interests of power rather than the interests of truth.

Selected
Bibliography

Literature on the higher learning and on America during World War I is vast. This bibliography is composed of selected sources, most of which have been cited in the book.

MANUSCRIPT SOURCES

Adams, George Burton. Papers. Historical Manuscripts Collection, Yale University Library, New Haven, Conn.

Ames, Herman V. Papers. University of Pennsylvania Archives, Philadelphia.

Beveridge, Albert. Papers. Library of Congress, Washington, D.C.

Burgess, John W. Papers. Special Collections, Columbia University Library, New York.

Burton, E. D. Papers. University of Chicago Archives.

Cattell, James McKeen. Collection. Special Collections, Columbia University Library, New York.

Columbia University Archives. Low Memorial Library, Columbia University, New York.

Coolidge, Archibald Cary. Papers. Harvard University Archives, Cambridge, Mass.

Davis, William Stearns. Papers. University of Minnesota Archives, Minneapolis.

Dean of Students Papers. University of Minnesota Archives, Minneapolis.

Department of History Papers, Intrafaculty Correspondence, 1910–1924. University of Chicago Archives.

Department of Political Science Correspondence. University of Minnesota Archives, Minneapolis.

Divinity School Correspondence. University of Chicago Archives.

Dodd, William E. Papers. Library of Congress, Washington, D.C.

Ely, Richard T. Papers. State Historical Society of Wisconsin, Madison.

Faculty Documents. University of Wisconsin Archives, Madison.

Fish, Carl Russell. Papers. State Historical Society of Wisconsin, Madison.

Ford, Guy Stanton. Papers. University of Minnesota Archives, Minneapolis.

Harper, Samuel N. Papers. University of Chicago Archives.

Hart, Albert Bushnell. Papers. Houghton Library, Harvard University, Cambridge, Mass.

History Department Correspondence, 1916–1920. Harvard University Archives, Cambridge, Mass.

House, E. M. Collection. Historical Manuscripts Collection, Yale University Library, New Haven, Conn.

Inquiry Archives. National Archives, Washington, D.C.

Jameson, J. Franklin. Papers. Library of Congress, Washington, D.C.

Lowell, A. Lawrence. Papers. Harvard University Archives, Cambridge, Mass.

McLaughlin, Andrew C. Papers. University of Chicago Archives.

National Board for Historical Service Papers. Library of Congress, Washington, D.C.

Perry, Ralph Barton. Papers. Harvard University Archives, Cambridge, Mass.

Presidents' Papers. Historical Manuscripts Collection, Yale University Library, New Haven, Conn.

Presidents' Papers. University of Chicago Archives.

Presidents' Papers. University of Minnesota Archives, Minneapolis.

Presidents' Papers. University of Wisconsin Archives, Madison.

Royce, Josiah. Papers. Harvard University Archives, Cambridge, Mass.

Schaper, William A. Collection. Western History Collections, University of Oklahoma Library, Norman.

Schaper Case Papers. University of Minnesota Archives, Minneapolis.

Seligman, E. R. A. Collection. Special Collections, Columbia University Library, New York.

Shotwell, James T. Papers. Special Collections, Columbia University Library, New York.

Sisson, Edgar. Papers. National Archives, Washington, D.C.

United States Committee on Public Information Papers. National Archives, Washington, D.C.

Van Tyne, Claude H. Papers. Bentley Historical Library, Michigan Historical Collections, University of Michigan, Ann Arbor.

Villard, Oswald Garrison. Papers. Houghton Library, Harvard University, Cambridge, Mass.

War Aims Lectures. Michigan Historical Collections, Bentley Historical Library, University of Michigan, Ann Arbor.

PRIMARY SOURCES

Adams, George B. "America's Obligation and Opportunity." *Yale Review*, n.s., V (October, 1915–July, 1916).

———. "The British Empire and a League of Peace." *Nation*, CVI (April 4, 1918).

———. "The Duty of the United States in International Affairs." *Columbia University Quarterly*, XIX (September, 1917).

———. "The English Background of American Institutions." *Historical Outlook*, IX (November, 1918).

———. "History and the Philosophy of History." *American Historical Review*, XIV (January, 1909).

———. Letter to the Editor. New York *Times*, October 13, 1914.

———. Letter to the Editor. New York *Times*, January 24, 1915.

———. Letter to the Editor. New York *Times*, December 3, 1916.

———. "The Present Problems of Medieval History." In Howard J. Rogers, ed. *Congress of Arts and Science, Universal Exposition, St. Louis, 1904*. Boston and New York: Houghton, Mifflin and Company, 1905–1907.

Ames, J. S. "The Trained Man of Science in the War." *Science*, n.s., XLVIII (October 25, 1918).

Aydelotte, Frank. *Final Report of the War Issues Course of the Students' Army Training Corps*. Washington, D.C.: Government Printing Office, 1919.

Barnes, Harry Elmer. *A Preliminary Syllabus for a Study of the Issues of the Present War*. Pt. 1, Historical. Worcester, Mass.: Clark University Press, [1918].

Beard, Charles A. "A Call Upon Every Citizen." *Harper's*, CXXXVII (October, 1918).

———. "The Function and Possibilities of an International Legislative Body." New York *Times*, January 21, 1916.

———. "Mine Eyes May Behold." *New Republic*, LXXXIX (January 19, 1938).

———. "The Perils of Diplomacy." *New Republic*, XI (June 2, 1917).

Beard, Charles A., and William C. Bagley. *The History of the American People*. New York: Macmillan Company, 1918.

Becker, Carl. *America's War Aims and Peace Terms*. U.S. Committee on Public Information, George Creel, chairman, War Information Series, No. 21. Washington, D.C.: Government Printing Office, 1918.

———. "German Historians and the Great War." *Dial*, LX (February 17, 1916).

———. "The Monroe Doctrine and the War." *History Teachers Magazine*, IX (February, 1918).

Bell, Julian, ed. *We Did Not Fight: 1914–18 Experiences of War Resisters*. London: Cobden-Sanderson, 1935.

Billington, Ray Allen, and Walter Muir Whitehill, eds. *"Dear Lady": The*

*Letters of Frederick Jackson Turner and Alice Forbes Perkins Hooper,
1910–1932.* San Marino: Huntington Library, 1970.

Boas, Franz. "Kinship of Language a Vital Factor in the War." New York
Times, January 3, 1915.

———. Letter to the Editor. New York *Times,* January 8, 1916.

Boston University. *World War Record.* Boston: Earnshaw Press, [ca. 1920].

Bourne, Randolph S. "Those Columbia Trustees." *New Republic,* XII (October 20, 1917).

———. "The War and the Intellectuals." *Seven Arts,* II (June, 1917).

Breasted, James H. "The Bridgehead of Asia Minor." *Nation,* CVI (June 8, 1918).

Burgess, George K. "Science and the After-War Period." *Scientific Monthly,*
VIII (February, 1919).

Burgess, John W. *America's Relation to the Great War.* Chicago: A. C.
McClurg and Company, 1916.

———. *The European War of 1914: Its Causes, Purposes, and Probable
Results.* Chicago: A. C. McClurg and Company, 1915.

Butler, Nicholas Murray. *Across the Busy Years: Recollections and Reflections.* New York: Charles Scribner's Sons, 1935.

Carman, Harry J. "The Columbia Course in Contemporary Civilization."
Paper delivered before the Association of History Teachers of the Middle
States and Maryland, Bryn Mawr, May 2, 1925.

"The Case of Columbia Professors." *Nation,* CV (October 11, 1917).

Clark, John B. "Americans Urged to Enter Fight for Liberty." New York
Times, March 4, 1917.

Clark, Victor S. "The German Press and the War." *Historical Outlook,* X
(November, 1919).

Clendenning, John, ed. *The Letters of Josiah Royce.* Chicago: University of
Chicago Press, 1970.

"College Presidents Polled." New York *Times,* January 24, 31, 1915.

"The Colleges and the War." *Outlook,* CXX (September 11, 1918).

Colter, John R. "The Government Surprises the Colleges." *Outlook,* CXXIII
(September 17, 1919).

Columbia University. *Outline of the Course on Issues of the War for the
Students' Army Training Corps.* Pt. 1. New York: Columbia University
Press, 1918.

Columbia University Annual Reports, 1917–1920. New York: Columbia
University Press, 1917–20.

Commons, John R. *German Socialists and the War.* New York: American
Alliance for Labor and Democracy, 1918.

———. *Myself.* New York: Macmillan Company, 1934.

———. *Who Is Paying for This War?* New York: American Alliance for
Labor and Democracy, 1918.

———. *Why Workingmen Support the War.* New York: American Alliance
for Labor and Democracy, 1918.

Coolidge, Harold Jefferson, and Robert H. Lord. *Archibald Cary Coolidge: Life and Letters*. Boston and New York: Houghton Mifflin Company, 1932.

Corwin, Edward S. "The Right of Retaliation." *Nation,* CIV (March 1, 1917).

Coulter, John M. "The Contribution of Germany to Higher Education." *Chicago University Record,* VIII (March, 1904).

Creel, George. *Complete Report of the Chairman of the Committee on Public Information, 1917, 1918, 1919*. Washington, D.C.: Government Printing Office, 1920.

————. *How We Advertised America*. New York and London: Harper and Brothers, 1920.

————. "Military Training for Our Youth." *Century,* XCII (May, 1916).

————. "Propaganda and Morale." *American Journal of Sociology,* XLVII (November, 1941).

————. "Public Opinion in Wartime." *Annals of the American Academy of Political and Social Science,* LXXVIII (July, 1918).

————. *Rebel At Large: Recollections of Fifty Crowded Years*. G. P. Putnam's Sons, 1947.

Davis, William Stearns. *The Roots of the War*. New York: Century Company, 1918.

————. "The Study of the Roman Republic Today." *History Teachers Magazine,* IX (January, 1918).

Davis, William Stearns, ed. *The War Message and the Facts Behind It*. U.S. Committee on Public Information, George Creel, chairman, War Information Series, No. 1. Washington, D.C.: Government Printing Office, 1917.

Dewey, John. "Academic Freedom." *Educational Review,* XXIII (January, 1902).

————. "Conscience and Compulsion." *New Republic,* XI (July 14, 1917).

————. "Conscription of Thought." *New Republic,* XII (September 1, 1917).

————. "The Cult of Irrationality." *New Republic,* XVII (November 9, 1918).

————. "The Discrediting of Idealism." *New Republic,* XX (October 8, 1919).

————. "In Explanation of Our Lapse." *New Republic,* XIII (November 3, 1917).

————. "Fiat Justitia, Ruat Coelum." *New Republic,* XII (September 29, 1917).

————. "Force, Violence, and Law." *New Republic,* V (January 22, 1916).

————. "The Future of Pacifism." *New Republic,* XI (July 28, 1917).

————. *German Philosophy and Politics*. New York: H. Holt and Company, 1915.

————. "In a Time of National Hesitation." *Seven Arts,* II (May, 1917).

————. "Morals and the Conduct of States." *New Republic*, XIV (March 23, 1918).

————. "Universal Service as Education." *New Republic*, VI (April 22, 1916).

————. "What America Will Fight For." *New Republic*, XII (August 18, 1917).

————. "What Are We Fighting For?" *Independent*, XCIV (June 22, 1918).

"Discussion of Problems Presented by the Students' Army Training Corps, and the Future Military Training of Students." *Association of American Universities Journal of Proceedings*, XX–XXIII (1918–21).

Dodd, William E. "The United States of Tomorrow." *Nation*, CIV (January 18, 1917).

Dooley, C. R. *Final Report of the National Army Training Detachments, Later Known as Vocational Section S.A.T.C.* Washington, D.C.: Government Printing Office, 1919.

Dunn, Arthur Wallace. "Military Camps for College Students." *American Review of Reviews*, XLIX (March, 1914).

Ely, Richard T. *Ground Under Our Feet.* New York: Macmillan Company, 1938.

————. *The World War and Leadership in a Democracy.* New York: Macmillan Company, 1918.

Erskine, John. "The Scholar in the Crisis." *Columbia Literary Monthly*, XIV (February, 1917).

Facts About the War. Compiled or written by members of the faculty of the University of Minnesota. Minneapolis: University of Minnesota Press, 1917.

Ferguson, William S. "The Crisis of Hellenism." *History Teachers Magazine*, VIII (November, 1917).

Fish, Carl Russell. "Internal Problems During the Civil War." *History Teachers Magazine*, IX (April, 1918).

Ford, Guy Stanton. *On and Off the Campus.* Minneapolis: University of Minnesota Press, 1938.

Giddings, Franklin H. *Americanism in War and Peace.* Worcester, Mass.: Clark University Press, 1917.

————. "The Basis of an Enduring Peace." *International Conciliation*, No. 113 (April, 1917).

————. *Democracy and Empire; with Studies of Their Psychological, Economic, and Moral Foundations.* London: Macmillan and Company, 1900.

————. "The Democracy of Universal Military Service." *Annals of the American Academy of Political and Social Science*, LXVI (July, 1916).

————. "Intellectual Consequences of the War." *Transactions of the Royal Canadian Institute*, XII (May, 1919).

————. *The Responsible State: A Reexamination of Fundamental Political Doctrines in the Light of World War and the Menace of Anarchism.* Boston and New York: Houghton Mifflin Company, 1918.

————. "What the War Was Worth." *Independent,* XCIX (July 5, 1919).

Gray, William D. "The Great War and Roman History." *History Teachers Magazine,* IX (March, 1918).

Greene, Evarts B. *American Interest in Popular Government Abroad.* U.S. Committee on Public Information, George Creel, chairman, War Information Series, No. 8. Washington, D.C.: Government Printing Office, 1918.

————. "The American Revolution and the British Empire." *History Teachers Magazine,* VIII (November, 1917).

————. "Co-operation Between Colleges and Secondary Schools in Promoting Education for Citizenship." *Association of American Colleges Bulletin,* V (April, 1919).

————. *Lieber and Schurz: Two Loyal Americans of German Birth.* U.S. Committee on Public Information, George Creel, chairman, War Information Series, No. 19. Washington D.C.: Government Printing Office, 1918.

Hadley, Arthur T. "The Political Teachings of Treitschke." *Yale Review,* n.s., IV (January, 1915).

Harding, Samuel B. *The Study of the Great War.* U.S. Committee on Public Information, George Creel, chairman, War Information Series, No. 16. Washington D.C.: Government Printing Office, 1918.

Harper, Paul V., ed. *The Russia I Believe In: The Memoirs of Samuel N. Harper.* Chicago: University of Chicago Press, 1945.

Hart, Albert Bushnell. "Arms and the Ship." New York *Times,* March 12, 1916, Sec. 6.

————. "Austrian Fear of Serb Empire Is Real War Cause." New York *Times,* August 2, 1914, Sec. 5.

————. "Baker and His Task." New York *Times,* April 7, 1918, Sec. 7.

————. "Can Allies Afford to Make Peace Now?" New York *Times,* December 24, 1916, Sec. 5.

————. "The Essential Points of Belgian Neutrality." New York *Times,* December 27, 1914, Sec. 5.

————. "Germany's 'Law of Necessity' Vivesected." New York *Times,* February 18, 1917, Sec. 5.

————. *The Monroe Doctrine: An Interpretation.* Boston: Little, Brown and Company, 1916.

————. "Nations' vs. Belligerents' Laws." New York *Times,* March 21, 1915, Sec. 5.

————. "Neutrality, Armed Neutrality, and War." New York *Times,* March 4, 1917, Sec. 5.

————. "Peace With Honor." New York *Times,* January 28, 1917, Sec. 5.

————. "Popular Government as 'Made in Germany.' " New York *Times,* October 27, 1918, Sec. 8.

————. "Rocky Road to Permanent Peace." New York *Times,* January 6, 1918, Sec. 7.

————. "The U.S. Note to England." New York *Times,* November 14, 1915, Sec. 4.

————. *The War in Europe: Its Causes and Results.* New York and London: D. Appleton and Company, 1914.

————. "The Way of the Neutral Is Hard in This War." New York *Times,* October 22, 1916, Sec. 5.

————. "What Next for Germany?" New York *Times,* May 14, 1916, Sec. 5.

————. "What President's Peace Plan Has Accomplished." New York *Times,* December 31, 1916, Sec. 5.

Hart, Albert Bushnell, ed. *America at War: A Handbook of Patriotic Education References.* New York: George H. Doran, 1918.

Hart, Albert Bushnell, and Arthur O. Lovejoy, eds. *Handbook of the War for Readers, Speakers, and Teachers.* New York: National Security League, 1918.

"Harvard and Preparedness." *Outlook,* CXII (January 12, 1916).

Hawkes, Herbert E. "A College Course on Peace Issues." *Educational Review,* LVIII (September, 1919).

Hayes, Carlton J. H. "Which? War Without a Purpose? Or Armed Neutrality With a Purpose?" *Survey,* XXVII (February 10, 1917).

Hazen, Charles D. *Alsace-Lorraine Under German Rule.* New York: H. Holt and Company, 1917.

————. *Fifty Years of Europe, 1870–1920.* New York: H. Holt and Company, 1919.

————. "Germany, Last Stronghold of Autocratic Monarchy." New York *Times,* July 1, 1917, Sec. 8.

————. *The Government of Germany.* U.S. Committee on Public Information, George Creel, chairman, War Information Series, No. 3. Washington, D.C.: Government Printing Office, 1917.

Heckel, Albert Kerr. "The War Aims Course in the Colleges." *Historical Outlook,* X (January, 1919).

Hibben, John G. "The Colleges and National Defense." *Independent,* LXXXII (June 28, 1915).

Hibben, John G., and Jacob G. Schurman. "The University Cantonment, Princeton and Cornell." *Bookman,* XLVIII (November, 1918).

Horwill, Herbert H. "Anglo-American Interpreters." *Nation,* CVII (July 20, 1918).

James, Edmund J. "The Colleges and Our National Ideals." *Association of American Colleges Bulletin,* V (April, 1919).

Jameson, J. Franklin. "Historical Scholars in War-Time." *American Historical Review,* XXII (July, 1917).

Kallen, Horace M. "Politics, Profits, and Patriotism in Wisconsin." *Nation,* CVI (March 7, 1918).

Keppel, Frederick P. *Columbia.* New York: Oxford University Press, 1914.

———. *Some War-Time Lessons*. New York: Columbia University Press, 1920.

———. *The Undergraduate and His College*. Boston: Houghton Mifflin Company, 1917.

Kerner, Robert J. "The Historic Role of the Slavs." *History Teachers Magazine*, VIII (November, 1917).

Lee, John. "Drafted Universities." *Nation*, CVII (December 7, 1918).

"A Legacy of the War to Our Colleges." *Outlook*, CXX (September 11, 1918).

Lovejoy, Arthur O. "German Peace Drives Rightly Named 'Traps.'" New York *Times*, July 28, 1918, Sec. 6.

———. Letter to the Editor. *Nation*, XCIX (September 24, 1914).

———. Letter to the Editor. *Nation*, XCIX (November 5, 1914).

———. Letter to the Editor. *Nation*, C (March 4, 1915).

———. Letter to the Editor. *Nation*, CVI (April 4, 1918).

———. Letter to the Editor. New York *Times*, March 30, 1916.

———. Letter to the Editor. New York *Times*, September 17, 1917.

———. Letter to the Editor. New York *Times*, December 3, 1917.

———. Letter to the Editor. New York *Times*, June 28, 1918.

Lowell, A. Lawrence. *At War with Academic Traditions in America*. Cambridge: Harvard University Press, 1934.

Mabry, W. Alexander, ed. "Professor William E. Dodd's Diary, 1916–1920." *John P. Branch Historical Papers of Randolph-Macon College*, n.s., II (March, 1953).

MacCracken, John Henry. "Federal Leadership in Education." *Association of American Colleges Bulletin*, V (April, 1919).

McLaughlin, Andrew C. *America and Britain*. New York: E. P. Dutton and Company, 1919.

———. *The Great War: From Spectator to Participant*. U.S. Committee on Public Information, George Creel, chairman, War Information Series, No. 4. Washington, D.C.: Government Printing Office, 1917.

———. "Historians and the War." *Dial*, LXII (May 17, 1917).

McLaughlin, Andrew C., *et al*. *The Study of History in Schools: Report to the American Historical Association by the Committee of Seven*. New York: Macmillan Company, 1899.

Mather, Frank J. "Culture vs. Kultur." New York *Times*, November 8, 1914, Sec. 3.

———. Letter to the Editor. New York *Times*, October 9, 1914.

———. Letter to the Editor. New York *Times*, October 12, 1915.

———. Letter to the Editor. *Nation*, CIII (December 28, 1916).

———. "The Philosophy of the War." *Unpopular Review*, III (January–March, 1915).

———. "Rear-Rank Reflections." *Unpopular Review*, V (January–March, 1916).

————. "Sentimentalism—Soft and Hard." *Unpopular Review,* IV (October–December, 1915).

————. "The War, by a Historian." *Unpopular Review,* II (July–December, 1914).

————. "What Is Militarism?" New York *Times,* January 12, 1915.

Meiklejohn, Alexander. "The Colleges and the S.A.T.C." *Nation,* CVII (December 7, 1918).

————. "A Schoolmaster's View of Compulsory Military Training." *School and Society,* IV (July 1, 1916).

"A Mere Professor." New York *Evening Post,* October 23, 1918.

"Military Training at Columbia University." *School and Society,* VII (July 20, 1918).

"The Military Training Camps for 1916." *Outlook,* CXII (April 12, 1916).

Millikan, Robert A. "The New Opportunity in Science." *Science,* n.s., L (September 26, 1919).

Munro, Dana C., George C. Sellery, and August C. Krey. *German War Practices: Part I, Treatment of Civilians.* U.S. Committee on Public Information, George Creel, chairman, Red, White, and Blue Series, No. 6. Washington, D.C.: Government Printing Office, 1917.

————. *German War Practices: Part II, German Treatment of Conquered Territory.* U.S. Committee on Public Information, George Creel, chairman, Red, White, and Blue Series, No. 8. Washington, D.C.: Government Printing Office, 1918.

Notestein, Wallace. "The Interest of Seventeenth Century England for Students of American Institutions." *History Teachers Magazine,* VIII (December, 1917).

————. Letter to the Editor. *Nation,* CIII (August 24, 1916).

Notestein, Wallace, and Elmer E. Stoll, eds. *Conquest and Kultur.* U.S. Committee on Public Information, George Creel, chairman, Red, White, and Blue Series, No. 5. Washington, D.C.: Government Printing Office, 1917.

Ogg, Frederic A., and Charles A. Beard. *National Governments and the World War.* New York: Macmillan Company, 1919.

"Our Militarized Colleges." *Literary Digest,* LVIII (September 28, 1918).

"Our Military Propagandists." *Nation,* XCIX (July 16, 1914).

Patten, Simon N. Letter to the Editor. *New Republic,* I (November 14, 1914).

Paxson, Frederic L., Edward S. Corwin, and Samuel B. Harding, eds. *War Cyclopedia.* U.S. Committee on Public Information, George Creel, chairman, Red, White, and Blue Series. No. 7. Washington, D.C.: Government Printing Office, 1918.

Perry, Ralph Barton. "Fatalism and War." New York *Times,* February 21, 1915, Sec. 5.

————. *The Free Man and the Soldier.* New York: C. Scribner's Sons, 1916.

————. *The Present Conflict of Ideals: A Study of the Philosophical Back-*

ground of the World War. New York: Longmans, Green and Company, 1918.

————. "Students' Army Training Corps." *National Service, with the International Military Digest,* VI (August, 1919).

————. "The Universities in War Time." *University of California Chronicle,* XX (1918).

————. "What Is Worth Fighting For?" *Atlantic Monthly,* CXVI (December, 1915).

[Perry, Ralph Barton.] "The Demobilized Professor, By One of Them." *Atlantic Monthly,* CXXIII (April, 1919).

Pitkin, Walter B., and Roscoe C. E. Brown, eds. *Columbia War Papers.* Ser. 1. New York: Division of Intelligence and Publicity of Columbia University, 1917.

"The Plattsburg Idea." *New Republic,* IV (October, 1915).

"President James and the Land Grant College." *Outlook,* CXII (March 8, 1916).

"The Princeton Offensive." *Nation,* CVI (January 10, 1918).

"The Professors in Battle Array." *Nation,* CVII (March 7, 1918).

"Professor Sloane Warns America Against War Meddling." New York *Times,* September 20, 1914, Sec. 4.

Read, Conyers. "The Evolution of Democracy in England." *Historical Outlook,* IX (November, 1918).

"Report of the Committee on Academic Freedom and Academic Tenure." *American Association of University Professors Bulletin,* I (December, 1915).

"Report of the Committee on Academic Freedom in Wartime." *American Association of University Professors Bulletin,* IV (February–March, 1918).

"Reserve Officers' Training Corps in the Colleges." *School and Society,* VIII (December 28, 1918).

"The Revolution in the Colleges." *Nation,* CVII (September 28, 1918).

Robinson, James Harvey. "The Conception and Methods of History." In Howard J. Rogers, ed. *Congress of Arts and Science, Universal Exposition, St. Louis, 1904.* Boston and New York: Houghton, Mifflin and Company, 1905–1907.

————. "The Last Decade of European History and the Great War." Supplement to *The Development of Modern Europe* by Robinson and Beard and *An Introduction to the History of Western Europe* by Robinson. Boston: Houghton Mifflin Company, 1918.

————. "War and Thinking." *New Republic,* I (December 19, 1914).

Robinson, James Harvey, and Charles A. Beard. *Outlines of European History: Part II, From the Seventeenth Century to the War of 1914.* Boston: Houghton Mifflin Company, 1918.

Rohner, Ronald P., ed. *The Ethnography of Franz Boas.* Chicago: University of Chicago Press, 1960.

Royce, Josiah. "Belgium as the Teacher of the Nations." New York *Times*, December 20, 1915.

―――. *The Duties of Americans in the Present War*. Address delivered at Tremont Temple, Sunday, January 30, 1916. N.p., n.d.

―――. *The Hope of the Great Community*. New York: Macmillan Company, 1916.

Rushton, Wyatt. "Training College Students." *American Review of Reviews*, LIII (February, 1916).

"The S.A.T.C.—A Comedy." *Outlook*, CXXI (February 5, 1919).

Schmitt, Bernadotte. *England and Germany, 1740–1914*. Princeton: Princeton University Press, 1918.

―――. Letter to the Editor. *Nation*, XCIX (August 27, 1914).

―――. Letter to the Editor. New York *Times*, November 11, 1914.

―――. Letter to the Editor. New York *Times*, April 22, 1917, Sec. 2.

Schurman, Jacob Gould. "The Effect of the War on Education." *Association of American Universities Journal of Proceedings*, XX-XXIII (1918–21).

―――. "Every College Should Introduce Military Training." *Everybody's Magazine*, XXXII (February, 1915).

Schuyler, Robert Livingston. "History and Public Opinion." *Educational Review*, LV (March, 1918).

Scott, George W., and James W. Garner. *The German War Code*. U.S. Committee on Public Information, George Creel, chairman, War Information Series, No. 11. Washington, D.C.: Government Printing Office, 1918.

"The Secret Treaties." *Nation*, CVI (February 7, 1918).

Seymour, Charles. *The Diplomatic Background of the War, 1870–1914*. New Haven: Yale University Press, 1916.

Shepherd, William R. "Common Sense in Foreign Policy." *Political Science Quarterly*, XXXI (March, 1916).

Sherman, Stuart P. *American and Allied Ideals*. U.S. Committee on Public Information, George Creel, chairman, War Information Series, No. 12. Washington, D.C.: Government Printing Office, 1918.

―――. "Why Mr. Roosevelt and the Rest of Us Are at War." *Nation*, CV (November 15, 1917).

Shotwell, James T. *Autobiography*. Indianapolis and New York: Bobbs-Merrill, 1961.

―――. Introduction to Charles Altschul, *The American Revolution in Our School Text Books*. New York: Doran, 1917.

―――. "The National Board for Historical Service." *History Teachers Magazine*, VIII (June, 1917).

Sioussat, St. George L. "English Foundations of American Institutional Life." *History Teachers Magazine*, VIII (October, 1917).

Sisson, Edgar. *One Hundred Red Days: A Personal Chronicle of the Bolshevik Revolution*. New Haven: Yale University Press, 1931.

Sisson, Edgar, ed. *The German-Bolshevik Conspiracy*. U.S. Committee on

Public Information, George Creel, chairman, War Information Series, No. 20. Washington, D.C.: Government Printing Office, 1918.

"The Sisson Documents." *Nation,* CVII (November 23, 1918).

Small, Albion W. "Americans and the World Crisis." *American Journal of Sociology,* XXIII (September, 1917).

————. "Germany and American Opinion." *Sociological Review,* VIII (April, 1915).

Smith, Edward C. "The S.A.T.C. from the Military Viewpoint." *Educational Review,* LIX (May, 1920).

Smith, Munroe. "Aspects of Submarine War Against Merchant Vessels." New York *Times,* August 27, 1916, Sec. 2.

————. *Bismarck and German Unity.* New York: Columbia University Press, 1923.

————. *Militarism and Statecraft.* New York: G. P. Putnam's Sons, 1918.

————. *The Society of Nations Versus Germany in the Case of Captain Fryatt.* N.p.: [American Rights League, ca. 1916].

[Smith, Munroe, ed]. *Out of Their Own Mouths: Utterances of German Rulers, Statesmen, Savants, Publicists, Journalists, Poets, Businessmen, Party Leaders, and Soldiers.* New York: D. Appleton and Company, 1918.

Soule, George. "Military Training as Education." *Dial,* LVI (January 25, 1919).

Sperry, E. E., and W. M. West. *German Plots and Intrigues.* U.S. Committee on Public Information, George Creel, chairman, Red, White, and Blue Series, No. 10. Washington, D.C.: Government Printing Office, 1918.

"A Statement by Charles A. Beard." *New Republic,* XIII (December 29, 1917).

Stowe, A. Monroe. "The S.A.T.C. Idea: A Possible Solution of Some of the Social and Military Problems of Democracy." *School and Society,* VIII (December 28, 1918).

Stowell, Ellery C. *The Diplomacy of the War of 1914.* Boston: Houghton Mifflin Company, 1915.

————. Letter to the Editor. *Nation,* CV (November 15, 1917).

————. "U.S. Should be Chief Guardian of Neutrality." New York *Times,* August 16, 1914.

Sumner, Francis B. "Some Perils Which Confront Us as Scientists." *Scientific Monthly,* VIII (March, 1919).

Tatlock, John S. P. *Why America Fights Germany.* U.S. Committee on Public Information, George Creel, chairman, War Information Series, No. 15. Washington, D.C.: Government Printing Office, 1918.

Thwing, Charles F. "The Colleges as War Camps." *Independent,* XCVI (October 5, 1918).

————. "Gains and Losses of the College Revolution." *Independent,* XCVI (December 14, 1918).

"Towards Academic Freedom." *Nation,* CVI (February 14, 1918).

Turner, Frederick Jackson. "Problems in American History." In Howard J. Rogers, ed. *Congress of Arts and Science, Universal Exposition, St. Louis, 1904*. Boston: Houghton, Mifflin and Company, 1906.

United States House of Representatives, *Sundry Civil Bill, 1919: Hearings before Subcommittee of House Committee on Appropriations*. 65th Cong., 2nd Sess., Pt. 3. Washington, D.C.: Government Printing Office, 1918.

United States War Department, Committee on Education and Special Training. *Questions on the Issues of the War*. Washington, D.C.: Government Printing Office, [1918].

———. *A Review of Its Work During 1918 by the Advisory Board*. Washington, D.C.: Government Printing Office, 1919.

The University of Chicago War Papers. Chicago: University of Chicago Press, [1918].

Van Tyne, Claude H. Letter to the Editor. New York *Times*, September 23, 1915.

———. Letter to the Editor. New York *Times*, September 6, 1916.

———. Letter to the Editor. New York *Times*, August 21, 1917.

Veblen, Thorstein. *Essays in Our Changing Order*. Edited by Leon Ardzrooni. New York: Augustus M. Kelley, 1964.

———. *Imperial Germany and the Industrial Revolution*. Ann Arbor: University of Michigan Press, 1966.

———. *An Inquiry into the Nature of Peace and the Terms of Its Perpetuation*. New York: Macmillan Company, 1945.

"The War and the Schools." *North American Review*, CVIII (October, 1918).

War Book of the University of Wisconsin: Papers on the Causes and Issues of the War. By members of the faculty. Madison: University of Wisconsin Press, 1918.

Westermann, William L. "The Roman Empire and the Great War." *History Teachers Magazine*, IX (February, 1918).

"What the War Means to America." New York *Times*, May 19, 1918.

Whipple, Leon. Letter to the Editor. *Nation*, CV (December 20, 1917).

Whitelock, William W., trans. *Modern Germany in Relation to the Great War*. By various German writers. New York: Mitchell Kennerley, 1916.

Wilson, Woodrow. "The Variety and Unity of History." In Howard J. Rogers, ed. *Congress of Arts and Science, Universal Exposition, St. Louis, 1904*. Boston and New York: Houghton, Mifflin and Company, 1905–1907.

Winslow, John B., Charles R. Van Hise, and E. A. Birge. *Report Upon the Statements of Professor Robert McNutt McElroy and the Executive Committee of the National Security League Relating to the University of Wisconsin*. N.p., [1918].

Wood, Leonard. "Universal Military Training." *National Education Association Addresses and Proceedings*, LIV (1916).

Woodbridge, F. J. E. "The 'Issues of the War' Course in the S.A.T.C. Schedule." *Columbia Alumni News,* X (November 15, 1918).

The World Peril: America's Interest in the War. By members of the faculty of Princeton University. Princeton: Princeton University Press, 1917.

Yerkes, Robert M. "Psychology and National Service." *Science,* n.s., XLVI (August 3, 1917).

Zeitlin, Jacob, and Homer Woodbridge. *Life and Letters of Stuart P. Sherman.* New York: Farrar and Rhinehart, 1929.

SECONDARY SOURCES

Abrams, Ray H. *Preachers Present Arms.* New York: Round Table Press, 1933.

Allen, Harry C. *Conflict and Concord: The Anglo-American Relationship Since 1783.* New York: St. Martin's Press, 1959.

Angoff, Charles. "The Higher Learning Goes to War." *American Mercury,* XI (June, 1927).

Baird, Carol F. "Albert Bushnell Hart: The Rise of the Professional Historian." In Paul Buck, ed. *Social Sciences at Harvard, 1860–1920.* Cambridge: Harvard University Press, 1965.

Barber, Bernard. "Some Problems in the Sociology of the Professions." *Daedalus,* XCII (Fall, 1963).

Baritz, Loren. *The Servants of Power: A History of the Use of Social Science in American Industry.* Middletown, Conn.: Weslyan University Press, 1960.

Becker, Ernest. *The Lost Science of Man.* New York: George Braziller, 1971.

Ben-David, Joseph, and Awraham Zloczower. "Universities and Academic Systems in Modern Societies." *European Journal of Sociology,* III (1962).

Bestor, Arthur E., Jr. "The Study of American Civilization: Jingoism or Scholarship?" *William and Mary Quarterly,* IX (January, 1952).

———. "The Transformation of American Scholarship, 1875–1917." *Library Quarterly,* XXIII (1953).

Billington, Ray Allen. *Frederick Jackson Turner: Historian, Scholar, Teacher.* New York: Oxford University Press, 1973.

Binkley, William C. "Two World Wars and American Historical Scholarship." *Mississippi Valley Historical Review,* XXXIII (June, 1946).

Bishop, Morris. *A History of Cornell.* Ithaca: Cornell University Press, 1962.

Blakey, George T. *Historians on the Homefront: American Propagandists for the Great War.* Lexington: University of Kentucky Press, 1970.

Boardman, Fon W., Jr. *Columbia: An American University in Peace and War.* New York: Columbia University Press, 1944.

Brubacher, John S., and Willis Rudy. *Higher Education in Transition: A*

History of American Colleges and Universities, 1636–1968. New York: Harper and Brothers, 1958.

Bruce, Philip Alexander. *History of the University of Virginia, 1819–1919.* New York: Macmillan Company, 1922.

Buchler, Justus. "Reconstruction in the Liberal Arts." In Dwight C. Miner, ed. *A History of Columbia College on Morningside.* New York: Columbia University Press, 1954.

Burton, David H. "Theodore Roosevelt and his English Correspondents: The Intellectual Roots of the Anglo-American Alliance." *Mid-America,* LIII (January, 1971).

Capen, Samuel P. "The Effect of the World War, 1914–18, on American Colleges and Universities." *Educational Record,* XXI (January, 1940).

Cheyney, Edward Potts. *History of the University of Pennsylvania, 1740–1940.* Philadelphia: University of Pennsylvania Press, 1940.

Clapp, Margaret, ed. *The Modern University.* Ithaca: Cornell University Press, 1950.

Coats, A. W. "American Scholarship Comes of Age: The Louisiana Purchase Exposition, 1904." *Journal of the History of Ideas,* XXII (July–September, 1961).

Cohen, Warren I. *The American Revisionists: The Lessons of Intervention in World War I.* Chicago: University of Chicago Press, 1967.

Curti, Merle. *American Paradox: The Conflict of Thought and Action.* New Brunswick: Rutgers University Press, 1956.

———. "The American Scholar in Three Wars." *Journal of the History of Ideas,* III (June, 1942).

———. *The Growth of American Thought.* New York: Harper and Brothers, 1943.

———. "Intellectuals and Other People." *American Historical Review,* LX (January, 1955).

———. *Peace and War: The American Struggle, 1636–1936.* New York: W. W. Norton and Company, 1936.

Curti, Merle, ed. *American Scholarship in the Twentieth Century.* Cambridge: Harvard University Press, 1953.

Curti, Merle, and Vernon L. Carstensen. *The University of Wisconsin.* Madison: University of Wisconsin Press, 1949.

Dallek, Robert. *Democrat and Diplomat: The Life of William E. Dodd.* New York: Oxford University Press, 1968.

Doob, Leonard W. "The Utilization of Social Scientists in the Overseas Branch of the Office of War Information." In Daniel Lerner, ed. *Propaganda in War and Crisis.* New York: George W. Stewart, 1951.

Dorfman, Joseph. "The Role of the German Historical School in American Economic Thought." *American Economic Review: Papers and Proceedings,* XLV (May, 1955).

————. *Thorstein Veblen and His America.* New York: Viking Press, 1961.

Dupree, A. Hunter. *Science in the Federal Government.* Cambridge: Harvard University Press, 1957.

Fox, Daniel M. *The Discovery of Abundance: Simon N. Patten and the Transformation of Social Theory.* Ithaca: Cornell University Press, 1967.

Fox, Dixon R., ed. *A Quarter Century of Learning: 1904–1929.* New York: Columbia University Press, 1931.

Galpin, W. Freeman. *Syracuse University.* Syracuse: Syracuse University Press, 1960.

Gelfand, Lawrence E. *The Inquiry: American Preparations for Peace, 1917–1919.* New Haven: Yale University Press, 1963.

Grattan, C. Hartley. "The Historians Cut Loose." *American Mercury,* XI (August, 1927).

Gray, James. *The University of Minnesota.* Minneapolis: University of Minnesota Press, 1951.

Haines, George H., IV. *Essays on German Influence Upon English Education and Science, 1850–1919.* Hamden, Conn.: Archon Books, 1969.

Haines, George H., IV, and Frederick H. Jackson. "A Neglected Landmark in the History of Ideas." *Mississippi Valley Historical Review,* XXXIV (September, 1947).

Halsey, Albert H. "British Universities." *European Journal of Sociology,* III (1962).

Haynes, Roland. "The Colleges in the Preparedness Program, 1917–18 and 1940." *Educational Record,* XXI (October, 1940).

Hendricks, Luther V. *James Harvey Robinson: Teacher of History.* New York: King's Crown Press, 1946.

Herbst, Jurgen. *The German Historical School in American Scholarship: A Study in the Transfer of Culture.* Ithaca: Cornell University Press, 1965.

Herman, Sondra. *Eleven Against War: Studies in American Internationalist Thought, 1898–1921.* Stanford: Hoover Institution Press, 1969.

Higham, John. "The Schism in American Scholarship." *American Historical Review,* LXXII (October, 1966).

Higham, John, *et al. History.* Englewood Cliffs, N.J.: Prentice-Hall, 1965.

Hirschfeld, Charles. "Nationalist Progressivism and World War I." *Mid-America,* XLV (July, 1963).

Hofstadter, Richard. *Anti-Intellectualism in American Life.* New York: Alfred A. Knopf, 1963.

————. "The Revolution in Higher Education." In Arthur M. Schlesinger, Jr., and Morton White, eds. *Paths of American Thought.* Boston: Houghton Mifflin, 1963.

Hofstadter, Richard, and C. DeWitt Hardy. *The Development and*

Scope of Higher Education in the United States. New York: Columbia University Press, 1952.

Hofstadter, Richard, and Walter P. Metzger. *The Development of Academic Freedom in the United States.* New York: Columbia University Press, 1955.

Hoxie, R. Gordon. "John W. Burgess, American Scholar: Book I, the Founding of the Faculty of Political Science." Ph.D. dissertation, Columbia University, 1950.

Hoxie, R. Gordon, ed. *A History of the Faculty of Political Science, Columbia University.* New York: Columbia University Press, 1955.

Hughes, H. Stuart. "Is the Intellectual Obsolete?" *An Approach to Peace and Other Essays.* New York: Atheneum, 1962.

Hutchinson, William T. "The American Historian in Wartime." *Mississippi Valley Historical Review,* XXIX (September, 1942).

Jones, Rufus M. *Haverford College: A History and an Interpretation.* New York: Macmillan Company, 1933.

Kandel, Isaac L. *The Impact of the War Upon American Education.* Chapel Hill: University of North Carolina Press, 1948.

Kennan, George F. "The Sisson Documents." *Journal of Modern History,* XXVIII (June, 1956).

Kerr, Clark. *The Uses of the University.* Cambridge: Harvard University Press, 1963.

Kevles, Daniel J. "Testing the Army's Intelligence: Psychologists and the Military in World War I." *Journal of American History,* LV (December, 1968).

Kolbe, Parke R. *The Colleges in War Time and After.* New York: D. Appleton and Company, 1919.

Kris, Ernst, and Nathan Leites. "Trends in Twentieth-Century Propaganda." In Bernard Berelson and Morris Janowitz, eds. *Public Opinion and Communication.* Glencoe, Ill.: Free Press, 1953.

Lasch, Christopher. *The American Liberals and the Russian Revolution.* New York: Columbia University Press, 1962.

————. *The New Radicalism in America, 1889–1963: The Intellectual as a Social Type.* New York: Alfred A. Knopf, 1965.

Lasswell, Harold. *Propaganda Technique in the World War.* New York: Peter Smith, 1938.

————. "The Theory of Political Propaganda." In Bernard Berelson and Morris Janowitz, eds. *Public Opinion and Communication.* Glencoe, Ill.: Free Press, 1953.

Lubin, Isador. "Recollections of Veblen." In Carlton C. Qualey, ed. *Thorstein Veblen.* New York: Columbia University Press, 1968.

Ludlom, Robert P. "Academic Freedom and Tenure: A History." *Antioch Review,* X (March, 1950).

Lurie, Edward. "An Interpretation of Science in the Nineteenth Century." *Journal of World History,* VIII (1964–65).

————. "Science in American Thought." *Journal of World History*, VIII (1964–65).

Lutz, Ralph H. "Studies of World War Propaganda, 1914–33." *Journal of Modern History*, V (December, 1933).

McCarthy, Charles R. *The Wisconsin Idea*. New York: Macmillan Company, 1912.

Metzger, Walter P. "Expansion and Profession." Paper delivered before the Committee on the Role of Education in American History, Symposium on the Role of Education in Nineteenth-Century America, Catham, Mass., June, 1964.

————. "The German Contribution to the American Theory of Academic Freedom." *American Association of University Professors Bulletin*, XLI (Summer, 1955).

Miller, J. Hillis, and Dorothy V. N. Brooks. *The Role of Higher Education in War and After*. New York: Harper and Brothers, 1944.

Miner, Dwight C., ed. *A History of Columbia College on Morningside*. New York: Columbia University Press, 1954.

Mock, James R., and Cedric Larson. *Words That Won the War: The Story of the Committee on Public Information, 1917–1919*. Princeton: Princeton University Press, 1939.

Nevins, Allan. *The State Universities and Democracy*. Urbana: University of Illinois Press, 1962.

Nichols, Roy F. "War and Research in Social Science." *American Philosophical Society Proceedings*, LXXXVII (1944).

Odum, Howard, ed. *American Masters of Social Science*. New York: Henry Holt and Company, 1926.

Paxson, Frederic L. "The Great Demobilization." *American Historical Review*, XLIV (January, 1939).

Perkins, Bradford. *The Great Rapprochement: England and the United States, 1895–1914*. New York: Atheneum, 1968.

Pierson, George W. *Yale College: An Educational History, 1871–1921*. New Haven: Yale University Press, 1952.

Playne, Caroline E. *Society at War, 1914–1916*. Boston and New York: Houghton Mifflin Company, 1931.

Pole, J. R. "The New History and the Sense of Social Purpose in American Historical Writing." *Transactions of the Royal Historical Society*, Ser. 5, XXIII (1973).

Quandt, Jean B. *From the Small Town to the Great Community: The Social Thought of Progressive Intellectuals*. New Brunswick: Rutgers University Press, 1970.

Rader, Benjamin B. *The Academic Mind and Reform: The Influence of Richard T. Ely in American Life*. Lexington: University of Kentucky Press, 1966.

Randall, Mercedes M. *Improper Bostonian: Emily Greene Balch*. New York: Twayne Publishers, 1964.

Ringer, Fritz K. *The Decline of the German Mandarins: The German Academic Community, 1890–1933.* Cambridge: Harvard University Press, 1969.

Rudolph, Frederick. *The American College and University: A History.* New York: Random House, 1962.

Rudy, S. Willis. *The College of the City of New York: A History, 1847–1947.* New York: City College Press, 1949.

Schuyler, Robert L. "War and Historiography." *American Philosophical Society Proceedings,* LXXXVII (1944).

Sellery, Charles G. *Some Ferments at Wisconsin, 1901–1947.* Madison: University of Wisconsin Press, 1960.

Shryock, Richard. "The Academic Profession in the United States." *American Association of University Professors Bulletin,* XXXVIII (Spring, 1952).

Small, Melvin. "The American Image of Germany, 1906–1914." Ph.D. dissertation, University of Michigan, 1965.

Speier, Hans. "Morale and Propaganda." In Daniel Lerner, ed. *Propaganda in War and Crisis.* New York: George W. Stewart, 1951.

Storr, Richard J. *The Beginnings of Graduate Education in America.* Chicago: University of Chicago Press, 1953.

Strout, Cushing. *The American Image of the Old World.* New York: Harper and Row, 1963.

Thwing, Charles F. *The American and the German University: One Hundred Years of History.* New York: Macmillan Company, 1928.

————. *The American Colleges and Universities in the Great War, 1914–1919: A History.* New York: Macmillan Company, 1920.

Todd, Lewis P. *Wartime Relations of the Federal Government and the Public Schools, 1917–1918.* New York: Bureau of Publications, Teachers College, Columbia University, 1945.

Trow, Martin. "The Democratization of Higher Education in America." *European Journal of Sociology,* III (1962).

Veysey, Laurence R. *The Emergence of the American University.* Chicago: University of Chicago Press, 1965.

Ward, Robert D. "The Origins and Activities of the National Security League." *Mississippi Valley Historical Review,* XLVII (June, 1960).

Weinberg, Sydney Stahl. "Wartime Propaganda in a Democracy: America's Twentieth-Century Information Agencies." Ph.D. dissertation, Columbia University, 1969.

White, Morton G. *Social Thought in America: The Revolt Against Formalism.* New York: Viking Press, 1949.

Wilkins, Burleigh T. *Carl Becker: A Biographical Study in American Intellectual History.* Cambridge: M.I.T. Press and Harvard University Press, 1961.

Wilson, Logan. *The Academic Man: A Study in the Sociology of a Profession.* London: Oxford University Press, 1942.

Yeomans, Henry A. *Abbott Lawrence Lowell, 1856–1943.* Cambridge: Harvard University Press, 1948.

Index

DATE DUE